THE JUDAICA IMPRINT
FOR THOUGHTFUL PEOPLE

REBBETZIN TZIPORAH HELLER

How to bring the power and passion of Torah into our homes, our children — and ourselves

The Balancing Act

© Copyright 2012 by Shaar Press

First edition – First impression / November 2012

ALL RIGHTS RESERVED
No part of this book may be reproduced in any form, *photocopy, electronic media, or otherwise without* written *permission from the copyright holder, except by a reviewer who wishes to quote brief passages in connection with a review written for inclusion in magazines or newspapers.*
THE RIGHTS OF THE COPYRIGHT HOLDER WILL BE STRICTLY ENFORCED.

Published by **SHAAR PRESS**
Distributed by MESORAH PUBLICATIONS, LTD.
4401 Second Avenue / Brooklyn, N.Y 11232 / (718) 921-9000

Distributed in Israel by SIFRIATI / A. GITLER
6 Hayarkon Street / Bnei Brak 51127

Distributed in Europe by LEHMANNS
Unit E, Viking Business Park, Rolling Mill Road / Jarrow, Tyne and Wear, NE32 3DP/ England

Distributed in Australia and New Zealand by GOLDS WORLD OF JUDAICA
3-13 William Street / Balaclava, Melbourne 3183 / Victoria Australia

Distributed in South Africa by KOLLEL BOOKSHOP
Northfield Centre / 17 Northfield Avenue / Glenhazel 2192, Johannesburg, South Africa

ISBN 10: 1-4226-1322-4 / ISBN 13: 978-1-4226-1322-1

Printed in Canada
Custom bound by Sefercraft, Inc. / 4401 Second Avenue / Brooklyn N.Y. 11232

Table of Contents

Foreword   9

PART 1: THE QUESTIONS WE HAVE, THE ANSWERS WE NEED

Chapter 1: Living Our Lives
- Self-Improvement   15
- Coping With Today's Challenges   43
- On Being a Jewish Woman   62
- Marriage   86

Chapter 2: Building a Relationship with Hashem
- Serving Hashem   109
- Shabbos and Yom Tov   127
- Tefillah: The Power of Prayers   137
- Tzniyus   147

Chapter 3: Raising Our Children
    Questions of Chinuch   161
    Our Lives as Mothers   175
    Raising Happy Kids   193

Chapter 4: Understanding the World
    Tough Questions About Judaism   209

PART 2: BRINGING TORAH TO LIFE: ESSAYS ON DEEPENING OUR CHILDREN'S JEWISH EXPERIENCE

Chapter 5: Shabbos, Yom Tov, and Kids
    Making Shabbos Come Alive for Our Children   239
    Elul, Rosh Hashanah, and Yom Kippur   243
    Succos and Simchas Torah   246
    The Beauty of Chanukah   248
    Teaching Our Children the Essence of Purim   251
    The Seder Night: Inspiring and Involving Our Children   260
    Making Pesach Meaningful   265
    Sefiras HaOmer and Lag BaOmer   271
    Shavuos   277
    Tishah B'Av   283

Chapter 6: Teaching Our Children Middos
    Teaching Children to Be Givers   293
    Helping Children Feel Content   298
    Sibling Rivalry   303
    Helping Children Make the Right Choices   309
    Teaching Children the Power of the Tongue   313
    Emes and Sheker   317
    Teaching Children Kibud Av Va'eim   321
    Building Parent-Child Relationships   327
    Meaningful and Productive Summers for Our Children   334

Tefillah: Opening the Gates	340
Relating to Torah Leaders	344
The Value and Sweetness of Torah	348
Glossary	355

Foreword

Dear Reader,

When you ask yourself how you got to where you are in life, you may find yourself saying, "It was my family," or "It was my education" or (worst of all) "I always just happened to be in the right place at the right time."

Hashem has given me so much! He has sent me people who gave me the access to learning and growing from their example and their teachings. He gave me the opportunity to meet some of today's famous greats, and some of today's hidden greats. When I think about the lasting imprint that Neve Yerushalayim has left on the world, I can't help but being full of wonder for Hashem's kindness in letting me be part of it. In many ways the students have educated me far more than I educated them. I have met young women who are brilliantly talented, spiritually refined, and who today have taken their place in the world of *kiruv* and every form of community activism.

Others are less well known to anyone except the most important people in their lives, their families. Naaleh, the world's largest seminary with thousands upon thousands of online students has enabled me to reach out still more, and to share with them whatever I have learned from my mentors and from the *sefarim* that are the legacy of our rabbis throughout the ages. Hashem has given me the sort of family that made teaching possible. My husband and children are my partners in every sense of the word.

It is with gratitude to Him that this book was written.

Part 1:

The Questions We Have, the Answers We Need

Chapter 1

Living Our Lives

Self-Improvement

CHANGING OTHERS BY CHANGING YOURSELF

Q *I heard of a Rabbi who wished to change the world. Then, realizing that was impossible, he thought to change his community. Then, seeing that this too was a daunting task, sought to transform his family. Until he finally realized that his real goal in life was to change himself. He accomplished just that, which I think is the point of the story. He wouldn't have gotten around to changing himself if all his efforts had been invested in others.*

How do we as women and mothers go about changing ourselves when most of our lives are dedicated to influencing others? Don't we need to focus primarily on developing our husbands and children?

A Ultimate self-improvement is best accomplished by giving. Being a developed person means finding the part in yourself that is in Hashem's image and giving it a voice. The most accessible of all of Hashem's attributes is *middas hachessed*, our capacity to give. Working on yourself without *middas hachessed* is almost impossible. Therefore, the more you give of yourself to help develop others, the more you awaken the transcendental and compassionate aspects of your soul.

The aforementioned Rabbi could just as easily have said the same thing in reverse. The more one gives, the more one grows. It seems to work in both directions, provided you are giving in an honorable way. It is very easy to develop others out of the desire to give forth and not as an act of kindness, allowing your ego to find its satisfaction through doing whatever needs to be done. Just as we enjoy watering plants but don't necessarily want to be "watered" (i.e., inspired to grow), we can make the mistake of wanting to change others but not wanting to change ourselves. However, a person who approaches the act of giving in an honest way will definitely change as she changes others.

I'M NOT A NATURAL HOSTESS

Q *Hachnasas orchim does not come easily to me. When people ask me for a favor my automatic reaction is to say no. How can I become a more giving person?*

A Some people are extremely social. They dread being alone. You seem to be a person who has an inner life and enjoys order and control. Your *middah* is restraint rather than outpouring. Don't be hard on yourself. *Gevurah* is just as holy as *chessed*.

However, *Maharal* says that *gevurah* is most easily corrupted, so you have to be careful. When you manifest your desire for restraint on other people, instead of using it on yourself, it can get distorted. Invite guests who need an invitation. Don't host people for the sake of company. Take your eyes off yourself and focus more on others. If you need thinking space, do it when people aren't around. If someone comes to you for a favor, treat it as an opportunity for self-development. Tell yourself, "This is how I'll build my *chessed* and become more balanced. This is how my *gevurah* will be tempered."

You have to learn to be more spontaneous and giving rather than disciplined and in control. When Hashem sends *chessed* your way He is really telling you to broaden your horizons. You're a person of restraint, which is a holy *middah*. Use your self-control to perfect yourself, but be expansive and giving with others.

ADAPTING LESSONS FROM THE SAGES TO OUR LIVES

Q *How does a person know which of the many lessons of our sages to adapt to life? For example, when studying about the importance of chessed, should one push for the maximum and make plans to open ten gemachim? I find that while these values are inspiring, I'm never sure how far to go with them.*

A Go for the maximum. Life is short. If you have the money, time, and space, open ten *gemachim*. You know what your limits are. If we only knew the value of the good acts we perform, we would invest everything we had.

There is a famous parable about a man who was given a sack and was told to put in as many gems as he wanted. Of course, he stuffed it with as many precious stones as he could carry. Obviously we have needs such as sleeping, eating, and occasional breaks. But idealizing the breaks as life is idealizing death. Use every minute to its fullest. The people who do that are the ones who are the most happy and fulfilled.

If what's driving you isn't the desire to pick up gems, but to compete with some invisible or visible person, stop. Don't compete with anyone. Compete with the time and abilities Hashem gave you and maximize them to the limit.

WHAT DEFINES TIME THAT IS ACTUALLY LIVED?

Q *In a shiur you gave on Sarah Imeinu, you mentioned that when we come to the next world we will be asked our name and age. Our age will not be measured by the amount of time we actually lived. Can you clarify what this really means?*

A At a minimal level, age will be calculated based on days that were actually filled with purposeful activity. For example, the man who spent most of his life earning more money than he possibly could spend in his lifetime will have accrued years of wasted hours. There are many things we do that are purposeless. The half-hour phone calls that border on or even go over the edge of *lashon hara*, the "*yenta*" stuff" that could take two hours in some circles, and the endless discussions of politics are all a huge waste of precious time.

You have to ask yourself, "Am I really doing something meaningful right now?" It doesn't have to be "*tafkid*" with a capital "T"; it can be "*takfid*" with a small "t," like doing the laundry so your kids have clean clothes the next day or preparing supper for your husband, or rejoicing with a bride at a wedding, or lending a listening ear to a friend in need.

Doing small acts of kindness, snatching a quiet moment to pray, listening to an inspiring Torah *shiur* are the puzzle pieces that make up a meaningful life.

IS MY IDENTITY WHAT I DO?

Q *I am a single woman currently enrolled in a full-time master's degree program in college. I am also involved with a chessed organization. I find that people automatically tend to associate who I am with what I do, and their first question usually is, "How is school?" How can I detach my identity from my actions?*

A Our window into another person's world is usually by what they do. If you were married with children and someone asked you what you did, you would naturally say that you were a full-time mother or a housewife. The way we learn about other people is through their speech and actions. If you want people to get to know you better, you need to speak to them more at length so they can develop a sense of who you are. The need to reveal your deeper self is not necessarily important or good. In fact, having a secret place in your heart, an inner life that isn't judged or exposed to other people, is a precious thing.

I suppose that your real question is, who am I as a single woman? Your education might have told you that a woman's fulfillment is achieved through her husband and children. That is true, but in addition, there is an identity that is unique and specific to each individual. You need to develop that by asking yourself, "Who should I be at this moment in time in terms of Hashem's Will for me? How can I bring light into the specific space that Hashem placed me in?"

Your soul can take you in many directions. Let it lead you on the right path and let it help you fill your present moments with love of Hashem, His people, and His Torah.

HAVING A HARD TIME WITH SELF-DEFINITION

Q *I am afraid to be as religious as I can be because I don't want people commenting on it. The more irreligious the person I'm with is, the more irreligious I claim to be. I'll hold myself back from doing good just so that I can feel accepted. I know this is hurting my soul. What can I do to improve?*

A Read the section in *Mesillas Yesharim* that discusses arrogance. Ramchal explicitly writes about this problem. The *yetzer hara* is very clever. He tries to convince you not to seem too good so people won't perceive you as arrogant. If you adjust yourself to other people you'll be normal. We all like acceptance.

The Rambam says that this is human nature. Most people want to be like the people around them, because it eliminates borders and makes us feel more accepted.

You're behaving normally, but it doesn't mean you're on the right path. You have to bite the bullet and say, "Hashem created me as an individual with a unique background and way of thinking. I will be myself, not because it's good for me (which it is), but because I want to serve Hashem with the abilities He gave me."

If you've studied the mitzvos and have integrated them into your life, make a commitment to keep them. You're Hashem's servant. This issue is between you and Him, not between you and others. It's not a psychological problem, it's a spiritual one.

Study the chapter in *Mesillas Yesharim* well. It will give you the direction and courage you need to change.

FIGURING MYSELF OUT

How do I know who I really am or what I really should be? Am I limiting myself by remaining at the level that I am when I really could strive for higher levels? Am I deluding myself by thinking I can be better? What can I do to figure out where I belong?

You don't need to think that much about where you are. You need to think more about where you are going. The Rambam gives us a five-step formula to consider:

1. Your biological makeup. This includes your physical appearance, nature, strengths, and weaknesses. You need to think about how you can use the specific qualities Hashem endowed you with to improve yourself and the world around you on Hashem's terms.

2. Your environment. Take a trip down memory lane. Travel back to your high school years, your childhood, and to the teachers and friends you knew. Ask yourself what you learned from the specific places, incidents, and people you encountered.

3. Study the decisions you made in life and where they got you. What inspired you to choose the good decisions and what pulled you to the bad decisions? This makes you aware of what to look out for in yourself and what to nurture.

4. Examine your potentials and the things to which you are naturally drawn.

5. Scrutinize your habits and how you respond to specific situations on a knee-jerk level.

Applying this formula will give you a new sense of self-awareness and will be an eye-opener in terms of how you are unique. Your personality and *middos* are meant to be filtered through the Torah. You should look at your potential and what Hashem specifically set before you and ask yourself how you can give expression to it in the best possible way.

Self-Improvement / 21

DEVELOPING EMPATHY

Q *Does it really matter what my intent is or what I feel as long as I am doing what is right? Does it make a difference if I don't have a kind heart or that I don't feel empathy or love toward my fellow man if I still behave respectfully toward others?*

A I'll give you a very Jewish answer —"It depends." My grandmother would always say, "It is better to do the right thing with the wrong intent, than to do the wrong thing sincerely." This is true. However, it still does not equal doing the right thing with positive intent. Intent is enormously important, not so much for the recipient, but for you.

To illustrate this, if you saw someone jump into a burning car and drag out the passengers, you would be impressed at the man's daring rescue. However, if the rescuer's intent was to choke the passengers and steal their money, that would change the picture entirely. External action can be defined very differently depending on the person's specific intent.

The Baal Shem Tov said, "You are where your mind is." The recipient may never know the difference, but you as the giver would be gaining a great deal by becoming a more loving person and transforming yourself into someone who appreciates and learns from other people.

I'M TOO SELF-ABSORBED

Q *I don't feel much when it comes to the lives of those around me. I'm not materialistic or shallow, but I'm very self-absorbed, since I have so much to deal with in my own life. How do I develop empathy toward my fellow Jews?*

Self-absorption is not a good *middah*. There could be physical, psychological, or spiritual reasons why one has to be self-involved. Still, a person has to learn to focus beyond himself. The Gemara says that Pharaoh was as tall as a little finger. It doesn't mean that he was physically small, but that he was so petty that his entire world was as big as a finger. We all start out that way. Ideally, as we grow, more people besides our parents and close friends should enter our circle. Nobody is alone on an island. Even if you are physically sick, you will still come in contact with other patients, nurses, and volunteers. Part of spiritual living is connection with other people.

How do you develop feelings of attachment? Practice imagery. If you receive a wedding invitation in the mail, instead of noting the date down and tossing the card in the trash, try to visualize the joy of the *chasan* and *kallah* and their parents. The more you can envision what people are feeling, the more you'll be there with them at their *simchah*. If someone is in pain, put yourself in their position. If your neighbor broke her leg, try to think about the difficulties of getting out of bed with a cast, trying to take a shower, preparing meals, and taking care of children. Become the person.

There are many stories of great *tzaddikim* who perfected themselves in this *middah*. Reb Aryeh Levin would sometimes feel a person's pain even more acutely than the person himself did. During the British mandate in Israel, Reb Aryeh would visit the Jewish women's prison in Bethlehem. When he would see the young girls standing under the burning sun, surrounded by vulgar Arab women guards, he would burst into tears. He would stand there crying until it was time to leave.

When the Lubavitcher Rebbe married, his parents could not attend his wedding because the borders were closed. His father, Rav Levi Yitzchak, who was a great Kabbalist, spent the evening vicariously celebrating his son's *chasunah*. He arranged a mini wedding party in his home, complete with *l'chaim* and festive music. He was there at the wedding in his heart, picturing the joy of the *chasan* and *kallah*.

Challenges in your life should make you more sensitive to people's pain, not less so. The same way you would want a helping hand, validation, or acknowledgment while going through difficulties, people need empathy. It's not a matter of fixing things for others. Sometimes you really can't. Sensitizing yourself to a friend's pain and sharing his burden can make a huge difference. You can do this much more readily than someone whose life hasn't been so rocky. Your problem isn't shallowness, but rather a lack of imagination. If you learn to arouse your emotions through visualization, empathy will automatically follow.

HANDLING INSULTS

What does one do in the face of an insult when it is clear that you are right and the other person is wrong? It seems to me that having an ayin tovah (a good eye) and a certain amount of mesirus nefesh (self-sacrifice) goes along with developing this middah (character trait). How does it all fit together?

The best way to respond to an insult would be to use it to bring yourself back to a place of *"shiflus,"* to a position of saying, "Hashem, only You are larger than life, and it is good for me to know that I am small." Making an effort to judge the person with an *ayin tovah* and seeing the insult as a *kapparah* (atonement) will help you on the path to *avodas hamiddos*.

However, the other person is not necessarily benefiting by being allowed to insult you. Find the right moment and tell the person that it is not good for him to speak in this manner. It creates alienation and it makes people defensive. Ask the person why he is speaking this way and help him redirect himself to change.

If the person being insulted isn't you, your silence may be interpreted as acquiescence. Take the person aside discreetly and speak to him. For example, if a clever student insults a weaker student, it can create a defense mechanism within the weaker student that can ultimately take him off the *derech*. Talk to the superior student in a tactful way. Say to him, "Do you think it's okay to speak like this? If you had been R' Akiva's rebbi when he first started to learn, would you have humiliated him this way?" The weaker student should be aware that you have come to defend him. If reproach is delivered with sensitivity, discretion, and dignity, it can bear positive fruit.

HOW CAN I BECOME MORE POSITIVE?

I am a very negative, unforgiving, and emotionally needy person. My parents argued and yelled often, and I do the same with my husband. How can I avoid criticizing him? How can I become a more positive, giving person, instead of concentrating so much on what I am lacking?

Learn to tell your husband what you like and want as opposed to what you don't like or want. For example, if you want him to be more involved with the children, instead of complaining, "It's all on me," say, "I need your help." Then follow up with praise and thanks after he's helped you. He will feel accomplished and appreciated, and you're almost guaranteed an identical positive response next time. If there's an established pattern that needs to be broken, and it's hard for your husband, this approach may take months. But don't give up. Keep up the positive words and reinforcement. It will pay off in the end.

I will suggest a battle plan with three points of attack to shift your negative attitude toward positive change. First, begin keeping a gratitude journal where you commit to forty days of writing at least half a page of things you are grateful about each day. You may not repeat yourself, and there are no skipping days. This will open the door to greater positivity and will train your eye to look for what's truly important in life.

Second, learn to talk to Hashem. When you sense negative vibes coming on, tell Him how you feel and ask Him to help you see the positive side of whatever difficulty you are facing. Plead for strength to face your challenges.

Third, most negativity comes because our souls yearn for beauty, goodness, and harmony, and that is not what we are perceiving at the moment. Everything in this world has divinity. Hashem is the only Source from which goodness emanates. Learn to find the internal *sheleimus* (wholeness) and spirituality hidden in ordinary life experiences. For example, if you've just completed folding a towering pile of laundry and you feel that euphoric sense of achievement, connect that feeling to its spiritual source of positivity and harmony. Recognize that you can bring more of that feeling into your life by performing mitzvos with *simchah*. Commit yourself to say one *berachah* a day with extra joy, and watch your perspective change.

All this takes a lot of inner work, but keep at it and you will definitely see dramatic changes for the better.

SPIRITUAL SIGNIFICANCE OF HEBREW BIRTHDAYS

Q *Is there spiritual significance related to one's Hebrew birthday? Are our prayers more powerful or is there anything customarily done on this day?*

A One of the things related to *mazal* is one's day of birth. It says in *Tehillim*, "Ani hayom yelid'ticha, she'al mimeni v'etna — I have given birth to you today. Ask of Me and I will give."

Certainly one's *tefillos* are more potent on this day. The very elaborate birthday parties people sometimes make have no source in the Torah. The only birthday party mentioned in the Torah was Pharaoh's. The ultimate celebration is really the *hilula*, the day of one's death, when the soul returns to Hashem weighted down with achievements and accomplishments.

Just being born is not a cause for celebration, although it is cause for reflection, thankfulness, and new resolutions for the coming year.

GIVING UP SECULAR MUSIC

Q *I grew up listening to secular music (rock, among other genres), and I still enjoy it. I don't enjoy most of the modern Jewish music. Should I really be depriving myself of listening to what I like?*

A I understand what you mean about modern Jewish music, but there's a lot more out there than you think. I don't think being *frum* means depriving yourself. I think we have to be selective. The lives of people involved in secular entertainment are not good lives. It's not as black and white as you think. Wholesomeness and good-heartedness don't come from listening to rock. There is invisible power woven into music that can have both a positive and a deleterious effect on us.

Elevate your musical experience with pure and holy melodies. Listen to real music. I mean the Chassidic melodies of 200 years ago, such as those of Chabad, Belz, and Breslav. These are classics that are moving and beautiful. Try to get someone in a yeshivah to record a *Simchas Beis Hosho'eivah* or get a cassette of a *Simchas Chasan V'Kallah*. This kind of music is stirring and inspiring and will uplift your soul in a way that secular music never will.

BEING FLEXIBLE

Q *The Torah writes that one should be as flexible as a reed. How does one develop this trait and incorporate it into daily life?*

A The word I would use for this is "spiritual flexibility." It means realizing that Hashem has designed every particular moment especially for you in the same intricate detail as an ant's eye. You have to realize that your specific situation is part of Hashem's perfect plan and it needs to be exactly the way it is.

Here's an example to illustrate this point: The bank is closing at 1 p.m. You made it past the security guard 5 minutes before closing, with the intent to get your check cashed that day. The clerk however, shuts the window and refuses to accept any more arrivals. If you're reactive and inflexible, you will let everyone know your opinion of the bank and prevent the clerk from leaving on time just so she knows that you have been treated unfairly.

If you apply the principle of the reed, you will realize that this situation was specifically designed for you and you will try to accept it in a meaningful way. Whether this means that you will implore the clerk to do you a personal favor or contemplate what you can learn from the situation, you won't lose yourself, and that is where being flexible as a reed begins. It ends with being creative, thinking of other solutions, and stretching your mental muscles to frame situations in a positive way.

SENSIBLE NUTRITION

Q *I've heard you discuss a few times our responsibility for our health and safety. I understand that this falls under the Torah commandment of, "V'nishmartem me'od l'nafshoseichem ..." What about good nutrition? Is this optional or praiseworthy?*

A Nobody really knows what good nutrition is. When I was in elementary school, we all knew that balanced nutrition consisted of meat, milk, a green and yellow vegetable, and fruit. Butter was the health spread, margarine was iffy.

Times changed. By the time I reached my early teens, butter, red meat, and olive oil were all blacklisted. Margarine became the health spread. We were told there was no difference between fresh, canned, and frozen vegetables.

Time moved on. Today olive oil is healthy, milk and margarine are not. Meat and fish barely make the grade. Fresh fruits and vegetables have staying power, but even fruits should be consumed sparingly.

So I quote the Rambam's cardinal rule: "Don't overeat and don't eat when you're not hungry." Even if your eating habits are not ideal, if you exercise and eat in moderation, you're on the right track.

WHEN IS IT OKAY TO GIVE IN?

Q *Can you explain the proper boundaries of being a vatran?*

A *Vatranus* begins by seeing the other person as an extension of yourself. Parents instinctively do this with their children. You have to learn to bring more people into your world.

Being a *shmattah* means resentfully giving in when there are other possibilities. I would call this intentional martyrdom, which is what people choose when in some way they benefit from making others feel guilty and beholden. People with low self-esteem tend to give in, because they can't bring themselves to suffer even momentary disapproval from another person. There is a huge difference when there are other alternatives and when you are giving in because of unhealthy reasons. Martyrdom isn't good for anyone.

The boundaries of *vatranus* have to do with halachic priorities. A mitzvah comes before other obligations. Something only you can do comes before something other people can do.

For example, only you as your children's mother can put your kids to bed in a way that will make them feel loved and cared for. If someone repeatedly asks you to drive them somewhere at that hour, you have to learn to say no. A definable mitzvah cannot be forfeited at the risk of doing an *aveirah*. For instance, if right before Shabbos a friend requests a favor that might cause you to violate Shabbos, you are obligated to decline. Obviously, real emergencies and saving lives take precedence over almost everything else.

Use your good judgment and common sense. Giving in is commendable, but never at the expense of neglecting your priorities.

BALANCING PHYSICAL AND SPIRITUAL DESIRES

Q We live very simply due to my husband's careful spending habits and our desire for him to be learning half a day. However, sometimes I can't help wanting small luxuries. When I bring these things up to my husband, he becomes very discouraged, and I feel that I am dragging him down a level. If gadlus is the goal and gashmiyus pulls us down, it seems so simple that we should all live with the bare minimum. Still, it just doesn't feel right to me.

The things we like are usually what make our souls happy. More than anything else, we desire attachment to spirituality.

Appreciate what you have and use it to reach ultimate good. If you find yourself really needing those extras, there are *gemachim* that offer secondhand items gratis or for a small fee. If you don't want to be a charity case, you have to ask yourself honestly what gives you more spiritual pleasure, the feeling of not being a *mekabel* or the feeling of having aesthetically pleasing items. If receiving will make you feel even more deprived, learn to see beauty where you haven't until now. In a state of *simchah,* you can praise your worn-out couch, "This is a very good couch. I can sit on it and I won't fall on the floor."

You can rise above status and aesthetics and decide to use what you have to serve Hashem. Don't make your husband trade *Olam Haba* for *olam hazeh*. Ask Hashem to give you what you desire. He can help you nurture more acceptance in your heart or send you what you need in any of numerous ways. Ultimately, *berachah* comes from Hashem, not people. There are people with beautiful homes who are miserable. The suicide rate among the wealthy is higher than among any other segment of the population. Be happy and learn to see the *berachah* in what you have. Your children will remember the *simchah* in their home, not what the furniture looked like.

When you find yourself wanting things you can't afford, tell yourself, "Yes, the things other people have are nice, and maybe one day I will have them. It's all in the hands of Hashem, Who can send anyone anything if He so desires." You are fortunate that your husband is focused and directed and realizes the transience of this world. Explain to him that the same way he needs you to build him, you need him to build you. Tell him that his words of kindness and appreciation would make your life sweeter and more meaningful. With the right approach and your husband's encouragement, you can learn to find joy in what Hashem has given you.

PRACTICAL WAYS TO IMPROVE ONE'S MIDDOS

Q *Can you suggest a practical way to go about middos improvement and development? I am aware of keeping a cheshbon hanefesh. However, it does not help me to make practical changes. Is there a way for a person to create his own one-person mussar vaad?*

A There are many ways to improve one's *middos*. The first method is applying the Ramchal's dictum that says that a person must have an ultimate goal for himself, where he can say, "This is why Hashem made me. This is what I want to achieve in life." Various great Jewish thinkers have suggested different objectives, such as bringing light to a dark place, refining ones *middos*, and becoming more like Hashem.

The Gra says to keep the big picture in mind at all times. We all have little day plans, such as going to work, getting to the dentist, or attending PTA meetings. The challenge is to see that the little pieces of your small plan fit into the big plan. If your goal is to bring light, you'll radiate joy and you'll try to give people a sense of significance. If you want to improve your *middos*, you'll make an effort to be friendly and warm and go beyond the letter of the law to help others.

The Maharal depicts this world as a place where all the puzzle pieces are visible but the actual puzzle is not. It is an *olam hapirud*, a world of separation. Conversely, the world where everything is interconnected is the *olam ha'achdus*, the world of unity. I would suggest you start with working on seeing this world as an *olam ha'achdus*. When you are feeling stressed out, tell yourself, "This is a fragment of the picture. How can I connect it to the whole picture?"

A second way to work on self-improvement is to set aside a few minutes each day in a quiet place to speak to Hashem. Start by thanking Him for all the good He has given you. Tell Him about your struggles and what is lacking in your life. The joy you'll find in learning to talk freely to Hashem is indescribable.

A third way is to make your own personal *mussar vaad*, as you suggested. Select a *mussar sefer* to study, keep a *cheshbon hanefesh* notebook, and set specific goals for yourself each week. I would recommend you start with *Orchos Tzaddikim*, because it is the most accessible of all the *sifrei mussar*. Read a paragraph, write your weekly goal at the top of your notebook, and mark off each day as you achieve your objective. Alternatively, you can read *Mesillas Yesharim*, or *Alei Shur* by Rav Shlomo Wolbe. *Alei Shur* is wonderful because it presents concepts that lend themselves to *cheshbon hanefesh*, suggests goals for the week, and delineates the baby steps you'll need to take to achieve your aims. It is best to do this with a friend so you can give each other support and encouragement. If this is not possible, go for the "one-person *mussar vaad*" anyway.

May your efforts at achieving self-perfection bring you closer to Hashem.

I TALK TOO MUCH

Q *I speak lashon hara often. I have this deep inner need to state my opinions so that people can tell me that I'm right. I know it's wrong, but I can't stop. Can you suggest a plan of action?*

A Your most significant problem is that you don't feel heard or validated. The Maharal says that women have more difficulty with sins of speech because of their need to be understood. I would suggest you begin keeping a journal where you commit to writing down only good things about your life and the life of the people around you. Devote a minimum of 15 minutes every day for this. Writing will require you to change your mode of thinking

Self-Improvement / 33

and help you concretize and verbalize your experiences in a positive way.

At first it will feel as if you are whitewashing reality and being dishonest. However, if you keep at it and are careful to jot down only things that are true and positive, you will begin to feel validated and authenticated.

The Gra writes that one of the causes of *lashon hara* is our way of thinking. The barrier dividing thought and speech is very fine. By changing your mind-set you will automatically see changes in your way of speaking. Work on *hisbodedus*. Talk to Hashem as you would to a friend. Tell Him what is in your heart. He can alter reality and draw down blessing in the merit of your turning to Him.

Take on a *chessed* project. This will help you develop empathy toward others. Work on becoming a safe haven to which other people turn. Move forward from a feeling of victimization to a feeling of giving. Sync your mind to your heart by studying the Maharal's essay on *ayin tov* and *lev tov* in *Nesivos Olam*.

If you are committed to change, you will surely see improvement for the better.

SPIRITUAL DECLINE

Q *I feel as if I have declined spiritually over the last few years. I try to listen to shiurim, but I find that although I am inspired to grow in the short term, after a while I end up letting my observance slack again. What can I do to get back on track?*

A The *Navi* tells us that even among the angels there is a concept of *ratzo*, going forth, and *shov*, withdrawing. As humans, we all have periods when we feel low and periods when we ascend. It's a part of the rhythm of life. The function of these low periods is to help us solidify our spiritual levels through *mesirus nefesh*.

Buy a small notebook and write down two things you can do daily to bring yourself back to your previous level. Think of acts that will inspire you. Force yourself to do these acts so that you can check off both deeds every night. If you can get a friend to do this with you, that would be wonderful. Put money away for every check mark and buy yourself a treat at the end of the week. This may sound juvenile, but you need to fight the evil inclination with his own weapons. He is dragging you down to physicality and to living a life devoid of spiritual light. Beat him by bribing yourself with something material and commit yourself to not purchasing your reward until all the check marks are filled in.

I guarantee that you will soon find yourself doing the right thing not for the wrong reasons, but because it will make you feel good about yourself. Keep going for another month. At the beginning of the third month, move the focus from what you have already integrated and add two new practices to the list. Follow the same procedure. Keep changing the focus and adding new things. Slowly you will see yourself moving forward and regaining the spiritual levels you once had.

DEALING WITH FAILURE

Q *What is the correct hashkafic approach to dealing with failure? For instance, what does a person do when he commits a sin that he resolved not to do again, or when he destroys relationships he committed to build? How do we maintain our self-esteem in the face of feeling worthless inside?*

A We all fail at some point in life. The evil inclination's strongest weapon is despair. It says in *Mishlei*, "A *tzaddik* falls seven times and rises." There are seven attributes we share with Hashem. A person could fail at each one, but it doesn't give him an excuse not to get up again. The difference between a *tzaddik* and a non-*tzaddik* is not that a *tzaddik* never fails, but he rises up after falling the seventh time. You must get up and try again.

If you resolved not to do something and then did it again, that tells you that whatever method you used didn't work. Be creative. Devise a different plan of action. If that too fails, think of something else. Realize that Hashem will not judge you by your successes, but rather by your efforts. Failing is completely normal. Many times we look at spiritual people and think they were born righteous. In fact, most *tzaddikim* started out small and suffered many setbacks before they finally attained their elevated spiritual level.

ALONE IN A CROWD

Q*I feel empty and alone and very far from Hashem whenever I am in a crowd or in traffic or waiting on line. I can't comprehend how this dirty, noisy, unruly world, with all of these people, could possibly be the world Hashem envisioned. The last time this was bothering me, I looked up, and the bumper sticker on the car in front of me said, "One Human Family." Is this my answer? Should I look at everyone like he or she is part of me? Should I look at them like they belong here as much as I sometimes think that I do?*

AEvery person is as important, real, and purposeful as you are. The Gemara tells us, "Great is the king who mints many coins, each unique in its own way." There is no such thing as optional people. Every single person is absolutely special. When people mention faceless hordes it is usually in a racist context. The more you adapt yourself to seeing people as individuals, the easier it will be for you to bear crowds.

Did you ever wonder why Hashem chose Yerushalayim, a city teeming with people, as the holiest spot on earth? I would have chosen a majestic mountain or a breathtaking valley, because I sometimes tend to think like you. Although we view nature as beautiful and people as ugly, Hashem sees people as His most magnificent creations. The profound depth of the human mind, the capacity to feel, the desire to create and build, the ability to make moral choices, are expressions of the soul and a reflection of the Divine Image.

Every person you see is an entire universe with enormous content and beauty of purpose. I would suggest you get past your difficulties in viewing people by finding ways to reach out to strangers. It can be through visiting the sick, tutoring, or joining "Partners in Torah." In this way you will learn to change your mode of thinking from seeing people as a threatening, anonymous mass to viewing them as unique individuals, each with a special story of his own.

THE MEANING OF ACHDUS

Q *I've seen school-age girls who were lumped together and told to be friendly and it backfired very badly. It bothers me because it's all in the name of achdus. What is the Torah perspective, and where does achdus fit in here?*

A Our world is enormously complex. Every creation has its purpose, structure, and reason for being, with the common goal of revealing Hashem's glory. A lion and a frog are very different, but they share one factor — they show Hashem's greatness. The function of a Jew is to interpret the world and find Hashem's glory in every person, creation, or situation that he encounters. Every Jew is part of the collective of *Klal Yisrael*, and together we can give meaning to existence.

It says concerning the Jews, "*Becha espa'er* — I take pride in you." When you meet another Jew, ask yourself, "How does Hashem take pride in him in a way that is different from how He takes pride in me? How can I really know this person, what is his unique contribution to the world, how can I learn from him?" *Achdus* is when you ask, "Where do I see Hashem's *kavod* in this person?" Hashem's glory may be hidden under layers of pride and sinfulness. Your job is to see through that facade so that you and the person can connect by tapping into the *tzelem Elokim*. This is really what *achdus* means — seeing the spirituality within another person and feeling one with him.

Viewing different sectors within *Klal Yisrael* and seeing what is unique, admirable, and beautiful without necessarily feeling you have to be a part of that particular group is *achdus* manifested in reality. This is the way true *tzaddikim* have looked at other Jews, and it is this to which we should aspire.

I NEED APPROVAL

Q *I like when people show admiration for my spiritual endeavors. It is not enough for me to feel Hashem's approval. I need other people's respect as well. How can I work on this?*

A Welcome to the club. You are not entirely free of desiring honor. You're human. Don't be too concerned about it. Very few people have totally weaned themselves of enjoying *kavod*. If you really want to work on it, try to do a good deed and give someone else the acknowledgment, or don't demand any honor for a *chessed* you did. If you do this by choice, then, rather than feeling as you'd feel if someone robbed you of acknowledgment, you'll realize that you're still the same person and have done the same deed without necessarily needing the cheering thousands. Slowly you can develop more of a sense of the integral beauty of a spiritual act, rather than automatically searching for external approval.

WOMEN'S PERFORMANCES

Q *I was wondering about the proliferation of women's performances. Are they good, since they're allowing people to have a positive outlet for their talents, or are they just a product of being confused about where to channel our talents?*

A Productions provide an outlet for talented people, which is good in and of itself. They may also be inspiring to the audience, depending on what is being presented, which is also wonderful.

What isn't good and isn't given enough thought is the amount of honor bestowed on the stars of the show. We need to be on guard here, because we can easily create Frankensteins by giving the most prestige to the girls who are the most outgoing and successful on stage, while the real virtues of other girls are ignored. The problem isn't the production, it's the way we relate to it. This is what we have to correct.

GETTING RID OF BAD THOUGHTS

Q *How can I rid myself of bad thoughts, for example, wishing evil on someone but at the same time wanting it to be good for them? I know these thoughts stem from the yetzer hara. How do I fight it?*

You may not be able to prevent a bad thought from entering your mind, but you can decide if you want it to stay there. You can make a choice to say, "I don't want to be here. I want to think of something else," and consciously distract yourself by thinking of something important in your life at the moment. You can also take another approach. After the bad thought enters your mind, you can ask yourself, "What is this coming to correct in me?"

Rav Asher Freund once told a parable about a man who died. A tree began to grow right over his burial place. In the course of time, the roots burrowed deep into the ground until they pierced his body and drew nourishment from it. The tree grew and became very large. Hashem judged the man and decided that he had to come back to life again. In his second reincarnation, he was a carpenter. He ordered wood and the merchant delivered a big chunk of the tree that was in essence him. His life force had gone into it. It was old and bent, and he vacillated whether to make something out of it or just to discard it.

When Hashem makes something ugly come your way it's a reflection of yourself. You can either rectify it or discard it. Ask yourself, "What do I need to fix?" Let us say you are jealous of someone. Her life seems better than your life. She's connected, you're isolated. She's secure, you're insecure. She has a perfect marriage, and yours is less than perfect. You find yourself thinking, "She has everything and I have nothing." At that point you have to ask yourself, "If I'm jealous of her life, then Hashem is making me question something. How do I regard my own life? Do I see it with all its problems and challenges as coming from Hashem? Do I look at it with *simchah*?" This could be a call for some deep soul-searching and a step toward self-improvement.

SELF-GROWTH

When my kids were small I ached for some privacy and time alone. Now that I have it, I am having trouble structuring my day. I waste precious time shopping for things I don't need just because

I enjoy the thrill of finding bargains. I also spend a lot of time eating. When I see a food that I crave, I must finish all of it. I can't control myself. I feel there is a common thread here, but I need help putting my finger on it.

You need to develop a personal program of self-growth. The soul yearns for control, achievement, and nurturing. If it does not get it through meaningful ways, it will look for other avenues. Shopping for the best bargains is your soul's way of expressing its desire to achieve something. Find a more constructive mode of doing this. Call up the people in charge of *hachnasas kallah* in your area and offer to buy things for needy brides. Volunteer to shop for elderly people in your community. Do things that will help bond you with others and with the part of you that craves meaning.

Your uncontrolled eating is misguided self-nurturing. Be good to yourself in a different way. Physical self-nurturing can choke the part of you that wants spiritual self-nurturing. Learn to remove the heavy blanket of illusion that says food is pleasurable and nurturing. Before you begin a meal, give yourself permission to eat whatever you want. However, once you finish, decide firmly that you will not eat anything again until the next meal.

This spiritual exercise will move you away from impulsivity, which drowns out the mind, its yearnings, and its capacity to know. It will not necessarily make you thinner or healthier, but it'll make food smaller in your eyes.

Once you've done that, you can then think about how you can nurture yourself in ways that are authentic. What do you really want to be? What do you want to do? How will you achieve it? Don't go into stress mode; go into discovery mode. Think about what has made you happy in the past and what could bring you joy in the future. Work toward becoming something greater. Ask yourself how you can make the world a better place. Make a plan to channel your gifts positively. In this way you will attain the harmony and *sheleimus* your soul desires.

IS IT OKAY TO FOLLOW THE NEWS?

Q *I am confused about following the news. On the one hand, not knowing what is happening to fellow Jews around the world is bad for my ahavas Yisrael. On the other hand, hearing about too many tragedies makes me jaded. It can also be addictive, and much of what is reported is really unnecessary for me to know. What is the correct balance?*

A The Rabbanim are divided in their opinion on this. Rav Mordechai Gifter once said, "You have to look in the mirror and you have to look at the paper." You should know what you look like and what the world looks like. I agree that the news is addictive and most of it is superfluous. However, you need to stay informed and you need to care. Learn to cultivate the art of skimming. Scan the headlines instead of spending time on long news articles. Listen to the news roundup on the hour instead of wasting precious hours on talk shows or endless discussions. The news is alluring because it offers an escape from the tedium of daily life. Recognize this, and if you find yourself becoming addicted, look for meaningful activities to engage in that will make you unwilling to sacrifice your time on senseless things.

News addiction is more prevalent among men than women. If your husband shows signs of addiction, recognize that this is a problem for both of you, since you are one unit. Empathize with his pain and feel the emptiness within him that is driving him to this. Help him heal by guiding him to find other more purposeful avenues of interest. When you do hear of tragedies, commit yourself to recite a chapter of *Tehillim* and try to say it with *kavannah*.

Yes, you should stay informed, but don't spend more time on it than you have to.

Coping With Today's Challenges

MY SON IS OFF THE DERECH

Q *My 19-year-old son, who used to be a top bachur in yeshivah, has dropped most vestiges of Yiddishkeit and spends the bulk of his time in inappropriate and sometimes dangerous actions. I have gone to many people for advice but so far have not seen any changes for the better, only for worse. I spend most of my waking hours worrying and thinking about him. It's hard for me to find happiness in my life because I care so much. Children can give parents a lot of nachas, but the pain of seeing them fall is great. How can I lift myself above the situation and not allow it to pull me down?*

A You are going through one of the most painful and difficult *nisyonos* a person can face. Worrying about your child's fate in this world and the Next World is more difficult than suffering through illness or poverty. Practically every seeming mistake you ever made raising him seems huge, insurmountable, and impossible to rectify.

Our *Avos* struggled with similar challenges. Avraham had to contend with Yishmael, the child who behaved so wickedly that he was forced to expel him from his home. True, Yishmael repented in the end, but he was certainly not the child of whom Avraham had dreamed. Yitzchak had to struggle with Esav, the evil son who fooled him for so many years. How did they deal with their challenges? I would say the key was something Avraham said to Hashem, "*Lu yichyeh Yishmael lefanecha* — Yishmael should live before You." Avraham prayed that Yishmael should attain *yiras Hashem*, and to some degree his prayers were answered, as Yishmael did repent.

Take the energy you are now putting into blaming yourself, your son, his school, or his father, and put it all into prayer. The Baal HaTanya advises that if a person is worried about mistakes that he has made, he should allow himself to feel the pain up to a certain time limit, let's say from 11 a.m. to 11:30 a.m., and then he must go right back into living in the moment. Ask yourself, "What is Hashem telling me now, and what should I be doing at this moment?" Some people think that if they permit themselves to switch focus, they're somehow surrendering to despair. This is not true. Today you need to respond to today. Tomorrow may be a completely different day with a new set of challenges.

Turn to Hashem for help. King David says in *Tehillim*, "*V'nasata simchah v'libi.*" Ask Hashem to create joy in your heart. Appreciate all the goodness He did give you — your other children who provide you with *nachas*, your devoted spouse, and your loving friends.

Create a reality within yourself that is big enough and good enough so that when the long-awaited day comes and your son returns, you will be ready to welcome him, ennobled and strengthened by this *nisayon*.

MY FRIEND'S CHILD IS OFF-THE-DERECH

Q *What is the proper way to encourage a friend whose family member went off the derech? I'm not sure what to say, because I can't think of any kind of good that can come from this, apart from the unlikely chance that the person will come back.*

A First, take the word "unlikely" out of your vocabulary. Statistics show that many people come back as they mature.

Second, be there for your friend. Tell her, "I'm with you and I'm praying for your family member. Tell me how else I can be of assistance." She may be too paralyzed by grief to try to do something. Suggest ideas, such as getting *berachos*, seeking counsel, and going to the grave of a *tzaddik* to beseech Hashem in prayer. Guide her in finding the right people who can help. Prevent her from throwing up her hands in despair and saying, "This is how it is." Encourage her to trust in Hashem and never give up hope.

CULTIVATING SIMCHAH

Q *I'm single, in my 30's, and unemployed. I am looking for ways to increase my simchah and to be less controlled and defined by my external reality. Can you explain what simchah really is? How can I cultivate the spiritual courage to be happy? Often the nisayon itself is not the hardest part, but people's reactions. They often misinterpret my attempts at being happy as not dealing with my life. Doesn't Hashem want us to do what's within our power and trust Him to do the rest?*

You're exactly where you should be. People tend to forget that Hashem is really in control. Therefore, when they see you happy, they think you've somehow relinquished mastery over circumstances that are not really in our hands. The Sfas Emes writes that Hashem created the world for *birur*, to select good from evil. According to the *Zohar*, just as the Torah first narrates the creation of darkness and then light, so too Hashem created *nisyonos* and difficulties so we could use *birur* to discern Hashem's light in every situation.

The name *Yud Kei Vav Kei* means He was, He is, and He will be. When we integrate *birur* into our daily lives we are in essence stating that Hashem is with us at every moment. If you are in your 30's, single, and jobless, this is precisely Hashem's Will for you at this point, and you are meant to grow from the *nisayon*.

The Jews had to go through the pain of Egyptian servitude so they would return to Hashem from their point of suffering. Of course there were failures. They sank to the forty-ninth level of impurity, but ultimately they acquired enough faith to be redeemed. The verse says, "*Ki v'simchah seitzeiu* — With happiness you will leave exile." This refers to both collective and individual exiles.

For the world to fulfill its destiny, we must find Hashem within all the myriad shades of reality, whether they're pleasant or difficult. A person who is *b'simchah* is in essence saying, "Not only is this good, but it's the best that could possibly be." Genuine *simchah* is the smile on your face when the whole world thinks you're strange for being happy.

Although I have never stood in your shoes, I don't think any *nisayon* is harder than being single at 28 or older. I've seen people suffer through illnesses, terrible bereavement, and awful tragedies, but I still don't think there is anything as painful. The level of loneliness, despair, and the complete lack of sympathy has no parallel. Yet I've known people who were happy during these years because they used every day constructively and joyously. These are the people who were never in *galus*. You don't have to choose to be there. Keep smiling, stay upbeat, don't waste a moment, and you'll ultimately find your point of redemption.

SINGLE AND ALONE ON SHABBOS AND YOM TOV

Q *I constantly hear women asking how to stay inspired on Shabbos and Yom Tov when they have to meet the physical demands of marriage and a young family. I know so many single women, myself included, who would love to be married. We have ample free time to learn and daven, but Judaism is built around the family. It is heartbreaking to be alone during these times. Even if I do get invited out, it's still not my own family, no matter how nice the hosts are. I know we have to have bitachon and accept that this is what Hashem wants, but can you offer any other words of inspiration or encouragement?*

A When someone complains about something you don't have, it's like a dagger in your heart. When a childless woman hears a mother griping about her baby, or when a man who is unemployed listens to people complaining about the crowding on commuter trains, or when someone who is breaking his head over Gemara and is just not getting it hears people discussing the pros and cons of an exclusive yeshivah or *kollel*, it's not easy.

However, the problem here is really *kinah*, which the Maharal describes as the epitome of emotional dishonesty. Nobody knows what his purpose in life is and what the future holds. Someone else's tools will not get you closer to your mission in life. If you're single and Divine Providence led you to live far away from your family, then accept this as Hashem's Will, and use the opportunity to develop yourself. Attaining a higher level of *bitachon* may be your entire purpose for living. Of course you can say that your situation is not ideal. Your feelings are completely natural, but call it by its right name, which is *kinah*. Accept that life is a process and it takes a long time to get past this *middah*. In fact, many people never succeed.

How do you begin? The Ibn Ezra tells a parable about a country yokel who went to the big city one day and caught sight of the princess at a parade. Would the yokel ever consider the princess as his *bashert*? Of course not, because she lives in an entirely different world than he does. The Ibn Ezra says that every person is a complete universe. No one else's world has anything to do with your world. Look at your own universe and see what it offers. Open your eyes to the courage, self-sufficiency, and *deveikus* that you could potentially develop, and realize that for the moment this indeed is where you should be.

LONELINESS

Q I'm a baalas teshuvah, 38, and single. I am very lonely. I can't keep in contact with anyone from my former irreligious life. Most of the religious women my age are married with many children and act as if I have nothing in common with them. The younger girls are only interested in getting married and I seem too old for them. How can I find friends?

A The *nisayon* of loneliness is one of the most difficult challenges a person can face. You are not the only older single around. If you live in New York, try Ohr Naava, an amazing learning center where women come together for friendship and learning. You could make many new friends there.

If you don't live in New York, I would recommend you get involved in *kiruv* or *chessed*. You'll find things in common with the people you meet on the basis of your shared experiences.

Don't give up trying to find new friends, but make Hashem your friend. Everyone has periods of loneliness in their lives, whether before marriage, within marriage, or in the later years. At such times, Hashem is really telling us to turn to Him. "*Zeh dodi v'zeh rei'i* — This is my lover, this is my companion." Learn to talk to Hashem. Make time for Him every day. Speak to Him in your own words. Express your deepest feelings and longings. You can sing, shout, cry, or whisper. Begin with 5 minutes and move up to an hour. Before long, you will find that you have developed a profound relationship that will give you an inner sense of who you are and who Hashem really is. This will stay with you for the rest of your life and give you the strength to face all of life's challenges with faith and fortitude.

I'M LIVING IN A NON-RELIGIOUS HOME

I'm currently living with a non-religious family, with no hope of moving very soon. I try to use my time wisely by keeping a gratitude journal, learning, and working on my middos. However, I often find myself feeling resentful, lonely, and unfulfilled. My head and heart are in different places. I feel as if I am not in a situation where I can fully use my talents and reach my potential. How can I be mechazek myself to utilize this period of my life to grow despite the many challenges I'm facing?

Ask yourself, "What can I do?" not, "What can I not do?" I can give you several examples of people who were in worse situations than you are. Think of Daniel who lived in the palace of Nevuchadnezer. Visualize Natan Sharansky, who was put in solitary confinement in a notorious Soviet prison for nine years. Think of Esther, married to the wicked King Achashveirosh. Imagine yourself as the Maharam M'Rottenberg, who purposely told the Jewish people not to ransom him even after his death so that other great rabbis would be protected from kidnaping. What did they do with their days? They followed the rule, "If you can't do it on the outside, do it on the inside." Daniel became a prophet and a master of prayer. Esther developed into a model of modesty and *chessed*. If you read Natan Sharansky's book, *Fear No Evil*, you will see that he was very disciplined and tried to improve himself in every way possible even though he had scant knowledge of Torah. You have to stop comparing yourself to what you would be if you were living under different circumstances. Your heroes should be people who were in your place, who stood where you are.

Realize that your struggles are exactly the circumstances you need to become what Hashem wants you to be. Broaden your horizons and find new people to look up to. Tap into your talents and abilities. If you write well, sharpen your skills, and use your power to touch others. If you enjoy reading, take advantage of the plethora of excellent reading material available today. If you're a social person, reach out to the needy people in your community and use your talents for *chessed*. It may not be possible to affect the family you are living with, but you can work hard to use your gifts in the best possible way to become the person Hashem meant you to be.

UNDERSTANDING TRAGEDY

Q What is the right approach to enjoying life when there is such devastating suffering around us? We have been in exile for so long. I feel as if no matter how much I beg Hashem to end the galus, it is futile, much like a teardrop in the ocean.

In *Tehillim*, we read how things will be when the exile ends. "*Hayinu k'cholmim* — We will be like dreamers." The redemption will be so unbelievably wonderful that it will seem like a fantasy. On a deeper level, in hindsight, our exile will have been like a dream. A dream is a message from above. The way it is interpreted determines its outcome.

I was very moved by the eulogy of the father of the Mumbai victims. [In 2008, Rabbi Gavriel Noach and Rivka Holtzberg were killed during a terror attack on the Chabad House in Mumbai, India.] His message was that there had to be a positive meaning behind the tragedy. The depth of our pain was caused by the nobility of the people whose lives were lost. The Holtzbergs were like Avraham and Sarah. We aren't meant not to mourn what was destroyed, but we must also recognize that the reason the pain is so great is because of the beauty of the lives that were destroyed. We have to let that move us forward.

In *Koheles*, King Shlomo tells us, "It is better to go to a house of mourning than to a house of celebration." Death awakens us to what we should aspire to be. Mourning the exile is not enough. We have to go beyond what happened and ask ourselves what it is atoning for. We should take upon ourselves to emulate the extraordinary love for every Jew that the *kedoshim* of Mumbai had. We should rid ourselves of the sectarianism and nonsense that divide us. We have a lot to do. Of course we must pray for Mashiach's arrival, but coupled with that we must show Hashem with our deeds that we are indeed worthy of his coming.

THE MITZVAH OF GETTING WELL

I learned that Rabbi Yisrael Salanter said that if someone is sick, there is only one mitzvah, namely to get well. Is this an absolute ruling? How do I know if I'm too sick to do anything else? How do I find a balance between taking care of myself and taking care of others?

Whatever Rav Salanter said, he meant. However, I'll differentiate between physical and mental illnesses. There are physical conditions that require rest. If your situation warrants it, you must rest so that you can get back on your feet again.

On the other hand, my observation has been that for mental illnesses, doing is inherently part of recovery. I've seen people move beyond what anyone could imagine was their capacity by being active and giving to others. There are physical illnesses that don't require rest, and indeed, in that situation you won't get better by focusing on yourself rather than on others. Doing *chessed* might actually help you. Seeing yourself as functional, needed, and useful is probably one of the most important things you could do toward your own recovery.

If you are suffering from a mental illness, I would advise you strongly to try to do as much as you can for others without wearing yourself ragged, of course after consulting with your mental health professional. See that you get enough sleep, don't become overly anxious, and don't have unrealistic expectations in terms of gratitude from the people you've helped.

CONNECTING THROUGH SICKNESS

How can I use my illness to connect to Hashem?

Just wanting a relationship with Hashem means a lot. I would suggest that you encourage your visitors and friends to read to you and discuss with you some of the many books available on *bitachon*. I would recommend *Chovos HaLevavos, Shaar HaBitachon*. If you'd prefer something easier, *Pirkei Machshavah* by Rabbi Ezriel Tauber on *emunah* and *bitachon* is great. You can ask friends to bring you books from the library or buy them if you can afford it.

Don't just study these books. Talk to your friends about the concepts you have learned and share with them ways of applying them to daily life. Encourage them to discuss with you their own personal struggles and challenges with *bitachon*. This will benefit both you and your friends as you share and grow together. I would also recommend that you study the meaning of *Tehillim*.

Strengthening your *bitachon* by learning and sharing and deepening your understanding of *Tehillim* will surely bring you closer to Hashem.

GIVING VERSUS RECEIVING

I'm recovering from a long-term illness. I am trying to get completely better but nothing seems to be working. I have a constant stream of problems coming my way. My relatives and friends who are supposed to be helping me are critical and unsupportive. What is Hashem trying to tell me? Why can't I move on?

Everyone likes acknowledgment. Maybe some very great people have weaned themselves off it somewhat, but ordinary people need it a great deal. There are different ways to get it. One way is to do things that people admire. Another way is to act needy so that others will extend themselves and give them a feeling of validation and being cared for.

We all start out as recipients. Our sense of importance comes from being nurtured. As we get older, the balance shifts. The pleasure one gets from achievement overpowers the pleasure of receiving. By the time we reach adulthood, the balance shifts even more. We want acknowledgment but despise being cared for because it makes us feel small, which is what it should do.

I remember once visiting a Yerushalmi *tzaddekes* after her husband passed away. She seemed not only dispirited, but physically weakened, and I asked her what I could do to help her. The idea of my giving and her taking was repugnant to her.

When a person hasn't been given a lot of acknowledgment for who he is and what he does, the balance never shifts. In the face of authentic illness, there is a rediscovery of the pleasure of being cared for. This is not healthy. The pleasure of being and doing is much greater than the pleasure of receiving and needing.

Train yourself not to complain more than once a day, to one person. This will force you to speak about things other than what you are lacking. You need to be nurtured, but it must come from within you, not from other people. If you don't have the physical energy to do for others, learn to be a listener and offer others validation instead of subtly demanding it from people.

Something will change inside you. What Hashem may be trying to tell you in the discontent mode that you are in now is that you can be more and do more and live more by becoming a giver.

WIDOWHOOD: WHAT DO I DO WITH MY SUFFERING?

Q *I lost my husband at age 29 and now I am alone with my 18-month-old daughter. I haven't been searching for answers to the questions — "Why did this happen?" and "How could Hashem do this?" What I have been asking is what to do with my suffering. I feel that I can't just continue being the way I was before. Real cheshbon hanefesh is difficult, and when I try to think of ways to improve they seem trivial in light of what happened.*

A Suffering makes a person acutely aware of how painful certain situations can be. It awakens a kind of compassion that only someone who has been there can feel. I would suggest you transcend your suffering by using this empathy for something purposeful.

Somewhere out there, there are other young widows just like you. When the time is ripe and when you have the inner space to do so, create a support group for widows. You obviously have the sensitivity and the ability to move beyond "why" to "what." Helping others in a similar situation can be a very great *chessed*, and may it bring you fulfillment and *nechamah*.

SHOULD MY HUSBAND STAY IN AN UNFULFILLING BUT SECURE JOB?

Q *My clever, talented husband is stuck in a dead-end job with very little stimulation and hope for promotion. I don't know if Hashem wants him to leave his job without knowing whether he will find something better, or make do with feeling unfulfilled at work. How can I help him?*

A If you examine the lives of some of our great leaders, you'll find that many of them were ordinary craftsmen and shopkeepers. Rashi was a wine merchant, the Ohr HaChaim was a goldsmith, and the Chofetz Chaim ran a grocery for a short period of time. Do you think their work gave them fulfillment? They did it to support their families, which is a noble goal in and of itself.

We don't know the end of our life stories. It could be that at this point in your husband's life, he is meant to find satisfaction, like Rashi, in activities outside of work. To make that happen, he will need to organize his day. It could be this is just a transient period in his life. His main test may be withstanding the many *nisyonos* prevalent in the workplace, such as maintaining integrity, judging others favorably, and observing *shemiras einayim*.

A final possibility is that he is meant to feel the discontent so that it will propel him to move on to something else. Obviously, he cannot leave his existing job without having a comparable position waiting for him. If you can keep your ears open for job possibilities available in his field or other opportunities in which his time could be spent productively when he is not working, that would be a great help.

CHILDLESSNESS – IS IT YISSURIM SHEL AHAVAH?

Q *You once mentioned that childlessness is not considered yissurim shel ahavah. If so, what is the reason for the suffering of childlessness? In addition, if affliction comes from Hashem in order to help us get closer to Him, how can one person make another person suffer through ayin hara?*

A Hashem sends suffering upon a person not only out of love, but also for the sake of *tikkun*. According to the Arizal, most of us have already been in this world before and are here again to correct previous mistakes. Childlessness draws a person closer to Hashem, which is why all the *Avos* and *Imahos*, except for Leah, were childless at the beginning. Therefore, it's fair to understand that the trial of childlessness is probably for the purpose of *tikkun*. *Tikkun* doesn't necessarily mean putting your finger on what is broken and fixing it. It means looking at the options that are open to you and consistently choosing the best ones. In this way you will eventually arrive at your *tikkun* whether you know what it is or not.

Suffering comes from Hashem. However, He uses different mediums as his agents. There are many ways to achieve the same end. If suffering is meant to occur through human choice, placing someone who needs to suffer within close parameters of a person who will bring that about may be part of the master plan.

Unlike a human who can shoot only one arrow at a time, Hashem can aim at many targets at the same time. Every detail of a person's suffering — the way it comes about, the duration of the suffering, and its effect on other people — are all part of Hashem's master plan.

WHAT TO SAY TO A CHILDLESS FRIEND

I have a close friend who has been married for about four years and has no children. I would like to know what words of chizuk and emunah to offer her. How does one comfort someone in such a difficult situation, especially a woman who was put on this earth to be a mother?

How do you know what this woman was put on earth to do? It could be that her purpose is to be a mother, and it may happen eventually. But obviously Hashem sends people into the world for other reasons too. Our own *tafkid* is difficult to pinpoint, let alone someone else's. There may be things she is meant to accomplish specifically because she has no children to distract her. She may need a certain amount of freedom for self-development, or she may need to contribute something to the world before she has a child. Certainly she has a worthwhile purpose, even if she never becomes a mother.

You can give your friend *chizuk* in subtle ways, not by discussing childless couples who were helped, but by telling her how Hashem is there for people in difficult times. You can tell her stories of situations in which people were aware of Hashem's capacity to help them. Offer her support through non-judgmental listening and by being empathetic.

SUFFERING — ARE THERE NO CHOICES?

Q *In one of your classes, you mentioned that when we suffer we have no choices. Does that mean we have no choice in how to accept the suffering?*

A What I meant is that we obviously have no choice whether to suffer or not. What we do with the suffering is up to us. We can become embittered, we can choose not to act, or we can grow and develop and reach unimaginable spiritual heights precisely because of the suffering.

FIGHTING ADVERSITY WHILE BECOMING OBSERVANT

Q *I teach a class to a group of young women who are growing in their knowledge and observance of Judaism. What practical advice can I give them to stay motivated when faced with opposition and discouragement, both at home and in their social circles? At this early point, their commitment to Judaism and to further observance is still very fragile.*

A There are several things you have to do. The first step is to normalize their difficulties for them through using humor and sharing personal experiences. If you ever encountered opposition, had embarrassing moments, or know anyone who did, share it with them. Make the problems appear less insurmountable and scary. Tell them about other people who went through the process and survived.

Try in subtle ways to get them to support one another. Have them form their own little nucleus or social group so that they can give each other strength. Make it clear to them that they can forgive themselves if they slip up. Everyone has ups and downs. Nobody moves straight up.

If your students are having problems at home, teach them to give their family members brief, reasonable explanations for what they are doing. Tell them to admit when they do not know instead of fudging it. Refer them to programs that will help them deepen their knowledge so they will have more of a basis to fall back on when they are called upon to explain their new practices.

DOES HASHEM WANT TO HEAR FROM ME?

Q *I've learned that Hashem gives nisyonos to those who can grow from them and to those whose prayers He longs for. Baruch Hashem, my life is running smoothly. Does this mean that Hashem doesn't want to hear from me? I thank Hashem all the time, but I also can't help constantly feeling that something bad may be looming on the horizon. Does this fear stem from a lack of emunah, or from an inaccurate view of Hashem as a loving Father, or from a low self-esteem that's inhibiting spiritual growth?*

A The Rambam tells us that we are all in the midst of a *nisayon*. Even people who are living seemingly easy lives face the test of not taking credit for achieving the blessings they have been granted. Continue thanking Hashem for all the good He's provided you with. Give Him the *nachas* of serving Him with joy. When you wake up in the morning, say *Modeh Ani* with passion and enthusiasm. Call out to Hashem with the same kind of force and emotion as a poverty-stricken person would cry out to Him for his basic needs.

Your joy should be infectious. When people would ask Rav Noach Weinberg, "What is the most important *kiruv* tool?" he'd answer, "Happiness." You can save countless lives just by teaching people the art of appreciation and gratitude.

The Rambam says, as you feel intuitively, that our life spans are like circles that go around and around. A person may be up today and down tomorrow. We should all expect that life will present us with different challenges. Few of us will face the same *nisayon* forever. But the same loving, caring Father Who gives us *nisyonos* that are obviously good also gives us *nisyonos* that may appear bad. Even if Hashem decides to test you with a daunting trial, hold on to your sense of gratitude and love for Him.

Despair stems from a lack of *emunah*. It comes from failing to believe that whatever Hashem does is good and compassionate, and that something painful may in fact be for *tikkun*. Your flaw in *emunah* is that though your *emunah* is real, it is not broad enough. It doesn't take into account that even the seemingly bad things that happen to us are in fact for our good and come from the same compassionate Source. Work on strengthening that, and then any challenge Hashem may send your way will only be a catalyst for growth.

THE JEWISH WOMEN IN MITZRAYIM

Q *How did the women in Mitzrayim bring new life into a world that looked so bleak? What do you think gave them the strength to have children during times of such great difficulty? It's hard to even minimally comprehend how they reached such great levels. Can you shed some light on this?*

A These women were on a very high *madreigah*. It is not for nothing that *Chazal* say that in the *zechus* of the *nashim tzidkaniyos* of Mitzrayim, the Jews were redeemed from exile.

Their merit was the merit of *emunah*. *Emunah* means believing that everything, even in their case the horrors of their existence in *Mitzrayim*, comes from Hashem and that it is all for *tikkun*.

They believed that there would be light at the end of the tunnel. Their children would have a different future, and the more souls the women brought down, the more holiness would come into the world. They were thinking thoughts of *emunah*. Hashem would ultimately bring what was good in the midst of all the blackness and horror.

This is the kind of *emunah* Avraham had during *bris bein habesarim*. Hashem showed him the entire future of the Jewish people, including all the suffering they would encounter. Avraham felt the pain of his children. He was more compassionate and full of *chessed* than we can ever comprehend. Yet he did not flinch at the tragedies. He understood that whatever *tikkun* was taking place made everything worthwhile.

Love of Hashem, belief in the future, and steadfast *bitachon* carried the women of *Mitzrayim* through the bitter exile. Indeed, in terrible times, Jews have chosen to marry and build families. Marriages took place in the ghettos during the bleakest era of World War II. It was not a small *madreigah*; it was awesome. But it is something that we can begin to grasp if we study what genuine *emunah* really is.

On Being a Jewish Woman

MANAGING THE HOME

I'm not good at running and managing my home. I find it boring and overwhelming. There's always another load of laundry to do and another set of dishes to wash. My family is on a budget that doesn't allow for cleaning help. I realize that housekeeping is an important responsibility. How can I improve?

You and I should meet. I don't enjoy housekeeping either. You're not a natural. Neither am I. However, it has to be done in order to keep a sense of order and cleanliness in the home. Read time-management and housekeeping books. I particularly recommend two excellent books, "It's About Time" by Chaya Levine and Nechamah Berg, and "Akeres HaBayis" by Sarah Chana Radcliffe. These books will help you organize your day so that you can painlessly put things together in a short time. Although their methods are different, you can study both books and adapt what works best for you.

Here are some techniques:

Don't begin with things that have to be done. Start with chores that will give you a feeling of orderliness. Begin with the front room or the kitchen. If you get the dishes in the sink (you don't need to wash them yet), the counters and tables clear, and the floor swept clean, the kitchen will look neat even though it's not yet entirely clean. Then go on to the living room. Clear the floor. Don't put things away room by room. Go through the hall and the kitchen and collect all stray objects on the main table. When you're done you can sort things out. Your living room will look orderly because there is nothing on the floor, couch, or table. Then go on to the bathroom. If the toilet is clean and there is toilet paper and nothing out of place, you're ready to move on. Go to the bedroom. Make the beds. Pick up the stuff from the floor. All this shouldn't take a long time and can be done between other things with a tape or CD player on. Once your house is reasonably in order, your mind-set will change.

In terms of having things really clean, make your own schedule for what works for you. Buy colored index cards. Go through what has to be done in your house and how many times. Write down everything and use different colors to mark jobs that have to be done weekly, jobs that must be done monthly, and jobs that must be done yearly.

Commit yourself to get through what has to be done. Every day, do some of the things that have to be done weekly. Every two weeks, do some of the things that have to be done monthly. Every month, do some of the things that have to be done yearly. You can choose to do the dishes once or twice a day. It doesn't have to be every time a dish gets dirty. You can mop the floor at the beginning or end of the day. You can do one room a day so that it's really clean.

Teach yourself the discipline of cleaning up as you cook. It may sound time-consuming but it really isn't. Learn the art of cooking and baking in bulk. Always make more than needed and freeze the rest. If you have a planned menu, you can go shopping once a month for the basics and then make little trips for perishables.

Don't let housekeeping take over your life. Get organized, learn to use your time effectively, and maybe one day you'll even come to enjoy it.

HOW DO I FOCUS ON SPIRITUALITY AS A WIFE AND MOTHER?

Q *I know intellectually that my role is to be a wife and mother, but I often get stuck in the shallow and superficial aspects of it. I try to listen to at least one shiur a day, I'm involved with different self-growth groups, and I am busy with various chassadim. Yet I still feel unfulfilled. What can I do to make sure that I am maximizing my spiritual potential and that when I go to sleep at night I don't feel that it was just a meaningless day?*

A You're doing everything right, but for some reason the spiritual messages you're getting are not entering your life. I would advise you to switch the topic of your *shiur* to something with *penimiyus* that will affect your attitude. Studying Chassidic works such as *Nesivos Shalom* is a good start. You will find that when you learn about *ahavas reyim* it will effect actual changes in your interaction with your friends, children, and husband. Alternatively, if you prefer something more challenging, I would suggest studying the first *Maamar* in *Likkutei Moharan*, not for the sake of intellectual stimulation, but to help you refocus on the way you look at things.

Let the learning flow down to who you really are, even when working on mundane tasks like sorting laundry or checking rice. Your soul, mind, emotions, and actions should ideally be on the same page. This was the level Yaakov Avinu reached, and this is why he was called

"*Ish Tam.*" Try to step out of yourself to see the beauty and preciousness in the little things in life. For example, when you are feeding the baby, don't try to finish quickly so you can move on to the next thing. Revel in the fact that you have a baby, that he can eat, and that he is delighting in his food. Realize that the light that you see here comes from a single Source, Who is the Power that energizes everything. Focus on the depth and intricacies of creation and its subtle meaning.

Internalize the inner meaning of Torah and you'll discover fresh profundity and purpose in your life.

BRINGING HASHEM'S SHECHINAH INTO THE WORLD

Q *After the sin of Adam, the Shechinah departed to a certain extent from this world. Avraham and Moshe brought it back somewhat. However, the sins of the subsequent generations caused it to distance itself once more. What can we as Jewish women do to bring the Shechinah down again?*

A When we refer to the *Shechinah,* we mean Hashem's Presence in this world as we experience it. *Gan Eden* is absolute *hashraas haShechinah.* When Adam sinned, he caused the first distancing of the *Shechinah.* The evil acts of Kayin, the generation of the Flood, and the people who built the Tower of Bavel caused the Divine Presence to move farther away. More *mechitzos* were created, fueled by rampant jealousy, lust, and the desire for honor. The *Avos* and the subsequent great leaders of the Jewish people, including Moshe, Amram, and Kehas, removed some of these barriers and brought the *Shechinah* closer. Avraham eradicated the *mechitzah* of idol worship and drew Hashem's Presence down through *chessed.* Yitzchak did battle with egoism and brought the Divine Presence into the world through prayer. Yaakov, who manifested truth and rejected falsehood, drew down the *sefiros*.

Women are exceptionally strong in *emunah*. Maintaining faith during difficult times draws down the *Shechinah*. Creating a home where serenity reigns is another way of bringing down the Divine Presence. This is connected to *emunah*, because the voice of anger is really saying, "Whatever is happening is not acceptable," as opposed to *emunah*, which says, "It is what it is. Let me use this for *tikkun*."

When a woman dresses with *tzniyus* she emphasizes that her external aspect is only a garment and not the essence of her reality. This too brings sanctity into the world. Each person's life is replete with opportunities for revelation. For one person, *simchah shel mitzvah* is a way to draw down the *Shechinah*. For another person, standing firm against difficulties increases revelation. It all depends on the life Hashem opens up for you. However, the most significant way for women to bring the *Shechinah* into their lives is to work on their *emunah*.

BALANCING CHESSED WITH A HEALTHY FAMILY LIFE

Q *I am a wife and the mother of a one-year-old boy. I work part-time from home for a Jewish outreach shul. I end up working a lot more than my official hours because I am constantly called on to help people. On the one hand, my child and husband suffer because of this, but on the other hand, how can I refuse to help people in need? I'm so often put in situations in which I can do so much good at the expense of myself and my family. How do I know when to stop and how?*

A I would suggest you dedicate two hours every day during which you don't answer the phones at all. These hours should be the hour that your husband is expected home and one hour during the day that you devote exclusively to your son. It's not much, but it will take self-discipline to give both of them your full attention. This can change things. If you keep these hours sacred for your family, then you won't have to worry so much about the other times. It's okay to do *chessed* over the phone while holding your baby or cooking for Shabbos. It may also help if your shul has a congregant who would be happy to volunteer. You can delegate work to her, which will save you time and benefit her.

Make sure to give yourself focused time too, so that you don't become distracted and stressed out. Have your babysitter stay an extra hour and grab a nap during the day. Improving your home organization and time-management skills can also make a big difference. Don't worry about the little things. Put your family first, mentally and emotionally. When they talk, really listen to them. When they need you, be responsive. As long as your husband and child feel beloved, they will participate with you instead of trying to disengage you.

I believe that children grow up unhappy not because they were never given enough attention but because they felt unloved. You need to develop enough *bitachon* to realize that if you cannot accomplish something in terms of where your priorities are, then Hashem does not want you to do it. You can do only as much as your limited time and strength allow. Leave the rest up to Hashem.

THE LIFE TASK OF A CHILDLESS WOMAN

I am childless, happily married, about to turn 50, and quite honestly feeling very lost since I got laid off from my job almost a year ago. I can relate to the story of Lech Lecha and feel Hashem has said to me – "Pick up. Go ..." But to where? What is my mission? Why am I here? If a woman's primary function is to be a mother, what is the purpose of a woman who will never be one?

"*Lech Lecha*" means "go to you." Hashem sometimes presents us with situations that force us to figure ourselves out and thereby move beyond what we were before. A person can do this on several levels.

"*Artzecha*" — your land, the part of you that's earthy, lazy, depressed, or tied down to external order. Hashem has forced you to step out of this by taking your job away. You can no longer submerge yourself in routine material efforts.

"*Moladetcha*" — your inborn traits. Hashem made you childless and thereby moved you beyond the biological destiny of most women.

"*Mibeis avicha*" — your father's home. A father provides a child's form — the ideas and principles that shape his life.

You need to broaden your horizons and discover new interests. In order to find yourself, you have to know your abilities and what is accessible and needed in your particular area. Think about what you're good at and what you like to do. That may be what your destiny really is. You may argue that you need a job that pays and that doing what you like might not be all that lucrative. Still, you should make room for this. It may mean combining it with a regular job, but begin to walk in that direction.

In addition, work on developing "*birur.*" The idea of *birur* is finding the element of divinity in a situation and letting that become revealed. For example, if you are a real estate broker, you can focus on concerning yourself with people's needs and taking pleasure in helping them. Obviously this is not a broker's key motive, but if you succeed in making *birur* a part of your life, you can transform ordinary work into something eternal.

LIVING A KOLLEL LIFESTYLE AND STRUGGLING TO BE B'SIMCHAH

Q *Being responsible for cooking, cleaning, and childcare, along with pursuing a demanding career to support my husband's learning, at times leaves me sad and angry, as I feel unable to succeed in any area. Do you have suggestions for how I can be b'simchah even when I am tired, frustrated, and overwhelmed?*

A You do not always have to be *b'simchah*. It's okay to be frazzled when Shabbos comes in at 4 p.m. and you're racing against the clock to finish on time. You don't have to start dancing in the supermarket when you notice that the *treif* chickens cost a fraction of the price of the kosher ones.

It says, *"Lefum tzara agra."* This means that your values are such that you're willing to suffer a certain amount of frustration and difficulty to get something you want very much. *Kol hakavod* that you find it worthwhile to struggle so that your husband can dedicate himself to Torah. Of course, a person should work at acquiring *simchah shel mitzvah*. Appreciate that the trade-off you're making is worth it. Look forward to reaping the fruits of your labor — a worthy husband, children who value Torah, and a home where the *yetzer hara* is defeated because *"Torah tavlin lo."*

It's okay to find the going rough at times. Try to make it easier by drastically lowering your standards. Your house does not have to look perfect. Prioritize what needs to get done. I've spoken to respected rebbetzins who told me that there was a good deal of disorder in their homes when they were raising young children and supporting their husbands in learning. You need to work *b'emunah* at your job, but you don't have to be the star of the team. Give yourself permission to define success as working within the parameters of your real goals, which are to build a warm Torah home, support your husband in his spiritual growth, and raise happy, healthy, well-adjusted children.

KOLLEL AT THE CHILDREN'S EXPENSE

Q *For many women who are not superwomen, working at a demanding job in order to keep their husbands in kollel means that these mothers simply don't have the same emotional energy, patience, and enthusiasm to invest in their children. Shouldn't families be encouraged to reprioritize kollel if it is at the expense of their children?*

A This is a very individualized issue. I don't think there's anyone who would say it's the wife's problem if she isn't coping and the children are suffering. It is the husband's responsibility to provide for his family. Most Rabbanim would recommend that the wife drastically reduce her expenses so that she does not feel compelled to work so many hours. If this is not feasible, moving to an area where the standard of living is lower may help. A third option would be for the husband to leave *kollel* so that the wife can raise the children. Women working hard is not a new phenomenon. Women not working hard and spending their days at home in a leisurely fashion is at most a phenomenon of the last two generations.

I don't think there is one specific reason why children go off the *derech*. Many people struggle with their children, even the most committed and wonderful families. Despite this, the home often factors in such problems.

I would say the highest percentage of children at risk are those from families with limited commitment to Torah observance where both parents work. The next-largest category includes children whose parents' own Judaism is hazy and less defined. These children don't have a strong sense of what's expected of them, and they are therefore unsure exactly where they fit in. When the message they get at home is not the same as what they get in school, problems naturally develop. Having a father who works and a mother who stays home doesn't necessarily produce children who are less affected by the outside world. Children from wealthy families seem to do less well than children from more modest backgrounds. Kids from *kollel* families where the parents truly want the life they're living usually turn out happy.

If the children are suffering, the husband should go to work. If the wife is managing and would like to continue working, then there's no reason why she shouldn't. However, there is a lot of gray area here, and each individual situation should be judged on its own.

PERSONAL GROWTH VERSUS FAMILY OBLIGATIONS

In order to work on my deveikus b'Hashem, I get up early in the morning to daven, learn, and think. As a mother of six children, this is difficult, as it forces me to go to sleep early, making me less available to my husband and my older children. If I try to be more "down to earth" and skip my morning sessions, I end up feeling depressed and empty. Getting someone to care for the children at certain times so I have time for myself is not an option, as I don't want to sacrifice my children's welfare for my selfish spiritual needs. Dissociating from what I am doing and thinking lofty thoughts as I care for my family won't work, as they need me to focus on them. Doing mundane tasks and relying on Hashem to reward me with spiritual fulfillment doesn't satisfy me, as I want a relationship that I can build. Can you give me some guidance?

With six children, you won't be able to do things exactly the way you want to. However, you have to nurture yourself, so I would recommend that you set aside small nuggets of spiritual time to pray and learn.

Say the *Birchos HaShachar* and *Ahavah Rabbah*, which contain the components of praise, request, and thanks. Say these with real devotion and depth. Study some commentaries on these prayers and write down the explanations that move you. Make your davening, even if it is only 10 minutes, creative and meaningful.

Set aside time to learn every day. Learn less, but learn what inspires you. If Chassidus speaks to you, I would recommend studying the daily portion of *Tanya* because it's easy to do in small segments in a short amount of time. Alternatively, *Sfas Emes* can be broken down into sections so that you can finish one section in a week. Focus on what you've learned and ask yourself how you can apply its lessons to your daily life. If *Chumash* is what moves you, I would recommend *Peirush HaRamban Al HaTorah* or the *Stone Chumash*.

In everyone's workday at home there are times when they are interactive and times when they are not. You can move your thinking time to those latter hours. *It* says in *Shir HaShirim*, "Al mishkavi ba'leilos — I sought You Hashem on my bed at night." When your children are sleeping, lie down or sit down on a chair and think and speak to Hashem.

Your relationship and verbal interaction with your husband and older children is critical. Don't go to sleep early and miss this precious time to build a close connection with them. Learn to make your 10-minute spiritual breaks count like an hour. This is what Hashem wants from you at this point in your life, and ultimately you'll be doing His Will.

DOMESTIC WORK AND OUTSIDE EMPLOYMENT

I am very much looking forward to being a wife and mother, and I want to give my future family all the love and care they need. However, I find housework boring and draining. People I have dated have been strongly opposed to a woman "neglecting her duties" by working outside the home and expecting a husband to share the household work. I feel that I can be at my best only when I have time outside the house for other pursuits, and I think I'd feel resentful of a husband who expected that the responsibility for the majority of domestic work should fall on me. What is the Torah outlook?

There is no halachah requiring you to engage in domestic work. You do, however, have a responsibility to build a Jewish home. If you're willing to invest a significant amount of your salary into hiring help and buying yourself the best that technology offers, so that the maid mops the floors and the dishwasher washes the dishes, that's fine. You don't have to do the actual work, but you have to see that it gets done.

When I mention this to some women, they counter, "Even if we can afford to hire help, why shouldn't our husbands do half the work?" Here the issue isn't disliking domestic work, but buying into the feminist myth that men and women are good at identical things and share the same desires. There's no reason why a husband should be obligated to help in the house unless his wife needs it. This is a *bedi'eved* situation. Most women with young children require their husband's assistance, whether they work or not. In this case, of course your husband should help.

But ideally you should come to a point where you can say, "This is my home and I am happy to take full responsibility for it."

JETLAGGED MOM

What is a standard range of mood or consciousness for a married woman with young children? I feel foggy when I get up and exhausted most of the day. My main goal is staying calm with the children and organized with the house. The truth is I've always worked outside the home, but this year I decided to stop. I wonder whether that is related to my state of mind.

If you ask people what gives them fulfillment, they will not answer leisure. Leisure is desirable as a way to recharge one's batteries, but it is not seen as an end in itself. Studies show that when people retire they experience physical and mental decline. The problem inherent in housekeeping is that there isn't enough structure. It is repetitive and never-ending. Fulfillment and achievement come from defined goals.

How do you create realistic objectives for yourself in the house? Learning organization and time management can help you set priorities. If you see yourself accomplishing externally, it will give you the inner space to have realistic goals in terms of who you're becoming as you keep house and what your children are experiencing when they're at home with you.

There are mothers with large families and small apartments who are able to create an atmosphere of serenity, enthusiasm, and joy. This isn't because they're good and you're bad. It comes from having a sense of what is *ikar* and what is *tafel*, and having the organizational skills to realize one's goals. The *ikar* is to have a home where you encourage creativity and growth, where your family is happy, and where their needs are fulfilled. All of this is achievable. If you saw yourself doing it, you wouldn't be as tired as you are now. Feeling foggy can be a consequence of lack of organization or burnout. You may have to reprioritize your time to nurture yourself physically and spiritually.

It is very possible that you would be happier working outside the home. Work comes along with definable goals, structure, and achievement, which can give you fulfillment. The question is whether you can get this same feeling in your own home or if you really need to work outside to make it happen. I truly believe that proper time management and believing in yourself can do it for you.

A WOMAN'S NEED FOR VERBALIZATION

Q *What is the most ideal way for a woman to use her strength of expression?*

A If you find yourself constantly talking about your life, you are running the risk of losing contact with your inner self.
If you feel validated only by talking to other people, you are in a sense interrupting the flow of your relationship with Hashem. A woman needs to learn to use her desire to express herself in a way that involves restraint and self-discipline. The purposeful and deep need for women to speak is meant to make other people feel understood. It is a great and meaningful gift. Expressing your thoughts and feelings can be a way of positively influencing others.

Women were given *binah yeseirah* in order to build. Indeed, the word *binah*, which is the source of a women's ability to understand and her need to be understood, is related to the verb *boneh*, to build, which is what this strength is meant to do.

FINDING TIME TO MAKE A UNIQUE CONTRIBUTION

Q *When I was younger and had more time, I used to think I had a mission to accomplish with my gifts and talents. Now family obligations consume most of my time and energy, and I wonder if I was wrong.*

There are three possibilities here: The first is the magic word called "later." If your present situation demands that a significant amount of your time be spent with your family, you need to stay focused. Now isn't the time to veer off in different directions.

I have a friend who is a book publisher. When she had more going on at home, she was a birthing coach, which required much less time commitment. In fact, when her children were really young, she didn't work out of the house at all. There's a time in life for everything. We see this with Yaakov, whose name was changed to Yisrael when his mission in life changed.

A second issue may be your purpose or your unique gift. People usually like to do what they're good at. If you find there is still room in your life for utilizing your gifts but you don't feel drawn to do what you've previously done, maybe you need to reevaluate what your mission really is.

A third possibility may be that you need to master the art of time management. I would recommend you read some books on the topic. This will help you de-clutter your life and find the space to do the things you really want to do.

CAREER OR CHILDREN

Although having children did not come easily to me, now, thank G-d, I have three school-age children. Sometimes I can't help feeling like I'm neither here nor there — not really immersed in child-rearing to the exclusion of everything else, but not entirely free to go back to school to pursue my interests. I can only imagine how betrayed women who planned careers as prospective mothers and were not fortunate enough to get married and have kids must feel.

It seems like you see only two possibilities of fulfillment. One is full-time employment in a demanding career, and the other is full-time mothering. However, there are many other ways to spend time that are fulfilling and interesting.

When people's basic physical needs are met, they usually pursue aesthetic pleasure. After that, they search for relationships. Think about the individuals you like the most. Ask yourself why you like them. The answers will probably be spiritual. You can't weigh devotion or measure thoughtfulness. Feeling loyal, kind, and positive when you are with a person makes you like him even more. This is called spiritual bonding, and it is a very deep pleasure.

You need opportunities for spiritual bonding. It can take place within your family, through *tefillah,* through *chessed,* or by taking a course that can equip you to help others. If Hashem gave you the ability to do more, then by all means do more.

Some single or childless women may feel betrayed, but the proper response is, "This is where I am supposed to be, and I am going to find the good in it." The Sfas Emes explains that when Hashem told Avraham, "*Lech lecha,*" He did not tell him where to go because He wanted to bring Avraham to the maximum level of *bitul haratzon,* negation of his own will. Hashem gave him the opportunity to say, "I will go where You will lead me, wherever that may be."

Everyone is told, "*Lech lecha,*" to go to Eretz Yisrael, in a theoretical sense, the place of *bitul haratzon.* Ask yourself, "How can I do Hashem's Will without questions?" By giving you time and space, Hashem is saying, "Go where I am leading you."

Don't waste this time. Fill it with meaning and depth by nurturing your relationship with Hashem and giving to others in a way that will expand your inner self.

BALANCING MY HUSBAND'S LEARNING AND HIS HELP IN THE HOUSE

Q *My husband works full-time and learns at night. Sometimes I don't push him out the door as quickly as I should in the evenings, because he offers to help with the kids, and that feels good. Can you give me more clarity on how valuable my husband's learning is and how I should be working on myself not to accept his help? I really want to move in that direction.*

A It is wonderful that you want to work on valuing your husband's Torah more. Some women would just say, "He's so helpful and kind," and not take it any further.

There are three things you should consider. First, a moment of learning can never be replaced. In contrast, under normal circumstances there is almost nothing your husband can do in the house that is indispensable. This world is very transient. The only thing that endures is Torah. If he doesn't help put the kids to bed, they will get to bed at some point anyway. Whatever he does to help, it still would have happened without him and it will happen again. However, Torah learning is eternal. It validates creation, turns the world into a good place, and brings rectification. There is so much evil in the world. Torah learning can make the difference in tipping the world's scale toward merit. So realize that you are exchanging something transient for something eternal.

Second, you are creating your portion in the World to Come, not just his.

Third, you need to understand the value of Torah itself. Torah is the bond with Hashem. It is the conduit through which Hashem makes His Presence felt in this world. By studying His Will and making it a part of our lives, we connect with Him in a very real way.

So when you sacrifice to help your husband learn, you become his full partner in enabling him to achieve eternity, realize his spiritual potential, and bring greater merit into this world.

SHOULD I HAVE MORE CHILDREN?

Q *Oftentimes I hear women saying, "That's it. I'm done having children." Sometimes these thoughts go through my mind too, just because our lives are so challenging and demanding. Can you give me the right perspective on the issue so that later on in life, when it's too late, I won't regret it?*

A It's very normal for a woman to say, "I've had it." In fact, it was so normal that long ago a woman had to offer a sacrifice after childbirth. But the prospect of later remorse is a big possibility. Each child is a world onto itself. When you see your grown children and how they've all turned into responsible human beings, it's hard to regret that you brought them into the world. If your emotional and physical health is good, it's a mistake to say, "That's it," because there's nothing you will treasure more in the end.

Of course, when the children are young, it's sometimes difficult. I don't miss the time my kids would climb into my bed in the wee hours of the morning. I remember having this dream when my children were little: "One day I will get up when I want to get up." It's fine. I don't yearn for those years. But Hashem has a plan. When you're young and energetic, that's the time to raise kids. These are the years to exert yourself, to run the race, to exercise your spiritual and physical muscles to the utmost. If you have five or six kids, what's wrong with having fifteen or sixteen? Don't limit Hashem's hand. There's a verse in *Koheles*, "… in the evening do not let your hand rest." This is telling us to continue our efforts even after we've brought forth our first crops. Rav Shach would often remind people that he was the thirteenth child. All of his siblings were killed in the Holocaust.

You never know which child will be the source of blessing. True, you also don't know how much effort and stress another child will bring. One of the curses Chavah received was raising children with anxiety. However, I don't think people with two children have less stress than people with ten children. There's a possibility of having tension from all sorts of directions, regardless of family size.

Worrying how you will support so many children is not a Torah outlook. It says in the Gemara that every creation comes into the world with its own source of sustenance. Put your trust in Hashem and rejoice with every new child you merit to bring into the world.

ALL THOSE KIDS — WHAT IS IT ABOUT?

Q. My very religious sister is depressed because she has "only" seven kids. According to her, most of her friends have at least ten to twelve children. Are religious Jews really expected to repopulate the world? Do you think that having all these kids is a trend or a competition or one more lifestyle choice turned into an absolute law?

A. You probably assume that your sister is depressed because she's somehow failing in the unstated competition to have as many kids as possible. There may be another reason. Maybe she sees intrinsic value in raising children and loves having them. This is not a lot stranger than the *Imahos* who yearned for children. When Leah already gave birth to her "fair share" of tribes, she was grateful when she was granted more. Avraham was 100 years old when he had Yitzchak.

Can you picture an artist saying, "I've had enough of art. No more paintings for me"? Can you imagine an accomplished lawyer who loves the give-and-take of law saying, "This is my last case"? What people treasure most of all is self-actualization and creativity. There's nothing that can hold a candle to raising a child — not art, not a professional career, not anything. However, this is conditional on being willing to invest yourself in your child. The external aspect of child-raising isn't all that exciting, but the soul stuff is awesome.

Every child that comes into the world brings a level of light that was never there before. There is no reason not to have more children unless there are physical or emotional issues, and we don't idealize such a situation.

FINDING TIME FOR MYSELF IN A VERY BUSY SCHEDULE

Q *My husband works a full day, and I work half a day running a day care center in my home in Yerushalayim. Recently my husband joined a night kollel, and I am very happy that he is learning. However, I feel stressed out watching other people's kids and my kids all day with no time for myself. I have one child in particular who is very challenging and will not fall asleep easily at night. I wish my husband was home in the evenings to discipline him. I feel extraordinarily guilty suggesting that he leave kollel so I can have a breather. What do you suggest?*

A Nothing happens if a kid doesn't fall asleep right away. Tell him he can read or do some other quiet pursuit as long as he stays in his room and doesn't wake the others. Eventually he'll fall asleep on his own.

As for you, no matter how you have to scale down — by buying simpler food, making do with less clothing, or giving up on small luxuries — you must designate one night a week as your own. Leave the kids with a babysitter and do something you enjoy. You need time for yourself. Go swimming, visit friends, travel to the *Kosel*. Spend whatever you need to for as long as you need to so that you have that breathing space. This is vital for you.

If none of this is possible, try to prepare for Shabbos on Thursday and have things done so you can take a breather Friday afternoon. I know women who really couldn't cut things out of their budget who would switch off with each other one afternoon a week so they could have some time without the kids.

You must have a break. Make it happen.

SHOULD I BE STAYING HOME?

Q *The Midrash relates that Dinah fell into the hands of Shechem because she was a "yatzanis," a woman who frequently left her home. The Midrash continues by stating the importance of a married woman remaining inside her home and not going out, lest she be a stumbling block for men. What does this mean practically for Jewish woman today? I love going outside; I like taking exercise walks, going to work, and even doing the occasional shopping, for a change of scenery. Should I limit my excursions?*

A The same Sarah who is praised, "Behold she is in the tent," is described as a full partner with Avraham in his efforts to draw people closer to Hashem. While Avraham converted the men, Sarah converted the women. Rashi also notes that because Yaakov concealed Dinah from Esav, Shechem took her. Even before she was a *yatzanis*, she was doomed.

It's important to differentiate between going out as a means of self-expression and going out for a specific purpose. A woman's strongest point is her innerness. It is the source of her *binah* and her willingness to understand herself and others. Going out because you're restless at home or because you have no strong sense of self is certainly not what a woman is meant to be. In fact, Hashem created Chavah from the inner part of Adam so that she would not be a *yatzanis*.

In the old days, when feminism was still strong, there was a apron with the slogan, "For this I went to college?," which really means, "Does it suit an educated person like me to be relegated to cooking, serving, and cleaning up?"

I'm all for technological advances that ease responsibility, but a woman's first duty is to care for the needs of her family. How she goes about doing it depends on the situation. Empathy and nurturing are a woman's virtues. You can't express caring for a child if his needs aren't met. A woman's role is to take her inner self and address it primarily, but not exclusively, to the home. Building people requires one-on-one contact. You can't do that if you're restless and unable to devote yourself to others. If there's this constant need to get away, if you feel like your home is a prison, if you don't like nurturing because negating the self and focusing on others is undesirable, there's a problem.

The smallest crack in the edifice of the *Avos* had implications forever. Indeed, something small Dinah did was judged severely. We do have to be wary of going out as an escape as opposed to a means to an end or for a purpose. The part of us that is a *yatzanis*, that could awaken positivity, can be used for good. Making friends feel appreciated, teaching a class, or working outside the home in order to help pay expenses are worthy pursuits. However, when it takes a woman away from her primary role as a focused, devoted nurturer, it is no longer commendable.

TORAH LEARNING FOR WOMEN BEFORE AND AFTER MARRIAGE

Before I was married I used to love studying Torah. Learning uplifted me tremendously. Now I would rather wash dishes than listen to a d'var Torah. I sit down to study only when my husband asks me to learn with him, and I'm eager to finish. I zone out when I hear speakers. Is this normal? Is it a yeridah? Do you have any suggestions for how to move in the right direction?

There's absolutely no essential reason for women to learn Torah for the sake of learning alone. For women, Torah is a means to an end. The end is developing a relationship with Hashem, oneself, and other people — on Hashem's terms. To accomplish this, you have to know the rules of the game, which is the intent of learning. You also have to have a repository of inspiration that will keep you in a state of *ahavah, yirah, and deveikus*. Think of it as flight school. Once you're behind the wheel, in the cockpit, you have to do your job. There is no more time to learn. Before you were married you learned. Now you're actualizing what you've studied.

I don't know where you are in life. I'm imagining you must be a busy mother with young children, a demanding job, and little extra time. You're taking the Torah you know and putting it into action. Don't feel guilty. You are where you should be. Still, there's a minimum you have to maintain. Study a halachah a day from a *sefer* or through Dial-a-Shiur. Stay inspired by reading a book, listening to a *shiur*, or going back to the notes you have from your seminary days and bringing them into your life.

There may be women who require more intense learning to stay on an even keel. For them, delving into *sifrei mussar* or Chassidus is their lifeline. It helps them come alive, rekindles their *ahavas Hashem* and *yiras Hashem*, and revitalizes their davening. For them, setting aside more significant blocks of time for in-depth learning may be essential for their *avodas Hashem*. They are not you. You're fulfilling your mission in your own special way.

WOMEN OR MEN AS FORMAL TEACHERS OF TORAH

Q *Are men better than women in formally teaching Torah? I know women are more nurturing and passionate, but I don't necessarily want to hear what they feel about Torah. I think I can gain so much more from men teachers, who have the breadth of knowledge that women don't have. Am I wrong?*

A The level of Bais Yaakov learning today has changed since 30 years ago. Today women are fully capable of going to the sources and differentiating between basic rules, stringencies, and varying opinions. There are many women who are excellent Torah teachers and can give over solid information without being swayed by emotion.

Women certainly have a lot of passion and are much more suited to giving other women *chizuk* and guidance on how to best channel their feminine emotional energies. There is nothing wrong with going to a *shiur* for that purpose alone. If you want to learn actual Torah, there are many competent women teachers who can teach you Rambam, Midrashim, and Maharal.

Rashi tells us that when the Torah was given to the Jews at Sinai, Miriam taught the women. There was a unique learning system set up for men and a different one for women. This is still true today. Women can best speak the language of women, which is what makes them the optimum choice to teach other women.

Marriage

WHEN A HUSBAND LEAVES LEARNING

Q *I have a friend who is a very spiritual, deep-thinking person. She always dreamed of marrying a man who would devote his life to learning, but was later disappointed to find out that her husband had chosen a different path. She now wonders what is her position as an eizer kenegdo. What happens when roles are reversed? On the one hand, the marriage provides for spiritual growth, as she can influence her husband from becoming too materialistic and shallow. Her husband too can keep her grounded. What words of advice or encouragement would you give to a woman in this situation?*

A Yaakov Avinu had twelve sons who were all learned *tzaddikim*. Yet certainly Yehudah wasn't Naftali and Levi wasn't Asher, nor were they meant to be. All men are supposed to learn, but not all are meant to sit and learn long term. Historically this has never been the case. Diminishing his accomplishments, putting him down, and pretending that he is a big learner and lying to others about it are all destructive acts. A woman's role in marriage is to build. She does this by discovering who her husband is, not what he isn't. If learning all day isn't his thing, she has to use her *binah yeseirah* to find out what does speak to him and then build on that maximally.

I know a woman whose husband is not an expert at Gemara learning. But he enjoys *hashkafah sefarim* and has become quite an authority on this topic. Is the husband good at *chessed* or fathering? Let the wife capitalize on it. Rashi says, "*Zocheh ezer, lo zocheh kenegdo.*" If a women feels her husband is unworthy because he is not a big learner, she will constantly be at war with him. Our Sages say that a foolish woman destroys her home. I know of many homes that were devastated by women who demeaned their husbands. The balance in marriage can work only if the wife shows respect for her husband. Reversal of roles isn't good. In *Tanach,* we see that although Devorah the prophetess was on a higher level than her husband, she didn't let him become her "wife," so to speak. She worked to make him into something greater.

When I was in seminary in Bnei Brak, a serious learning boy was considered a big catch for a Sephardic girl. Years later, I remember meeting an old friend and dorm-mate from seminary, who happened to be Sephardic. She spoke to me with such authentic pride about her husband. "My husband puts on *tefillin* every day," she said. "He has to be at the taxi station at 5 a.m. It doesn't matter, rain or shine, he won't forgo this mitzvah. And if there is time left, he will even finish davening with *a minyan.* He's a true *oved* Hashem." And he really is one. This man is bound to grow, because he has a wife who is wise enough to take pride in his positive accomplishments.

I have another friend who became observant early in her marriage. Her husband did not join her. She spoke to Rav Nissen Yagen, who told her to keep encouraging him. She told the Rav, "I tried, and there is no progress. I buy him books and he doesn't read them. I bought him a *Kiddush* cup. He uses it to make *Kiddush* and then switches on the TV." Rav Yagen answered, "Keep encouraging him. The day will come when you'll see him with a beard." And you know what? I've seen him and he has a beard.

Things can change. With encouragement and heartfelt *tefillah*, Hashem can open a husband's heart, give him more depth, and steer him to meet the right people who will touch him deeply and ignite his soul to grow.

SHOULD MY HUSBAND BE HELPING MORE?

Q *My husband is very hardworking and can go for long stretches without vacations, while I am the complete opposite. I would like him to sometimes initiate or plan a small getaway as opposed to my always doing it myself. We keep having conflicts around this issue. Should I just give up and stay home or continue planning things myself?*

A Do it yourself. You write that he works hard. It is enough that he is paying for the vacation. Just as you wouldn't wait for him to prepare your breakfast, don't expect him to organize your trips.

I can say this with certainty, because my husband and I also had very different ideas about vacation. I love traveling. He does not. After years of trying your method of wishing and hoping, I realized this was cruelty. Why try to fit a size eight foot into a size seven shoe?

The first day I went on vacation alone with the children, I felt terrible. The next day I had a grand time. The third day I thought, "What did I want all these years? The kids and I are enjoying ourselves, and my husband is happy at home." I realized that the whole issue was about *kavod*, not about vacations. *Kavod* means feeling a certain sense of importance. Because of the culture in which some of us grew up, a woman thinks she is respected when her husband takes over certain things having to do with chivalry and gallantry. Your sense of *kavod* should ideally come from being part of something larger than yourself, i.e., building your marriage, your inner self, and your children.

If you want to feel beloved and treasured, give your husband the feeling that you care about him the way you care about yourself. The message you are conveying now is that his desires are not important, only yours matter. This inevitably leads to conflicts and belittling on both sides and is definitely not a way to gain respect. Let go of this. Don't let go of vacations if you want them. Just plan them with your husband's wishes in mind and build your sense of self on aspects in life that are greater than this.

HOW TO BUILD WHEN A HUSBAND IS DEPRESSED

Q *My husband suffers from severe depression. He refuses to do anything constructive such as working, davening, exercising, or learning. What can I do to help him? How does one build if there is nothing to build on?*

A Depression is a very difficult problem. The question is why he is this way. Young children love puzzles that fit their developmental level. Give a 5-year-old child a 20-piece puzzle and he'll happily put it together and revel in that sense of achievement. However, offer the same child a 1,000-piece puzzle and he'll throw up his hands in despair.

In the same vein, when things feel overwhelming, adults too tend to retract. It seems as if he's being asked to answer a 100-page exam in

15 minutes. He must be feeling inadequate, unsuccessful, and defeated. That's really where depression begins for most people. Try to figure out what he can do or what he trusts himself enough to do.

For example, you can ask him to help with shopping or babysitting. If he succeeds, you've put a brick in place and you've begun the process of building. Move slowly and find opportunities to talk about what he's done, not about him personally.

Depression may also stem from internalized anger. In a sense he is saying, "This is not how I want it to be." Some people express their anger outwardly. Other people get past it with *emunah*. *Emunah* is saying with belief, "This is how it is meant to be. Now let me see who I should be in this situation." Undeveloped *emunah* and bottled-up anger can quickly spiral into self-blame and depression.

Try to mold yourself into a safe environment where your husband can feel free to vent his frustrations and disappointments without encountering criticism. Together you can then work toward *emunah*.

A third cause of depression may be a chemical imbalance. Your only option then is to seek the help of a psychiatrist.

Give yourself encouragement and validation. Don't devalue what you do. If your husband is unable to work you may find yourself supporting the family while juggling a home and children. That's a huge accomplishment. Be good to yourself. Take time out to do the things you enjoy. Strengthen your *emunah* and daven to Hashem to give you that extra *siyata d'Shmaya* and *binah yeseirah* to build your husband anew.

APPRECIATING ONE'S HUSBAND

I'm not sure I've ever liked or respected my husband. We've had windows of happiness, mostly in our early years of marriage, before the stresses and responsibilities of caring for our young children took over. My husband is unappreciative by nature, selfish, uncaring, and often feels sorry for himself. Many times he will refuse my requests for help with the kids. In his defense, he does work long hours, takes care of the bills, and helps with some shopping and minor tasks around the house. I don't think he means to be a bad husband. How do I learn to appreciate and respect him?

A: I think the problem here is not that your husband doesn't appreciate or understand you but that you don't appreciate and understand him. It seems that your husband is putting in more than a full day at work. He's doing his job. Your stress and tiredness are preventing you from feeling grateful to him. "There's never happiness where there's no gratitude." Your expectations have dulled your appreciation.

A man's joy in marriage stems from feeling acknowledged for the fact that he provides financially, intellectually, and physically. Lack of appreciation leads to feelings of failure, which will cause a husband to shut down. If your husband didn't sense your happiness when he did offer to help you, he may have become inclined to do less.

I don't think you're lazy or demanding. I think you've fallen victim to the American mentality that has trained women not to love, appreciate, or take pride in their husbands, but to redefine them as willing to be both a husband and half a wife. You have to question whether you're willing to maintain this role of victim forever. You are an adult. You have to take responsibility for your own health, peace of mind, and happiness. This is not your husband's responsibility. If it means forgoing a vacation or other luxuries so that you can hire extra help in the house, then go for it.

When a husband closes down and has to fight for respect, the marriage is in big trouble. You can change things around not only for his benefit but for your own. If you become more joyful, things can get better. You can have the pleasure of a husband who comes home to a happy wife. In turn, he will enjoy providing and being with you and will come to like the children more if he sees that you don't treat them as a burden. Things can change. Pray for *siyata d'Shmaya*, learn to enjoy your kids, and train yourself to always be grateful.

MEN'S AND WOMEN'S ROLES

Q *You often refer to the opinion of the Maharal that the role of man is to provide and the role of woman is to take what he provides and build with it. Is this the prevalent view of Chazal?*

A This is definitely what *Chazal* meant. The *kesubah* is a statement that the man will provide. When the bride accepts the *kiddushin* ring, she is taking upon herself not only to be her husband's exclusive wife but also to fulfill all the duties inherent in being a wife. This means accepting what her husband will provide and developing something from it. The Torah marriage is one where one's home and heart become a repository for the *Shechinah*.

I suspect that the reason why you think there are other views is because in today's world, the *kollel* lifestyle, where the wife works and the husband learns, has become the norm. Until very recently, this was unheard of. Rav Aharon Kotler, who popularized the *kollel* idea, saw it as a historic imperative in order to replace the generation of scholars that were decimated in the Holocaust. At the same time, Hashem enabled this to happen by dint of technological progress. It used to be that a woman's time and energy were all but consumed by such draining tasks as washing laundry at the pond, sewing clothing by hand, and baking the family's daily bread. Today women have far more leisure to train and work at various lucrative professions.

If the effect of this is that the woman becomes the *mashpia*, the one who gives and influences, and the man takes on the role of the *mekabel*, the one who accepts what she gives in order to build, one cannot say that this is a Torah marriage. If the husband is forced to take time off from *kollel* to fulfill the wife's responsibilities because she may lose money if she neglects her demanding job, then the children are getting the message that money outweighs Torah learning.

However, if the woman views her working as just another way of keeping things going in the home, and the central influence remains her husband's Torah learning, then the marriage is on a Torah footing.

Many women can pull off being a superwoman. They may work at a full-time job and then come home and move into the role of enabler. This requires a lot of self-discipline, respect for Torah, and physical stamina. A lot of women cannot manage this and end up becoming neurotic, unable and then unwilling to be good wives and mothers to their families.

The third situation is where the husband assists his wife in the home when she becomes overburdened, not because what he is doing has no value, but as a form of *chessed*. Both parties need to be careful about why there is a role reversal. There has to be honest *kavod haTorah* on the woman's part and genuine compassion to help his wife in her struggles on the man's part, without devaluing the husband's Torah learning. If both have a clear picture that Torah is their prime motive they will succeed.

PRACTICAL WAYS OF RESPECTING YOUR HUSBAND

Q: What does it mean to respect your husband? Can you explain what we have to do practically in our own home?

A: This is a big issue. In secular society, it's considered cute and sometimes even brave and honorable to be disrespectful to your husband. This attitude has rubbed off on us. What a man wants most is to provide. He wants to feel that he's giving something and that he's appreciated for that. Respecting your husband means showing that you believe in his efforts and that you value him.

A man wants a happy wife who smiles when she sees him and is sincere about it. Sometimes a problem arises in the marriage where the wife is unhappy because the husband is petty or unknowing or mistaken or not providing what she needs. That's between her and Hashem. He's trying to give her what he can. Her role is to be appreciative. That means taking him seriously because she thinks he is important.

It may be cutesy and daring for a woman to belittle her husband, but it would certainly not come across as such if she did the same to her employer. The degree of reverence she has for her employer should be reflective of her reverence for her husband, not because her husband's the boss and she's the worker, but because he provides for her intellectually, emotionally, and financially. It's okay to disagree with him, just as you would with anyone you respect, but do it by validating his view and then offering your own.

In your home, show your husband in every way that you respect him, by expressing appreciation, listening when he talks, and always speaking to your children about him with utmost *kavod*.

FAMILY VERSUS SIMCHAHS

Q. *I like to put my family first, and rarely participate in communal events and simchahs in the evenings. My husband feels strange going to all these places alone, even though they are all separate seating. Am I wrong in staying home and not allowing these events to take over my time? Do I need to respect my husband's feelings and make the effort to accompany him?*

A. Kudos for putting your family first. They do come before *simchahs*. I'm invited to a lot of *simchahs* because I teach marriageable-age girls. I've learned that it's okay to stay 5 minutes, wish the *baalas simchah* a hearty *mazal tov*, and leave. This means that, often, I manage to be back home within an hour. If this works for you, it's a good solution. I'm not advocating not going to *simchahs*, because it makes such a difference to the *baal simchah* to have people come and share in their joy. The need to belong to a group larger than oneself is very deep.

If it's important to your husband that you accompany him, set aside time for this either weekly or bi-weekly. As Rebbetzin Esther Greenberg, *a"h*, would often say: When you talk about family first, husbands are number one before children. You have to respect your husband's wishes, and your children should see you doing that.

SELF IMPROVEMENT WITHOUT HUSBAND'S SUPPORT

Q How does a woman who is striving to be a better person handle situations where her husband is not supportive of her changes? For example, what if the wife is working on shemiras halashon and the husband constantly speaks about others, or the wife goes to shiurim and the husband thinks it's over the top? What should she do?

A The only life you can live, and the one you're accountable for in heaven, is your own. Still, a woman's purpose is to build with what she receives from her husband. Tearing him down will only accomplish the opposite. So if you are in a situation where the person speaking *lashon hara* is someone you have to respect, and you can't change the subject (which you often can in marriage), you have to listen and not accept what was said. I've found that telling positive stories about real people can be just as entertaining as *lashon hara*. Try to plan ahead and have other good alternative discussion topics ready when a situation such as this arises.

If you go to a *shiur* every so often and you become a better person as a result, your husband will only like you for it. I have a dear friend who became *frum* in her 50's. Her husband didn't want any part of it. She did, however, discover that he could handle a festive Shabbos dinner with his wife dressed up, speaking to him in a refined regal manner.

If you're trying to work on your husband, there's a problem. If you are working on yourself, he will only approve.

MOTIVATING A HUSBAND TOWARD GROWTH

Q *What are some ways I can motivate my husband to think about Elul and Rosh Hashanah without sounding like an irritating seminary girl? He has a learning seder every day, so I'm not worried about his learning, but whenever I bring up the idea of change or growth, he gets annoyed.*

A Men don't learn a lot of the inspirational *sefarim* that women do. In high school or seminary, you probably studied *sifrei mussar* or Chassidus such as *Nesivos Shalom, Michtav MeEliyahu, Pachad Yitzchak,* and *Alei Shur*. During this time your husband was dissecting *Talmud Bavli* in yeshivah with maybe a brief *mussar seder* from time to time or an occasional *shmuess* from the *Mashgiach*. When you got married, you were probably a lot more *hashkafically* developed than your husband.

There are exceptions. Some men find satisfaction in the study of *hashkafah,* but most don't. Your husband is annoyed because no man likes to feel as if his wife is the provider and he is the receiver. There's hope, though. These *sefarim* were written by and for men, and many men will eventually study them. As men mature, they want to know more about how to put it all together. When they do study these *sefarim*, it will probably be with a lot more depth and perspective, and with a higher level of integration than women, because men are much more grounded in Torah learning. Be patient. By the time he's 38, he'll probably be motivating you, instead of the other way around. This is usually how it goes in most marriages.

However, let's say he's already 45 and you're still trying to get him to work on his inner life. Begin by asking some questions such as, "It's Elul, and I don't feel anything much different than I did in Av. Did they ever say anything about this in yeshivah? Is there anything I could learn that can give me insight?" Make him your teacher. Don't correct him even if he gets it wrong. Just listen. Since his skills are better, in the end his grasp will be much more profound.

It could also be that he's just not the *hashkafah* type at all. This doesn't mean that he doesn't have a yearning for spirituality. It's just that he doesn't have the ability to listen to the language. His means of communication may be *dikduk halachah*. His *ahavah* may be expressed through *tzedakah*. His *yirah* may be actualized by the level of *kashrus* he maintains. Let his deeds show you where he truly is.

BALANCING HUSBAND'S HELP WITH HIS TORAH LEARNING

Baruch Hashem, I have a husband who is always learning and I'm the mother of four children (born within a period of three years). We are very fortunate to live right next door to the yeshivah where my husband is a rebbi. He is happy to help me, but would rather be in yeshivah until I need him (versus being home just in case I do). However, if he is in yeshivah, I won't ever ask him to come home, because I don't want to interrupt his learning. How do I balance the two?

It is extremely unlikely that your husband will intuitively know when you need him. The burden is on you. You have to tell him when you require his help. As I can see from your question, you would like to receive as much assistance as possible, but you'd also like to be autonomous so your husband can sit and learn. You'd like to follow in the larger-than-life footsteps of Rebbetzin Elyashiv, who wouldn't call her husband home even for a health emergency. There's no easy answer here, but I can help you clarify the question.

Learning and teaching Torah is extremely important. Every moment a person learns, he is affirming Hashem's purpose in creating the world. On the other hand, Torah was meant to be put into practice. If the Torah obligates you to help unload your enemy's donkey when it buckles under a heavy load, surely there's no excuse for letting one's wife collapse under the burden of running a home single-handedly. Sometimes outside help or familial assistance is possible. Many times it is not. You have to ask yourself, "Is this something my husband must do right away that no one else can do?" If so, give him the opportunity to put his Torah learning into practice.

I know a *chashuv* Rosh Yeshivah who once complained about the *shalom bayis* issues that young couples bring him. The husband often believes that the wife should be inventive, independent, and strong enough to manage on her own. The Rosh Yeshivah pointed out that when his children were young, his wife would be busy feeding their many small children and he would be there at her side helping with whatever needed to be done.

We read in the *parashah* that Yaakov Avinu took his children and possessions across the Yabok River. He didn't ask the women to do it. Realistically assess what the priorities are at the moment, given what you can and can't do. Don't feel guilty for needing assistance. The *Orchos Tzaddikim* writes that if there's something you can't do, it's not meant for you to do. If your husband is happy to help, count yourself blessed.

DO MARRIED PEOPLE STILL NEED FRIENDS?

Q *What does Judaism say about friendship? Is my husband supposed to be my best and only friend? Although I have a good marriage, I find there are things I just can't share with my husband the way I used to with friends.*

A Our Sages say, "*Oh chavrusa oh misusa* — either companionship or death." Your husband is the one person who can give you things on every level that no one else will ever give you. However, he definitely should not be your only friend. He does not want to listen to feminine chatter, nor is he particularly interested in sharing his innermost feelings all the time.

Renew your old friendships. Make time for yourself. Go to a play, talk to your friends on the phone while you do laundry, straighten the house, or feed the baby. The social chitchat, the validation of emotions, experiences, and girl talk are meant to be shared with your friends, not with your husband. Be careful, though, not to cross lines or undervalue what your husband does give you. His loyalty, understanding, absolute caring, and commitment can never be filled by any friend, no matter how close.

MAKING WICKS FOR THE MIKDASH

Q *What can a wife do to steer her husband on the proper path? How can we apply to modern times Devorah the prophetess' method of making wicks for the Mikdash?*

The Maharal's paradigm, where the husband gives forth and the wife receives and builds, is the ideal situation. However, in less-perfect circumstances, a woman can still influence her husband positively. This can be accomplished by receiving what he does have and nurturing it, rather than continually reflecting on what he doesn't have and negating him.

Everyone has points of excellence. A wife's role is to find the place where her husband shines and build with it. There must be some reason she married him, after all.

For example, if he is a good provider, make him aware that he makes it possible for you to be home with the children, and point out to the children that he makes it possible for them to have what they want and need. If the husband feels good about his earning potential, the wife could then easily influence him to give *tzedakah*, which could be his point of excellence in *ruchniyus*. A husband with a good sense of humor can be influenced to make people happy by doing *bikur cholim*. Someone who is levelheaded can be steered toward making *shidduchim*, where having a good eye and being persistent is a virtue.

If a wife would like to see her husband learning more and he doesn't enjoy it, that may not be his point of excellence. Alternatively, she can help him find some area of learning that speaks to him, and then overtly express her appreciation and happiness when he does learn. Even if it's just reading the Midrash at the Shabbos table, it could motivate him to eventually want to study more.

BASHERT — THE SECOND TIME AROUND

How does the Torah explain bashert the second time around? Is it announced in heaven that Plonis bas Ploni will marry Mr. X the first time and Mr. Y the second time?

The Gemara says that forty days before a fetus is conceived, a voice declares, "This man's daughter will marry this man."

The Kabbalists and the Malbim explain that this is not referring to an actual marriage between a man and a woman, but rather to a match between a person's specific soul and his body. The specific soul, with all of its powers, is "introduced" to a specific body, with all of its capacities, tendencies, and background. This *zivug* between body and soul is ordained from heaven before a person is born.

The second *zivug*, which is the marriage between a man and a woman as we conventionally understand it — with its caterers, halls, and invitations — is determined according to merit. This does not mean that Hashem is unaware of what will eventually occur. However, we do have free choice. We need to take responsibility for these choices and have *bitachon* that Hashem will bring about whatever results need to be brought about for our benefit.

The first marriage — between body and soul — is determined by Hashem's vision of what will work for that person, what he needs to fulfill his *tafkid*. The second marriage, between man and woman, is based on what each person evolved into as a result of his or her choices.

MAKING SHIDDUCHIM THE RIGHT WAY

Can you give me some guidelines on questions I should ask singles before I try to set them up?

You should try to obtain as much information as you can about their background, nature, and goals. The more you get them to talk, the more you'll find out about them. The way they speak about their siblings, family, and life in general will tell you a lot about who they are. Are they effusive or reticent? Are they positive or negative? How do they feel about themselves? Do they hold their Rabbi in high regard, or do they tend to put him down? Asking a lot of background questions will give you a sense of what they will have in common with a prospective mate.

Inquiring about their goals and what they really want in life tells you who they really are and what their values are. It is also important to find out their *hashkafic* views and their level of religious observance. Ask about their economic background and what standard of living they will expect, so you can look for compatibility. It is your responsibility to find out if there are any physical or mental problems. You can then set them up with someone who is likely to be accepting of that.

There is a lot of "trophyism" in *shidduchim*. People are obsessed with inane issues such as "What will everyone say? Is he the best boy in yeshivah? Is he at the top of his profession? Is her family wealthy? Does she look right?" Answers to these questions don't really tell you who the person is, where they are coming from, and where they plan on going, which is really what will make or break a marriage.

THE KOLLEL SYSTEM

Q *My father-in-law works and also learns many hours a day and would like to find someone similar for his daughter, but it seems impossible. Most boys that are suggested for my sister-in-law want to stay in kollel "for as long as possible" and have no further plans. I am not against kollel and agree that some people should sit and learn forever, but surely not everyone. Why is the old way of working and learning no longer relevant today?*

A Very many authorities maintain that men should learn for at least two years after their marriage so that their homes are established on a solid Torah foundation and that they have some time to figure out where they truly want to go. Long-term learning really depends on the husband's nature, who he is, and what his capabilities are. In *shidduchim*, one should find out what the boy's real sense of self is, where he's headed, who he admires, who his rebbeim are, who he listens to, if he would be suited for the girl, and if they can build a home together.

The old way of working and learning is no longer viable today, because very few people have the stamina to do what people did two generations ago. In those days, men would get up at the crack of dawn, put in an 8-hour workday, come home, and then go out to a *shiur*. Most men don't live the life that *baalei batim* did long ago.

Today's society offers many more ways to spend time. People stay up later and don't get up as early. This is the work of the *yetzer hara*. Additionally, work today is more demanding than it once was. One can't compare being a lawyer with being a storekeeper. Full-time work doesn't lend itself to learning. Learning in terms of excellence will not jive with a demanding job.

So until the time comes when a husband is compelled to choose between work and *kollel*, either because of financial necessity or his own nature asserting itself, learning in *kollel* is a worthy goal.

IS KOLLEL PUTTING UNDUE PRESSURE ON PARENTS?

Q *The kollel lifestyle often puts a very stressful financial burden on parents, some of whom are having physical problems and are stressed out to the maximum. While it's a big mitzvah to learn, it's hard to hear that it's okay for others to get hurt in the process. How can we understand this?*

A There are parents whose greatest pleasure is to support their children in *kollel*. There are others who feel ripped off and pressured by society, but will give anyway. Parents can take delight in giving by saying, "I can go without because there are things in life that are bigger, more important, and more enduring to me." It's like trading a nickel for a dollar. Oftentimes, giving up a certain amount of leisure and staying on the job a bit longer because you really want to be a part of this life is commendable.

On the other hand, if the parents cannot physically handle it, the couple should make it their business to find another solution. If financial help doesn't come through parents, it can come in any number of other ways, many times through *tefillah*. We must have *bitachon*. If Hashem wants something to happen, He'll help us. Certainly if He's big enough to create heaven and earth, He can create the means to keep a promising *talmid chacham* in learning.

COMING TO GRIPS WITH "REQUIRED SUPPORT" IN SHIDDUCHIM

Q *Our oldest daughter is a wonderful bas yisrael, yet it seems that boys of her caliber will only say yes to a shidduch that comes with the promise of monthly support. My husband is already maxed out in his parnasah. I could work more hours, but it will be at the expense of the younger children, as I will then be less available to them. We already live modestly, so cutting back isn't an option. Can you offer some suggestions or words of chizuk?*

A It seems that the *shidduch* crisis is coming to a head. Both the supply of and demand for people who can give long-term support is diminishing. In Israel, a *chashuv bachur* may still be counseled to ask for an apartment so that he can sit and learn without the worry of meeting monthly mortgage payments. However, *Mashgichim* are becoming more realistic, and questions such as, "Can the boy's parents contribute? Can they live out-of-town where it's less expensive? Can both sides help with a down payment?" are becoming more common. There is more compromise, and there will be even more in the future, because the community is growing, and far more young men want to sit and learn.

Here's a personal story that will give you *chizuk:* By the time we were in the *shidduch parashah* with one of our daughters, we seriously had no money left. I told my daughter frankly, "You're going to have to learn to do a lot of different things, because we really can't help you." So she studied to be a *ganenet,* took a *sheitel* course, and learned sewing. We reassured the *shadchanim* that our daughter had three different ways to make a *parnasah* and she would keep her husband in learning come what may.

Soon after she started dating, she was set up with a boy from a family of seven sons. His father, a professional who had never had the opportunity to study Torah when he was young, made a vow to himself that his sons would not be prevented from learning because of money. She got engaged to him. His father ended up buying the couple's apartment. So after all our *hishtadlus,* Hashem showed us He would take care of us.

Keep your chin up, trust Hashem, do what you can, and it'll be okay.

Chapter 2
Building a Relationship With Hashem

Serving Hashem

WHAT DOES LOVING HASHEM MEAN?

Q *I've been fully observant for almost 11 years, but I think there's a root problem with my beliefs. I fear Hashem and I'm grateful for His many blessings, but I do not understand the idea of ahavas Hashem. What is it supposed to mean and what are some practical steps to attain it?*

A The first level is awareness. In order to develop love for Hashem, you have to fine-tune your sensitivities. Open your eyes and see Hashem's life force in nature, your children, your body, and in the profusion of *chessed* that He showers upon us daily. Study Hashem's intricacy of thought, His profound compassion, and the dazzling array of shades and colors He created for our enjoyment. Marvel at the beauty of the human soul and the profound joy we experience when we feel ourselves completely alive. This feeling is the soul overtaking the body. Learn to love Hashem with your soul.

The soul's favorite form of self-expression is giving, which leads to the next level: We say in *Shema*, "*V'ahvata es Hashem* —You should love Hashem." A person can reach this state by letting feelings of gratitude and oneness be expressed through one's heart, soul, and resources. Just as a bond between two people grows by giving, so too a relationship with Hashem develops by giving of ourselves.

The *Shema* continues, "*b'chal levavcha* — with all your heart." Love Hashem with the part of you that's creative and the part of you that's destructive, the part that needs to be rechanneled, and the part that gives you trouble. And love Him *b'cal meodecha* — with all your resources, with every character trait with which Hashem has endowed you. Find a way to reach Hashem by expressing your deeper inner self to Him, and this will ultimately lead to *ahavas Hashem*.

For further reading, I recommend "The Gate of Love" in *sefer Reishis Chochmah*, which is available in English translation.

BUILDING A PERSONAL RELATIONSHIP WITH HASHEM

Q *I've been told that Hashem has a personal relationship with every Jew. What does this imply and how do we get closer to Him?*

A A personal relationship means a connection that involves response and awareness. A blade of grass receives its energy from Hashem. It cannot exist for even a split second without Hashem's Will giving it life. Yet the grass does not have a real relationship because it cannot respond. It receives but all it gives back is its existence. There is no difference between one blade of grass and another. Hashem doesn't respond to each one individually. There is no such thing as a righteous blade of grass that deserves lots of rain and sunshine or a wicked blade of grass that has made major life mistakes. This is called *hashgachah klalis*, which means awareness without any involvement.

Hashem responds to every human being differently. A non-Jew who does good deeds may be rewarded, and he may be punished for his evil. However, there is no covenant with non-Jews. Therefore, they can reach a point where, like a tree or a blade of grass, they no longer have a relationship of awareness and response with Hashem.

Due to the covenant Hashem made with Yaakov, however, every Jew has a spark buried deep within him that remains eternally connected to Hashem. "Although they have sinned, they remain Yisrael." The spark can be so covered up with sin and bad choices that the person may barely be aware of it. This is one aspect of *galus haShechinah*, the Divine Presence — the G-dliness within us — in exile.

Getting closer to Hashem means becoming a more divine-like individual, just like getting closer to another person means developing communication and similarity. The way to build a relationship with Hashem is through keeping the mitzvos, emulating Hashem's *middos*, and attaching oneself to people who are already on the path to greatness.

HOW DO I SWITCH MY AVODAH TO THE PHYSICAL REALITY OF MANAGING A HOME?

Q I got married recently and I am trying to adjust to new responsibilities and priorities. Obviously my life now centers more on the physical reality of managing a home and family, and not so much on prayer and Torah learning. I feel as if my avodas Hashem has been diminished somewhat. Can you help me put things in the right perspective?

A I understand that it may not be easy switching your focus to the more mundane aspects of daily life. If supper needs to be fixed and a pile of laundry needs to be tackled, it's definitely not a time to be taking out your *sefarim*. If you find yourself feeling overwhelmed or stifled, ask your husband to share a Torah thought with you, or grab a few minutes and read a short essay on *hashkafah* together. It doesn't have to be anything too profound or lengthy, just enough to nurture you and keep you going.

Another way to grow during this period in your life is to learn to see Hashem in every situation in which you find yourself. The Arizal says that the holiest moment on Shabbos is during the Mussaf *Kedushah* prayer, when we say, "*Ayei mekom kevodo* — where is the place of His glory." Hashem's Being can be found wherever we look for Him.

Sensitize yourself to feel Hashem's Presence in the nourishing food bubbling on the stove, your children's smiling faces, a sink full of sudsy dishes, and clean laundry hanging on the line. In many ways, this is a higher level than perceiving Hashem from His place of holiness.

COMPARING HASHEM TO AUTHORITY FIGURES

Q *I tend to compare Hashem to the authority figures in my life with whom I do not have a good relationship. How can I learn to relate to Hashem without associating Him with people who evoke negative feelings within me?*

A It's true that having a difficult relationship with people in authority may make finding your way to Hashem that much more challenging. Some people say, "*Avinu Av harachaman* — Our Father, Father of mercy," and the words resonate with them. They see a vision of compassion, caring, and commitment. Other people unfortunately don't visualize this because this isn't what their father meant to them.

Many people say, *"Ribono Shel Olam* — Master of the World," and picture Hashem's glory, benevolence, and love. For others, the word "Master" immediately evokes the authority figures in their life, and it isn't a positive feeling.

The way to separate Hashem from people is to learn to become more aware of Him. The best and easiest way to do this is through *hisbodedus* — dedicating about 20 minutes to half an hour each day to talk to Hashem about your life. The critical factor here is speech, because words that come from the heart create a different level of awareness. Learn to see Hashem in nature, in your children, and in everything He provides for us. Once you do this, your vision of Hashem will change. Your challenges may still be harsh and painful, but it becomes as if you are writing on a beautiful, brilliant background on which there is a message that says, "I am Hashem, Who took you out of Egypt, both your own personal exile and the collective exile. I'm committed to you and I love you."

In addition, I would suggest keeping a gratitude journal. For this to work, you'll need to commit to keep it up for a few months and aim to fill at least half a page of regular-size notebook paper with new material every day. The first week will probably be a no-brainer. "Thank you, Hashem, for the tap water in my sink, the fresh air, the bright sun, the delicious variety of fruits and vegetables …"

By the time you get to week six, the mundane things that we normally take for granted will have already shifted within you to a new level of consciousness. You will feel that backdrop of mercy. Then you will begin to sense Hashem in a very profound way, in a way that expresses who you really are on the deepest level.

FEELING GUILTY ABOUT MY BLESSINGS

Though we are not rich, we are, baruch Hashem, comfortable. We give tzedakah generously, but also spend money on luxuries that my husband enjoys. We recently moved into a new house that is much nicer than the kind of place I'd choose to live in. It brings my husband much joy, but I can't help secretly feeling guilty. We are in galus and so many people are struggling. I appreciate what Hashem has given us, and try to focus on feeling thankful, but I also feel uncomfortable. What should my attitude and thoughts be regarding material blessings in my life?

People think that in order to be a *tzaddik* you have to experience privation. But the truth is there's more than one way to serve Hashem. One path is indeed through adversity and *mesirus nefesh*. Another way is through uplifting physicality.

For a wife this can mean many things. Seeing that there is *simchah* in your home, thanking Hashem, using your possessions wisely, encouraging your husband to give *tzedakah,* and opening your home to people in need are ways you can elevate the blessings Hashem has given you.

Wealth brings honor, and all men have an innate desire for it. Therefore, the more *kavod* you give your husband, the less he'll need to get it through external means. *Kavod* in and of itself can be used well in communal leadership and in being a role model for others.

I teach at Neve Yerushalayim, where the girls often get invited out for Shabbos. A home where the family is happy but impoverished gives them a feeling of dissociation from Torah life. A home that's aesthetically beautiful and exudes a feeling of largesse makes them feel entirely different about living a *frum* lifestyle.

There are lots of good things you can do with the wealth Hashem has given you, not the least of which is thanking Hashem for the *berachah* and training your children to be thankful, generous, and giving.

DEALING WITH FLEETING PHYSICALITY

Q *In one of your classes, you discussed how every physical thing is "hevel" because it will eventually end. Most of what I can perceive and experience in this world is physical. If this is so, how can I develop myself? What can I hold onto?*

A Spirituality doesn't mean cutting yourself off from the physical world. On the contrary, it is what you introduce into your interaction with this world.

My daughter volunteers for an organization called *Zeh LaZeh*. The woman who heads it is an incredible person. On Chol HaMoed Succos she arranges a "fantasy day" for widows and orphans. The magnificent experience ends with a *Simchas Beis HaSho'eivah* where the "Who's Who" in the Torah world attend. Great figures such as Rav Chaim Kanievsky, the Gerrer Rebbe, and many other distinguished personalities grace the affair. This huge undertaking involves hours of physical work, including countless phone calls, *shlepping* boxes, and cleaning up. It's *gashmiyus* all right, but it's *gashmiyus* concretized into action. This is genuine *ruchniyus*.

If you're cooking dinner for your family, think of it as a *chessed*. They are just as hungry as strangers would be. If your intention is to build a home of loving-kindness where you want to fill people's needs and create a healthy environment where people can draw closer to Hashem, this is *ruchniyus*. Don't let anyone ever deceive you into thinking anything other than that.

WHY DON'T I GET A "SPIRITUAL HIGH"?

Q *I try to make all the mitzvos I perform more meaningful by being mindful to bring Hashem into my life with my heart and concentrating on feeling grateful to Him. But despite this, I usually find myself just going through the motions. The feeling of real closeness to Hashem happens only once in a while and I feel like I need to sense it more.*

I have a non-observant sister who practices Eastern healing. She is able to get her spiritual high without the obligation of keeping Torah and mitzvos. Why can't I experience this same elation from davening and concentrating on berachos?

A I suspect your problem is that you don't see the connection between the mitzvos and how they bring a Jew closer to Hashem. I would suggest you study *Horeb* and Rav Hirsch's commentary on the Torah. It's difficult to learn, because it was originally written in German and the English translation is stilted. Get through it anyway. He will clarify how the connection works. Once you understand the mechanism, you'll feel different. The more you can comprehend the workings of a mitzvah and how Hashem's wisdom is an intricate part of it, the easier it will be to develop that spiritual bond. He Who knows our souls defined the mitzvos to create connection. If you include your mind in the experience, it will inform you more than you think.

Eastern healing does this inside out. There's the external sensation of meaning without reality. People think they are connected but they really aren't. You can have the feeling of *tikkun* without actual *tikkun*. On the other hand, you can have what really gives you *tikkun*, not necessarily with the accompanying feeling, unless you work hard to understand it better.

The numerical value of *Elokim* is *hateva* — nature. Nature is Hashem, but Hashem is not nature, He's far more. When you worship nature, which is the essence of Eastern religion, there are consequences. You make Hashem so small that there is no accounting, no World To Come, no direct link, and no prophecy. Embarking on that spiritual path will lead you only downhill.

Concentrate on developing a deep understanding of the mitzvos and use that as a springboard to come closer to Hashem.

LIVING IN A FRUM COMMUNITY VERSUS LIVING IN A KIRUV COMMUNITY

Q *When we were dating, my husband said he wanted to live in an established frum community in order to have access to the Torah learning readily available there. Although I had reservations, I ultimately told him I could live whereever he wanted and we'd make the most of our opportunities. Now that's it coming down to it, I'm afraid I'm not going to be happy in an established area. I realize there's plenty of community service to do even in a frum city, but it's not the same as living in a less religiously developed area, where I can be a part of actually shaping it.*

A It's up to you to be happy. *Simchah* is a *middah* and not a response to external circumstances. You can choose to develop your inner joy by believing that wherever Hashem put you, that's where your potential can be maximized. If you agreed to your husband's choice, you meant it and saw it as possible. You can be very happy in a *frum* community. Don't deceive yourself into thinking otherwise.

You don't have to be in Charan in order to make souls. I would suggest you get involved in Project Inspire, Partners in Torah, or any other suitable program. This way you can still be involved in creating a community by introducing people from the outside. We are naturally affected by our role models. Don't devalue the advantage of being in a *frum* environment. Your husband wants exposure to serious Torah learning and to people who are real *ovdei Hashem*. Seek out those people in your *frum* community who live bigger-than-life lives. Let them be your inspiration.

There is no reason for you to feel spiritually frustrated. There is plenty to do no matter where you live. In addition to *kiruv*, there are kids off the *derech*, women in distress, and families that need help coping. Be honest and ask yourself if your imagination is taking you to a place that you've fallen in love with, instead of falling in love with Hashem's Will.

Keep that promise to your husband. Make the most of your opportunities, and be happy wherever Hashem ultimately leads you.

TITHING TIME FOR KIRUV

Q *I have often heard in the name of a gadol that just as a person is required to tithe his money, he is required to give 10 percent of his time to kiruv. Although my husband is a serious Torah scholar, he does not feel ready to host non-frum guests at our table. He feels he still has so much more to learn. I know that on a spiritual level we are helping Klal Yisrael, but somehow I think we could be giving so much more.*

A I think your husband is more than likely to make a great contribution to *Klal Yisrael* in the long run. Hopefully when he is at the right stage in his life, he will make up for all those years of self-development.

You, probably more than your husband, will encounter many

opportunities to reach out to others. You can make a point of being a walking *kiddush Hashem*. Be pleasant and affable, whether it's on the bus, while shopping, or waiting at the doctor's office. You may not be the right address for hosting college students at the moment, but you should know where to send them. Strike up a conversation. Maintain a repertoire of Torah *shiurim* to which you can refer them. Be helpful and genuine. In your own small way you can make a difference.

Occasionally you might encounter people who are already somewhat observant who would gain an awful lot just from being at your Shabbos table. Seeing a family like yours interact can leave a lasting impression. You can show them what values are paramount in a Jewish home, what *chinuch habanim* is all about, how a husband speaks to his wife, and how a wife treats her husband,. Adopt an already *frum* couple who desperately needs an older sibling or a set of parents and be there for them. Be patient. Eventually, when your husband feels ready, you will both reap the dividends of your shared investment.

THE EFFECTS OF A DYSFUNCTIONAL CHILDHOOD ON AVODAS HASHEM

Q *Psychology sees negative influences in early childhood as directly correlating with later challenges in areas of trust and relationships. Would this include a person's connection with Hashem? Does Torah thought validate this theory?*

A The early years are certainly pivotal. The story in the Gemara about the mother of Rav Yehoshua ben Chananya who took her infant to the *beis medrash* to imbibe Torah teaches us that we believe that physical as well as spiritual influences leave a lasting impression on children.

The root of developing a relationship with Hashem is desiring to build one. Our history is filled with tragedy and suffering. There are so many Jews who lived through terrible times. Their early years were marred by insecurity, pogroms, and massacres.

One of the teachers in my daughter's school was hidden away in a tiny room during the Holocaust. She was a young child, probably in the pre-verbal stage, when trust is normally developed. Her friends were the ants who crawled around her hiding place. Nevertheless, she has extraordinary *bitachon* and *ahavas Hashem*. Where did this stem from? Probably in later childhood, she was told or understood on her own where goodness and evil really come from.

I know many people from abusive backgrounds who have a loving, secure relationship with Hashem. This is not to say that psychological help doesn't have its place when necessary. Nor is it easy to forget a traumatic past. However, it is definitely possible to overcome negative early influences and develop a deep and lasting bond with Hashem.

TRUSTING HASHEM INSTEAD OF PEOPLE

Q *I tend to put my trust in people rather than in Hashem. How can I change my perspective?*

A People are only people. You can love them and validate them for their efforts, but only Hashem can really be there for you. He knows what you are truly lacking, and only He can provide you with exactly what you need. Learn to trust Hashem. Focus on developing a higher consciousness by becoming more aware of what He does for you every day. The more you praise Him, the more *bitachon* you'll get. It doesn't mean mouthing clichés. View the good things in your life as gifts, because they truly are. Saying, "I can't believe the *hashgachah*," or "Hashem gave me so much energy today," turns Him from an abstract Being removed from your personal life into an intimate confidant Who will hold your hand along the circuitous road of life.

BALANCING AHAVAS YISRAEL WITH SERVING HASHEM

Q How can I practically go about working on my ahavas Yisrael while maintaining my own boundaries? Sometimes I feel guilty about being more frum than the people around me and I worry about whether I should be relaxing my standards in order not to hurt people's feelings. How can I be inclusive without being influenced by others?

A The Ramchal in *Mesillas Yesharim* points out that this feeling is one of the most artful tricks of the evil inclination. He wants you to lessen your *avodas Hashem* in the name of *ahavas Yisrael* or *anavah*.

There are three things you can do. Whenever possible, try to be inconspicuous. There are people who have very stringent kashrus standards who will pretend they are eating at a wedding so that other people will not notice anything. When you can't help being noticed, use humor to deflect tension. It works wonderfully. If humor is not your forte, use stage acting. Behave as if the other person is perfectly comfortable with whatever you are doing. It is not just that they'll pick up your vibes, but people naturally respond to other people's expectations. I've seen this happen many times in the *kiruv* world.

Don't let the *yetzer hara* convince you to lower your standards. Live up to your principles and others will respect you for it.

SETTING UP A LEARNING SCHEDULE

Q *I would like to work on developing my emunah and bitachon, improving my middos, and being same'ach b'chelko. Can you give me some advice on how to systematically set up a learning schedule? I enjoy studying Chassidus, mussar, and hashkafah topics. What books can I use? I would also like to do chessed, but I don't live near a Jewish community so I don't know of any resources. Can you suggest some ideas?*

A In terms of learning *mussar* and *hashkafah*, I would recommend you study *Michtav MeEliyahu*. If it's beyond your Hebrew textual skills, you can learn the English translation. There are many excellent books on *bitachon*. If you are intellectually inclined and would like to study the classical works, I would recommend you learn *Chovos HaLevavos* in a systematic way. Don't start at the beginning with *Shaar HaYichud*, which is difficult and philosophical and lends itself more to studying with a teacher. Learn the chapters on *middos* and *avodas Hashem*, such as *Shaar HaBitachon*. The vast majority of *mussar* books that were subsequently written draw a lot on *Chovos HaLevavos*, so you would do well to learn it in its original form.

As far as studying Chassidus, I don't know what your Hebrew skills and intellectual capacities are, but I would recommend you start with *Nesivos Shalom* by the Slonimer Rebbe. If you have no Hebrew language background, then try to obtain the four basic Breslov books: *Azamrah, Mayim, Ayei,* and *Tzohar,* translated into English by Rabbi Avraham Greenbaum. If you're at an advanced level and have more intellectual interests, I would recommend any of the excellent books available today on *Tanya*.

You can do numerous acts of *chessed* through the telephone. Contact Partners in Torah and offer to learn with a non-observant woman who is also interested in topics related to *hashkafah* and *bitachon*. This would benefit both you and your learning partner. Additionally, I would suggest you contact the nearest Jewish community and find out about elderly people who would enjoy phone visitations. You never know how a cheerful voice and a caring, listening ear can make a difference in a lonely person's life.

ERETZ YISRAEL VERSUS CHUTZ LA'ARETZ

Q *I know living in Eretz Yisrael should be every Jew's prerogative, but it doesn't seem to be the best place for my family right now. There are many reasons keeping us in chutz la'aretz, including health and financial considerations. Am I wrong for wanting to go only when Mashiach comes?*

A Our mission is to bring light into the darkness of the world through Torah and mitzvos. Eretz Yisrael is the place where we can fulfill our collective purpose. The Maharal writes that we end the second blessing of *Bircas HaMazon* with, "*al ha'aretz v'al hamazon,*" as opposed to thanking Hashem for what was mentioned in the actual *berachah*, i.e., *yetzias Mitzryim, bris milah,* Torah …, because all of these levels of elevation are meant to take place in Eretz Yisrael. The spiritual capacities of other countries are limited in that they cannot reveal Hashem the way He can be revealed in the Land of Israel.

Of course you can live a good life in *chutz la'aretz*, but it is in spite of where you are, not because of where you are. In a sense, you are working against your environment and the unique spiritual forces that define your country. No matter how holy a person in Lakewood may be, he can never fulfill the mitzvah of *maaser* from produce there. The land has no intrinsic holiness.

A meaningful question to ask yourself would be, "Where can I best accomplish my mission?" If there is no one to do what you or your husband are doing in *chutz la'aretz*, then you have to sacrifice and stay. If you have children, their *chinuch* obviously is an important issue: Until recently, the educational options for older children of people moving to Eretz Yisrael were limited. Thing are different now, but each family must consult with a Rav familiar with the *chinuch* options in Eretz Yisrael, who can discuss the specific needs of each child in depth.

But if what you're thinking is, "I'd rather be in *chutz la'aretz* because my family lives here, there's better shopping, I have a nicer home, and I'm emotionally comfortable with the language and culture," then there's a root problem with your reasoning. We shouldn't feel comfortable with *galus*. Our purpose is not shopping, consuming, or owning things. If Hashem *is* compelling you to stay in *chutz la'aretz* for *parnasah* or health reasons, that means you have to find your role and place there.

This indeed was the difference between the First Temple and the Second Temple. The First Temple had all the vessels and was an edifice of great light. During the Second Temple, everything was concealed. In a sense the First Temple had more sanctity. However, the Second Temple really brought forth greater holiness, because we were forced to reach into the dark place within ourselves to find the light.

May Hashem illuminate your path wherever it may lead.

WORRIED ABOUT THE SECURITY SITUATION IN ISRAEL

We made aliyah with our children about a year and a half ago. I think it's wonderful to be here, but I have doubts about the security situation. How do we know that we did the right thing? Should we feel guilty about having brought our children here? What should our mindset be as we live our mundane lives in the face of threats and terror attacks? Should we be worried or happy despite the danger?

During the Gulf War, when Israel was facing the threat of chemical warfare, someone asked Rav Elyashiv if it was permitted to stay in Israel. He thought awhile and then said, "We've been depending on miracles all along." I'd say the same thing here. There have always been threats and there always will be, but miracles have pulled us through.

Derech hateva has never had anything to do with Israel. It doesn't mean things will always be good for us, but it means that everything that happens occurs with absolute Divine Providence. Hashem conducts this world in two ways. One way is by response to our inner lives. If we make good choices, we draw down *shefa*. If we make bad choices, we cut ourselves off. *Shefa* comes from a higher place. It's Hashem's pure mercy, which is not always accessible to us by our deeds because we live in a world of free choice. It is our *bitachon* and *emunah* that will take us to far higher levels than our deeds ever will. We are all Nachshons jumping into the Reed Sea with our *bitachon*, because we know this land is not ruled by *derech hateva*. We're above nature, and we always have been. Natural cause and effect will not determine our fate.

By coming to Israel, you've made the choice of bringing up your children in a place where they will encounter *gilui Hashem*, a place where they'll be more alive than they will ever be in any country in the world.

Don't ignore the security situation, but don't worry either. Hashem doesn't put us in difficult circumstances without a reason. Every person has to ask himself how far his *emunah* will take him. Everything comes from Hashem, and there is purpose and *tikkun*.

Of course you should be happy. How can you not be? "*Ki v'simchah seitzei'u* — with *simchah* we will be redeemed." Having *bitachon* and believing that there is meaning in the moment creates true joy. This *simchah* should then take you to a higher manifestation of self. Ask yourself, "*Ma ashiv laHashem*" — How can I ever repay Hashem for bringing me to a Land that my ancestors only dreamed of reaching. Here we can attain higher levels of *emunah*, more *simchah shel mitzvah*, and greater commitment toward ourselves and others.

There's an excellent children's book about a child who was expelled from Gush Katif and was given a potato plant. This plant grows wherever it is transported because its roots are in water. The child realized that she was just like the plant. Hashem moves us where we have to be, and it's all taking us to redemption. As the Gra tells us, living in the Land of Israel brings the *geulah* closer.

Shabbos and Yom Tov

TAPPING INTO THE SPIRITUALITY OF SHABBOS AND YOM TOV

Q *How can a mother with small children tap into the spirituality of Shabbos and Yom Tov while she is constantly busy with physical preparation, the children, and the home?*

A Feeling uplifted on Shabbos and Yom Tov is contingent on achieving that state during the week. You can only give your kids what you are. Reaching this level requires training yourself to make each moment one of spiritual beauty. Doing this with young kids is much easier than it sounds. For example, when you dress or feed your baby, try to identify what is unique and special about him, and feel real gratitude to Hashem in your heart. Once you sense it, it will express itself at some point, either through a song or a story or even via the expression on your face. That's the backdrop. You have to become a spiritually developed person.

Once you've reached that state, you still have to wash the dishes and keep your kids busy. So do it, but plan ahead and take your inner self along. No matter where you are, Hashem is with you. Your task is to find Him.

The *Likkutei Moharan* explains how to do this by seeing, hearing, and feeling. Seeing is really noticing the moment and searching for possibilities. So when you're spending time with the children, ask yourself, "What's possible? Can I express love, boost their self esteem, teach them the rules of fair play, train them to speak nicely to one another, or tell them a story that will move them?" Hearing means really understanding. The more you hear and understand your children, the more opportunities will arise to give to them in a way that's meaningful and spiritual. Feeling is awakening your heart. Do everything with passion. Bring joy wherever you go. This may prove even more difficult than physical *chessed.*

See, hear, and go with your heart. It'll make tapping into the *kedushah* of Shabbos and Yom Tov a meaningful experience.

CANDLE LIGHTING WITHIN THE EIGHTEEN MINUTES

Q *Sometimes I am very busy Friday and I end up lighting candles within the 18 minutes. How bad is this?*

A We've lost a lot about what *Kabbalas Shabbos* really means. Ideally, we should bring in Shabbos in a calm and expectant manner. Make a less-fancy Shabbos, but be relaxed when it arrives. Do more on Wednesday and Thursday. The result of just having made it to the finish line isn't simply that you could accidentally break Shabbos if you're not careful, but it also means that on Shabbos itself your sense of sanctity and serenity isn't complete.

I'm not an organized person either. I tend to have hairline finishes. I'm the woman you see in the airport running with her suitcase on the moving staircase to catch her plane. Shabbos was a challenge for me, so I decided to bribe myself. If I finished everything I had to do by Thursday night, which often meant staying up very late, then I had Friday for me. I could spend the day doing the things I enjoyed such as visiting friends, going to the *Kosel*, or praying at Kever Rachel. It worked. My Fridays are completely different now. Hire a cleaning lady, organize your week. It's worth the extra effort and money so that Shabbos can be the day you'll look forward to all week.

SECULAR LITERATURE ON SHABBOS

I'm a big reader, and so are my husband and friends. I usually read at least three to five secular books during the weekend. Even though we don't pick out anything particularly inappropriate, even the tamest books have at least something that is probably not in the spirit of Shabbos. Should we put away the books on Shabbos? Should we stop reading secular literature altogether? What should we read instead?

The tricky thing about secular literature is that you become the characters of the books you read. The minority of non-Jewish people live decent, spiritually conscious lives. The vast majority are not wicked, but Hashem isn't relevant in their lives.

Secular reading can give you words to describe the world with great acuity and beauty. It can sensitize your heart to people that are different from you. However, it introduces you to a world where Hashem is irrelevant. So cut down on novels, even the best ones. Focus your reading more on nonfiction, but even there use a sifter.

Shabbos is an entirely different question. We can't begin to comprehend the holiness of Shabbos. On Shabbos Hashem's Presence comes down to this world, and He makes it possible for us to reach Him. Every moment of Shabbos is meant to be a moment of mindful awareness. If you find an area in Torah learning that excites you, Shabbos can be the most joyous and enlightened part of the week to study. Depending on your interest and textual skills, *Michtav MeEliyahu, Sfas Emes, Baal HaTanya, Maharal, Meforshei Peshat,* and *Meforshei Derash* are all excellent learning choices.

Shabbos is a time for truth, not escape. Use this precious day wisely.

MAKING SHABBOS MEANINGFUL FOR CHILDREN

Q *My kids spend most of Shabbos playing, fighting, and waiting for the day to be over. I almost wish davening in shul would take all day. What can I do to elevate the day?*

A The key is planning. Try to do as much as you can early in the week so that you can bring in Shabbos in a calm, relaxed manner. At night, the boys and your husband will leave for shul. In Israel it is quite common for women and girls to go too. Even if your daughters are very young or are not the shul-going types, they may enjoy *Kabbalas Shabbos,* which is short and has a lot of singing. If this isn't possible, try not to have the time disintegrate by taking a nap and leaving the kids to their own devices. Encourage your girls to participate in Friday night *shemiras halashon* groups and *Kabbalas Shabbos* clubs, if they are available in your neighborhood. At the evening *seudah,* involve all your children on some level in the discussion at the table. Prepare age-appropriate questions beforehand.

Try to put structure into the day. In the morning, give your children an *oneg Shabbos* breakfast with special treats. Buy board games and books and put them aside only for Shabbos. Don't make your kids sit through the entire day *seudah*. Involve them as much as their attention spans allow. Then let them play and come back for *zemiros* and *cholent*. Make the afternoon fun by telling stories and playing games. Take them out to visit friends or to the park. Encourage your older kids to join *Pirchei, Tehillim*, and *Bnos* groups.

Introduce some ritual to *shalosh seudos*. Ask your husband to save three or four inspirational songs for this meal. Whether or not the kids sing along, this will become a part of their *shalosh seudos* memories.

Rather than resent the long, unstructured hours of Shabbos, you can turn the day into a special opportunity to spend quality time with your children.

SHABBOS MEAL MENUS

Q *What are the parameters of cooking a Shabbos meal? In my circles, the women cook lots and lots of different, delicious foods. Then everybody can't help but overeat. I would love to know if there is a way to remedy this trend of stuffing ourselves silly for these special meals.*

A I cook very simply during the week, but I do cook a lot for Shabbos. One week I had thirteen salads on the table and my daughter mentioned that it was somewhat excessive.

The Shelah says that on Shabbos one should prepare many different kinds of food so that we can experience the varied flavors of creation. You can taste a bit of everything, but you don't have to eat a lot of anything. This way you won't walk away from the *seudah* stuffed, but you can still sample the myriad dishes that it is customary to eat on Shabbos.

HOW TO HANDLE NOT ATTENDING SHUL ON ROSH HASHANAH

Q *This will be the first year that I will not be able to attend shul for much of Rosh Hashanah and possibly Yom Kippur. There will be some (but probably very little) time for me to daven at home, as I have a little baby who needs constant care. I feel very defenseless. I realize that the nature of my next year will be determined at this time, and there is little opportunity for me to plead for myself. How can I handle this appropriately so that I can enjoy the Yomim Tovim and use the time to my advantage?*

A If you look at the Purim story, you'll see that Esther commanded the Jews to fast for three consecutive days, which happened to be Pesach. So you could ask, "What about the Seder? What about the mitzvah of *seudas Yom Tov* and *simchas Yom Tov*?" This is what the moment required. A *chacham* is someone who knows what to do at any given moment. This time of your life is precious. It will not come back. Be there for your baby and realize that when you are acting with compassion you are drawing down compassion from above.

My observation has been that people find time for what they want to do. Use the time you do have to learn what inspires you, so that the person you are while you're cooking or taking care of the baby is an enlightened, connected person.

There's a book called *Subota* by Yisrael Netzach that details how the author kept Shabbos in Siberia for 20 years. Oftentimes, he had no time to learn or daven, but he was *mekadesh Shem Shamayim* during those 20 years of brutal labor. Through his *mesirus nefesh*, he brought Hashem's transcendental reality into the world. I've seen everyday people do this. It's not easy.

My daughter told me about an acquaintance in Tzefas. This woman's little children all come home the same time she comes home from work. Instead of getting overwhelmed and frustrated, she makes sure the CD player is playing her children's favorite songs when they walk through the door. The focus on *simchah* that permeates that home is as good as *tefillah*.

When my second daughter was in seminary, she was assigned a *chessed* family with four young children. The mother was ill and could not manage the house and kids. Seminary girls would come in to help in the afternoon until the father came home at 5 p.m. to take over. When he arrived, he would immediately put up a big pot of cereal to cook (this was before the days of instant baby cereal) and sit and talk with his wife a bit. Then he would bathe and dress the kids, feed them their bottles, sing *Shema* with them, and put them to sleep. After all that, he would leave for his evening job as a waiter. This man and his family were full of *simchah*. This was a holy family. Would you say he was wasting his time when he could have been at third *seder* in yeshivah? This was serving Hashem on His terms, which is what *avodas Hashem* really is.

WOMEN AND SIMCHAS TORAH

Q *On Simchas Torah I have no particular desire to dance like the men, but I find just standing around and watching it very boring. It does nothing to develop my connection to Torah. What I've done for the last few years is spend the long morning learning Torah by myself, consciously valuing the experience and enjoying it. Is this okay, or should I really be in shul with the other women?*

A I understand your misgivings and I think your solution is excellent. Not all women would enjoy learning on their own, though. Many women are not so intellectually inclined.

Additionally, not all Simchas Torah celebrations are necessarily shallow. I've seen many with depth. I don't know where you live and what your opportunities are, but a fairly accurate measure of where genuine *simchah* can be found is where people really learn. There the celebration will be earnest.

In places where people learn less seriously they'll want to celebrate with the Torah and they'll do what they're supposed to, but it may sometimes come across forced or superficial. I've also seen the difference between yeshivos where the boys are young and those where the boys are more mature and real in their celebration.

I won't say watching the *simchah* has no effect, but I do understand that for some people, experiencing the Torah directly through learning may do the same thing or more. However, I would still recommend you try a place where true *simchah* is palpable.

CHANUKAH GIFTS AND THE TORAH HASHKAFAH

Q*Does giving Chanukah gifts have any basis in halachah? When I was growing up we received only Chanukah gelt (coins). New clothing and presents were reserved for the big Yamim Tovim like Pesach or Succos, which I think is more in tune with halachah.*

AWhile Chanukah *gelt* is an accepted *minhag*, Chanukah gifts are certainly not based on halachah. It has become somewhat of an imitation of the December holiday. However, if you live in a community where gift giving is expected, it is important that you not make your children feel different and deprived. Get them a small gift, but tell them clearly, "Chanukah is not really a time for presents. Erev Yom Tov is when we get the really beautiful and extravagant gifts." Point out that they already got their presents earlier for Succos. This will make them feel special instead of left out.

HAUNTED BY THE TRAGEDY OF ESTHER

Q *Every year when I listen to the Megillah, I am haunted by Esther's tragedy. How can we understand her personal suffering?*

A Esther's tragic saga is a living metaphor of the Divine Presence in exile. There was no exile worse than Esther's. She was a prophetess, righteous beyond anything we can imagine, and yet she was forced to marry the evil Achashveirosh and bear his child. Her fortitude in maintaining her identity in spite of all she had to contend with is similar to the reality at the time of the Second Temple. While the Divine Presence was apparent during the First Temple, it was hidden during the Second Temple. Finding Hashem in His place of concealment is in many ways greater than finding Him in His place of revelation.

At the end of time, the light of the moon will eclipse the light of the sun. The glow of those who absorbed only reflected light will equal those who gave forth light.

The Gemara tells us that the women of the tents — that is, our *Imahos* — will see that there were women who weren't of the tent who were as great as they were. This means that the women whose lives were more difficult and who held onto their *emunah* were in a sense even greater than the *Imahos*.

This is what Esther teaches us. Her life is an inspiration to all of us to hold onto our heritage despite the darkness and pain of exile.

FEELING LIKE A QUEEN AT THE SEDER

At the Seder night we're supposed to be like kings at our table. Does this refer only to men, or does it also refer to women? If I'm busy most of the evening serving and taking care of the kids and guests, how am I supposed to feel like royalty?

Perhaps you envision a king as luxuriating in repose. Today kings are little more than figureheads, but long ago they were powerful, active leaders. Being a king at the Seder doesn't mean relaxing. It means taking on an aura of regality. For a man, it's his ability to lead the Seder. For a woman, it's her capacity for making it happen in a way that's graceful, dignified, and beautiful.

Ideally, you should be able to look at your kitchen the way my *mechuteniste* once did. She was hosting a *Sheva Berachos* in her small Israeli apartment. The men were in the living room, and the women were in the bedroom, which was cleared out for the occasion. She was serving, and when I went to the kitchen to help her, she said, "This is my kingdom," and she wasn't all that anxious to accept my assistance. This is where you can try to put yourself. It's your kingdom. It's what you've been preparing for all along.

I would suggest that you try to simplify things so that you have time to sit down, say the Haggadah, and feel something of the evening. Delegate tasks to your kids and guests. Prepare things on trays before the Seder so they can just be taken out when needed. Plan simpler food without a lot of accompaniments. Try to streamline all the technicalities beforehand so that you can absorb as much of the magic of the Seder as possible.

Tefillah: The Power of Prayers

THE RIGHT APPROACH TO TEHILLIM

In your book, Our Bodies Our Souls, and elsewhere, you write about women and their special connection to Tehillim. I am new to Judaism and I would really like to become more familiar with Tehillim. How do I start? Are there any good commentaries that can help me really understand what I'm saying? I know some Hebrew, but I need to glance at the English translation frequently. I have an interlinear Tehillim but would love any suggestions you may have.

I don't know where you live, but certainly in Israel and in large religious Jewish communities in America, there are many organized women's *Tehillim* groups. Search for such a group near you. If there are none, align yourself with a particular group and recite *Tehillim* every day, at the same time they do. Even though you are not physically present, there is a certain spiritual energy you can connect to by being part of something larger than yourself.

Tehillim is about invoking the voice of King David. Adam, King David, and Mashiach are universal souls. King David and Mashiach have their root in the first man, Adam. Adam gifted 70 years of his life to King David so that David's soul, which was not destined to survive, could bring forth the exceptional potential that it had. Because of this, King David was able to write about every possible human experience a person could have in the course of life.

A good way to begin exploring the extraordinary power of *Tehillim* would be to study a good commentary such as that of Rav Samson Raphael Hirsch. I would recommend that you say a chapter of *Tehillim* a day. Reciting one chapter with devotion and focus is better than saying five chapters without the proper concentration. Realize that some chapters are long and some are quite short, so you may want to be flexible about this. Write down which chapters resonate with you. At the end of about three months you should have your own minibook of *Tehillim* complete with the chapters that really speak to you and reflect who you are.

Tehillim has phenomenal power. It was revealed to King David that his Five Books of *Tehillim* paralleled the spiritual force contained in the Five Books of the *Chumash*. That's huge. There's supernatural energy contained in every word of *Tehillim*. It's not just about how much emotion and focus you put into it as you say the verses; the inherent value of the words is also powerful. For that reason, *Tehillim* has become the second most popular Jewish holy book after the *Siddur*.

HOW MUCH SHOULD A WOMAN DAVEN?

Q *In one of your lectures, you discussed our struggle with the yetzer hara, and you spoke of a woman trying to daven a long Shemoneh Esrei as a negative thing. Since I'm new to prayer and trying to figure out what is appropriate, I wonder if you could elaborate on this idea. How long is "long"? How long is good? What should I expect of myself, and what is considered too much?*

It depends on each individual's life situation. Your list of priorities should be as follows — what is required and what is not required by Jewish law. Prayer is certainly a requirement, but a woman has other priorities. She is required to be her husband's wife first and then her children's mother. If she works, then she has ethical responsibilities to her employer that may preclude taking long breaks for prayer. No one can daven for you, but, just as certainly, no one can be your husband's wife or your children's mother. So you have to put a limit on davening when you see it is taking over the whole picture.

I know one responsible woman who takes very good care of her family and spends two hours each morning on prayer because she has those free hours. I know other women who have many responsibilities who can devote only 20 minutes to half an hour to *tefillah*. So it very much depends on your circumstances.

If you can daven only the minimum, at least in *Shemoneh Esrei*, think about who you are, Who it is you are addressing, where all blessings come from, and what you'll do with what you'll be given. Aim for proper *kavannah*. It is much better to say less in a way that's really focused than more because you have the mistaken idea that it's better to say everything in the *Siddur*.

PEREK SHIRAH

I would really like to start saying Perek Shirah, but I'm not sure how to go about it. Should I recite the entire tefillah each day, or is one chapter a day enough? Can you explain more about the origins and significance of Perek Shirah?

A There's no obligation to say *Perek Shirah*. However, if you do recite it, it should be said in its entirety and not one chapter at a time.

Its origin is ancient. It is considered a holy prayer. King David, King Shlomo, and the later Sages composed and compiled it. There are several commentaries on *Perek Shirah*, including one by the Chasam Sofer, who wrote extensively on it.

What *Perek Shirah* represents is the idea that everything we see is really making a statement. We perceive Hashem through free choice. Nature serves Hashem existentially, just by the fact of its being. Therefore, when we say, "*Shamayim ma hu omer*" or "*Kelev ma hu omer*," we are not asking what the sky proclaims or what the dog says. We know what thunder sounds like and the way dogs bark. What we are really asking is, "What is the statement made to us experientially by the existence of the sky and the dog?" *Perek Shirah* deepens and broadens our ability to look at nature and recognize Hashem.

The *Baal HaLeshem* says that in ancient times before the Torah was given, people knew Hashem the way we later perceived Him through *Perek Shirah*. This concept is especially relevant for women, who are more involved with the physical world. Our unique purpose is to find the spirituality within our everyday life and to utilize each moment as an opportunity to come closer to Hashem.

TEFILLAH — CAN IT CAUSE BAD REPERCUSSIONS?

Q *In Parashas Va'eschanan, Moshe prayed 515 prayers to be allowed into Eretz Yisrael. Hashem ordered him to stop praying. If Moshe would have continued, Hashem would have been "forced" to agree, which could have caused the destruction of the Jewish people during the Churban. How could evil possibly result from Moshe's* *tefillos? If by praying for the wrong thing, a person could receive something bad, how are we expected to know when to pray and when to stop?*

The *Nefesh HaChaim* discusses this issue. Hashem responds to us the way we conduct ourselves, as it says, "Hashem is the shadow of your right hand" *(Tehillim* 121*).* The same way the shadow follows the hand, so too an awakening from above is caused by an awakening from below. That is the idea of Hashem being, so to speak, "forced" to act in a certain way. This form of rulership is called "*Ohr Penimi,*" the inner light of a person, which draws Hashem's light into the world. Hashem also interacts with us occasionally through *"Ohr Makif,"* an all-encompassing light, where He gives because He so desires, unrelated to human action.

When Moshe prayed, Hashem asked him to stop, because if Moshe would have continued, it would have been bad for the future existence of the Jewish nation.

Why doesn't Hashem always intervene when *tzaddikim* pray? Anything a person does affects both him and the entire world. Therefore, a punishment may sometimes come not because of personal *tikkun,* but to help bring about *tikkun olam.* Only Hashem sees all the pieces of the puzzle; only He knows what the entire image of reality is meant to look like. Similarly, when a person cries out, it might bring down blessing. Additionally, the world may need to see the living example of a *tzaddik* suffering yet still maintaining his faith. The *tzaddik* may need the test of *bitachon* that comes from travail. A final possibility is that *tefillah* itself draws a person closer to Hashem. If the *tzaddik* could see things from a distance, he would ask for suffering in order to achieve that special relationship.

All the Matriarchs were barren except Leah. Hashem created this situation for *tikkun olam* and *tikkun tzaddikim.* When Hashem finally answered Yitzchak's prayers, the twins were born. Hashem caused Avraham to die five years earlier than originally planned so that he would not see Esav become evil. If Yitzchak's prayers had been answered earlier, Avraham would have died even earlier, which would not have been good for the world. Even if one would think that Yitzchak's prayers brought about a bad result, Hashem on His terms had a reason for Avraham's premature death, which had to do with both Avraham and the world.

Don't worry about negative repercussions. Your role is to pray. Hashem's role is to give you what's right for you, either because it fits your needs or because of *tikkun olam*.

ATTENDING SHUL ON SHABBOS

Q *I live in Jerusalem. I have a physically demanding job as a nurse, which frequently involves working long hours. On Shabbos morning, I am so happy not to have to get up at 5 a.m. that sleeping late is incredibly attractive. I really like davening on my own and I don't enjoy the social part of going to shul. Are these compelling reasons not to go?*

A There are several reasons why we go to shul. The main reason is that our prayers are more potent with a *minyan*. Some women find it more inspiring to pray in shul. However, since halachah never required women even without young children to attend shul, it is really up to the individual.

Since you are in Jerusalem, where there are a plethora of *minyanim*, I would suggest you try going to a shul that begins a bit later. If this won't work for you, then it is perfectly okay for you to stay home. You can attend shul on the *Yamim Noraim* or during times when you feel you need to draw down greater merits by connecting to Hashem through the power of a *tzibbur*.

INCREASING KAVANNAH IN TEFILLAH

Q *How can I increase my kavannah in tefillah? Can you provide some practical ideas?*

A Create an image that speaks to you and use it to guide you through *tefillah*. I'll suggest one but you can use your own.

Close your eyes and picture yourself as a young child, way before you realized that your parents didn't have much control over events. Imagine your father or mother telling you, "It'll be okay." Take that moment of absolute trust and transfer that feeling to Hashem. Only He cares for you in the ultimate sense, and only He can give you what you need. Any image that evokes a feeling of faith, love, reliance, and dependence will work. Take it along with you when you start davening.

Try to concentrate on the meaning of the words. It's difficult to move from an external, action-oriented world to an internal world where you have to feel absolute reliance on Hashem. When you say *Pesukei DeZimrah*, try to draw Hashem's infinity into your heart. When you get to *Shemoneh Esrei*, think about Hashem's Omnipotence and recognize that it's only His life force and essence that can give you anything at all.

DAVENING MINCHAH AFTER MARRIAGE

Q *I was a regular and intense Minchah davener for most of my life until I got married. Now I can hardly handle cooking, cleaning, and work, so I've basically given up davening Minchah for now. I did not consult a Rav about it. Is this okay?*

According to the Rambam, women are required to daven only once a day. Ashkenazim rule according to the *Mishnah Berurah*, who holds that a woman should daven Minchah. Therefore, not davening Minchah is *bedi'avad*, which means that you will need to learn to restructure your day to make room for it.

I know people with large families who work at serious jobs, have reasonably clean homes, and still find time to daven Minchah. It's really a matter of learning time control and organization. There are several excellent books on this topic. Buy them and study them. Make time your friend, not your enemy. Do this as soon as possible, because if you can't fit in Minchah now before you have kids, you won't be able to fit in Shacharis after you have kids.

Don't rely on the lenient opinion. As the *Kuzari* writes, our souls need *tefillah* the way our bodies require food. You have to bring Hashem into your heart and mind several times a day. It's not worth it for you to enter a state of malnourishment. Of course there are exceptional circumstances, where you can go by the Rambam. But, *l'chatchilah*, when the afternoon comes, you should have those precious minutes set aside for Minchah, so that you can remind yourself to always be reliant on Hashem before you trust yourself.

I CAN'T DAVEN IN PUBLIC

Q *I can't daven in front of people. I get very self-conscious, and I find myself unable to concentrate at all. I also don't like to bentch in public. This is a problem, since I eat at least two or three meals a week with others. I've been this way forever. How can I get over this problem?*

A Begin by taking the word "can't" out of your lexicon. Obviously you can. Unless there's something wrong with you physically, you can pick up a *Siddur* and say the words.

144 / The Balancing Act

Make Hashem a constant presence in your life by learning to speak to Him every day in your own words. It will take time, but eventually you will reach a point where focusing on people won't be an issue for you anymore. If Hashem is right there beside you, people become irrelevant.

A second approach would be to just do it. There are two ways to start swimming. You can spend a good five minutes getting used to the water, or you can dive right in.

The first thing you have to do is see that you can do it. The question is whether you will. People sometimes adopt rigid behaviors because they worry about what people will think of them. I think part of your insecurity with davening in public may have something to do with this. Your issue is not impressing others but not believing that you can address yourself to Hashem in the real world.

At the beginning of Avraham's life, when he came to Eretz Yisrael, he built various altars in close sequence. At the last altar he called Hashem *"Keil Elyon* — the Force of the world." He felt obligated to make the world aware of Hashem's Presence. Therefore, Avraham called out *"b'kol gadol* — with a mighty voice."

Every time you bentch in public, you strengthen people's belief that bread comes from Hashem. It says *"B'rov am hadras Melech* — the glory of the king is increased with many people." By being another voice, you will find another dimension of *l'shem Shamayim* in your bentching. Don't try to work on breaking this habit because it's unpleasant for you. Do it *"lemaan Shemo b'ahavah* — for the sake of Hashem's Name, with love."* Because of your love for Him, you'll thank Him for the good, not in spite of the fact that there are people around, but because there are people.

Create a new mantra for yourself to replace your old one. Your old one said, "I can't." Your new one should now say, "I have to."

PRAYING FOR OTHERS

Q *If the main purpose of prayer is to change the person who prays, how does it work when we pray for others?*

A Even though we see one another as separate individuals, Hashem sees us as one collective soul. From that perspective, when you daven for others, you are really davening for yourself. The more compassion you feel for the person you are praying for, the more compassion you will draw down from above. And indeed the effect can be very profound.

PRAYING ON SHABBOS

Q *I learned that we are not supposed to make requests on Shabbos. I am never sure exactly what I can daven for in the Shabbos Shemoneh Esrei prayer. Can you give me some guidance?*

A One should not pray for physical things on Shabbos except in situations that are life-threatening. Some *Poskim* rule that one may pray for spiritual things. Therefore, reciting *Techinos* or *Tehillim* on Shabbos, which express our longing for Hashem and for closeness to Him, is permitted.

Tzniyus

TZNIYUS IN THOUGHT AND SPEECH

Q *Can you suggest some practical ways to improve tzniyus in thought and speech? A friend of mine accidentally found herself discussing something with an inappropriate audience. In thinking about this incident and how it could happen, I realized that perhaps the problem didn't boil down to just not thinking about who else was in the room, but that maybe we are too comfortable talking about almost anything. Perhaps more subjects need to be off-limits, and maybe that is the real cause. How does one go about working on oneself to establish clearer boundaries in this area? What are some ways to gently give reproof to others regarding this issue?*

A The need to externalize and talk about everything comes from not having an inner life. It is certainly inappropriate to discuss everything, and more so in the presence of an audience. Personal matters such as issues relating to marriage, private life, and deep feelings about people should never be discussed in public. It is good to have one close friend with whom you can discuss almost anything, with the explicit intent that she serve not just as your sounding board, but also as your mentor.

In terms of yourself, the more you learn to pour out your personal and private feelings to Hashem, the less you'll need to involve other people. As far as others are concerned, my own experience has shown that people don't enjoy talking to a disinterested audience. If it becomes clear to you that your friend is venting not because she wants advice, but because she is involved in an ongoing inappropriate monologue about herself, looking bored will send her the subtle message to shift the conversation elsewhere.

RESPECTING TZNIYUS

Q *In my community, the standards of tzniyus are quite different from those espoused by the Chareidi community. Do you think I need to conform to the Chareidi rules when I visit my Chareidi relatives in order not to cause anyone discomfort?*

A Your problem is that you don't think *tzniyus* is a virtue. You wouldn't find it all that terrible if someone told your child to be kinder. You probably have no problem with people giving more *tzedakah*, being more honest, doing more *chessed*, and living a more righteous life than you do.

Yes, you would probably feel awkward, as I did when I was once visiting the Rachmastrivke Rebbetzin. Someone came to the door asking for *tzedakah*. She listened to the whole story, read the letter through completely (which I usually don't), and then began showering the man with *berachos*. She named a sum that she would give (which is a lot more than what I usually give) and apologized that this was all she could offer. She then went to the kitchen and returned with double the amount she had promised. I felt small and cheap in her presence. I'm willing to say that the experience was worth it because it ignited something inside me to want to grow in *chessed*.

If you have *Chareidi* relatives who are more modest, let that be an inspiration to you for greater refinement. Set your aspirations toward something higher than your status quo. *Tzniyus* is a virtue, and there's always room for growth. You don't have to content yourself with mediocrity; there's nothing admirable about doing so.

ARE SHEITELS OKAY?

Q *I recently read that sheitels are not tzniyus and anyone who wears one will not greet Mashiach. I need to know the emes. Are sheitels okay?*

A There are very reliable sources in halachah that maintain that *sheitels* are permitted. The Chazon Ish ruled in his times that wearing a *sheitel* should be encouraged. The Lubavitcher Rebbe also voiced the same opinion. Both came from a similar position, which held that women were more likely to cover their hair completely with a wig and would do it more joyfully if they felt they looked good.

There are a significant number of *Poskim* who ruled against wearing *sheitels*. Prominent among them were the *Badatz* of Yerushalayim and Rav Ovadia Yosef.

Today's wigs are often very immodest by anyone's standards. Don't constrain yourself. Do what you think is most modest. But be sure that the choice you make remains within the framework of *tzniyus*.

TZNIYUS AND REPROACHING OTHERS

Q *Sometimes I see people who are somewhat close to me dressed in a manner that is way beneath their level in other areas. Should I just daven that they overcome this challenge themselves, or should I say something?*

A The first step is to ask yourself whether you have a positive relationship with the person. If you don't, your comments may just make the other person defensive. The next step is to honestly consider why you want to correct the person. If it is because she doesn't make the family look good or it undermines your own *kavod*, then it will probably not work. However, if this is not where the person herself wants to be either, then you can give it a shot.

The best way to approach her would be to talk about yourself. You can say, "You know, after I had my third baby, nothing fit me either. I had to replace everything." Or, "I'm going shopping on Tuesday. Do you want to come along?" If it's a practical problem, try to come up with a solution. You can say, "I know this seamstress who is great at altering. The skirt I just bought is too short and I'm taking it over to her today. Do you want me to take yours too?" The idea is for your reproof to come from a place of friendship, caring, and honesty. Trust yourself. If you say what you need to, with warmth and respect, you can change things for the better.

PHYSICAL BEAUTY IN JUDAISM

Q *What does Judaism say about physical beauty? Since people are wired to think more positively about a good-looking person, should a woman use this quality to influence others for the good?*

A It doesn't say *"Sheker hachein v'hevel hayofi* — Charm is false and beauty is vanity" for nothing. Beauty fades with time. No one should build her identity on her looks. However, charisma has its place, such as when a woman speaks before other woman or teaches children.

You should certainly not consider using beauty as an asset in a secular career. On the contrary, if you work in the public sector, such as in the medical field or in the high-tech industry, you should take extra care to appear in a way that is extremely refined and modest.

TZNIYUS GUIDELINES IN RELATING TO MEN

Q *Can you give me some tzniyus guidelines on relating to men such as my brother-in-law, son's principal, or friend's husband? While I don't mean to come across as rude, I find that things can get too friendly too fast.*

A Talk *"l'inyan,"* which means stick to the matter at hand. If you're talking to your son's principal, it should be only about your son. After all, that is why you're speaking to him in the first place. If you're talking to your brother-in-law about a family matter, stick to the subject. Keep in mind why you are speaking to him.

There's nothing wrong with conforming to minimum social expectations, but keep conversations brief and to the point.

EMPHASIS ON EXTERNAL TZNIYUS

Q *I found your classes on tzniyus enlightening, especially the ideas of being focused on what's real, being aware of Hashem's Presence, and not needing to be the center of attention. Why have most of* us never heard of these concepts? What people might say is that *tzniyus* is not only about how we dress, but also about what we say, think, and do. But it's still always along the lines of physical appearance and attraction. The *middah* of *penimiyus* is so externalized today. I think that in order to work on something, we need to understand where it stems from within ourselves. Is it that *tzniyus* is so hard to get hold of because modern values are in the air we breathe?

The Gra tells us that at the end of time, the part of Torah we will treasure most will be *penimiyus HaTorah*, the inner dimension. Indeed, we are seeing more and more of our leaders spreading this aspect of Torah. Our generation is thirsting for this.

I would assume that there are two reasons why we hear so little about the *penimiyus* of *tzniyus*. The first reason may be that just about a generation ago, *tzniyus* was so internalized, so automatic, that no one had to explain why being refined, modest, and dignified was a virtue. It's the same way no one today has to justify *chessed*. You understand that someone is in need, and if you're a compassionate person, you'll respond as best as you can. Instinctive *tzniyus* is far from today's reality.

The second reason is that immodesty is so rampant and has damaged people in so many ways that we must put out the fire with emergency measures. This means at least keeping within the dimensions of external *tzniyus*. We're plugging the holes, which is why there is so much stress on the technical aspects of *tzniyus* today.

However, you are correct that learning about the *middah* is important too. I think both measures are necessary. While we work to enforce halachic standards, *tzniyus* groups such as Ateres for young girls and Bnos Melachim for women have done wonderful work in imparting the beauty and majesty of *tzniyus*.

JUDGMENTS BASED ON CLOTHING

Q *In today's era it seems like people decide if families are really religious based on very strict observance of tzniyus in dress, as if more covered and more austere is better. I follow halachah, but I do not conform to extra stringencies in tzniyus. I have no criticism for anyone who chooses to dress this way, but I don't think it's for me. I was brought up to believe that there are basic laws of modesty, and after that, the standards are determined by the individual, the community, and one's Rabbi. How should I react when people make judgments about me based on my clothing? Should I say something? Should I keep quiet? I am very uncomfortable with any remarks and assumptions.*

A Your goal should be to move beyond the level of your community. You should be a seeker. In a small Jewish community you won't find many people who are more than you in any regard. However, in a mid-sized community, you can meet new people with higher standards. That broadens your choices. It's not just you against the non-Jewish or non-religious backdrop. It's you against people who have developed to a higher level.

There are three responses you can have: You can resent them. "How dare they make me feel like number two?" Or, "Wow, new possibilities. I have to be me, but boy, it's so interesting to see higher standards." You can then seriously question what you can integrate into your own life, and how. A third response would be to outwardly integrate these stringencies. Two of these three options are self-limiting. If you wear the clothes and talk the talk but don't assimilate the values, you're creating a situation of profound inner conflict. Often this results in one of two negative outcomes — feeling so not at home with oneself that one slides all the way back, or having your own children perceive you as a hypocrite. The middle path is your best option. Say,

"Here's something more." Not being afraid of it and considering how much and when to integrate it into your life is the healthiest way to go.

There are different levels of modesty. Some have to do with refinement and sensitivity, and most are not related to pure halachah. It's not worth it for you to devalue *hiddur* in *tzniyus*, any more than you would devalue *hiddur* in kashrus or *chessed*. It's okay if the ceiling is higher. Just like you wouldn't feel resentful if you read about a great *tzaddik*'s accomplishments in *chessed*, you don't have to feel resentful if your neighbors are more modest than you are. Don't feel like you need to adopt standards you're not up to yet. Accept yourself and give it time.

Tzniyus is different from other mitzvos, because image and dress cannot be separated. Unlike kashrus, people see *tzniyus* as soon as they see you. Lesser standards means that you live in a world where the ceiling is lower, which may be accurate. Take the heat; it's not that terrible. If you don't want to, ask yourself, "How much of this can I take on, at what pace, and where?" If you keep growing, you'll never regret it.

I have a friend who came on *aliyah* from South Africa. She lived in Netanya for a while but then ended up in Meah Shearim. She's been living there for 22 years now. She's elegant, regal, but still very much in conformance with the standards of the women in her courtyard. She's happy because she's charting her own growth, and so can you.

WOMEN DANCING IN PUBLIC AND ON VIDEO

Q *Is there a difference between watching women dance at a wedding in person or watching them dance on video?*

A There is no difference. Therefore, most weddings in Yerushalayim have two photographers and videographers, a man for the men's side and a woman for the women. Often there are two separate videotapes. Women can watch the wedding with the women included, while men will see the videotape without. This doesn't cost much more and seems to be a very easy solution to the problem.

WEARING SHORT SLEEVES

Q *I have a friend who is an observant women and covers her hair, but for some reason she thinks it's okay to wear short sleeves. What is the best way to approach her so that she'll listen to me and not become defensive?*

A With friends you have to be open. Try to steer the conversation to head coverings. You can say something like, "What kind of *sheitels* do you have?" Or, "Do you know where they sell scarves that look nice?" Or, "I remember the time when so many women didn't cover their hair."

At this point she will no doubt be with you. From there, you can pick one of several options. You can say, "You know, there are so many opinions about things, even with hair coverings. Who do you ask about these things?" Odds are she doesn't ask anyone. You can then say, "There seem to be so many opinions about sleeves too. Who do you talk to about those issues?" No matter who she names, no Orthodox Rabbi will say that short sleeves are okay.

If she's not intellectual, she probably thinks long sleeves are a stringency, or she's simply not holding there. Don't try an intellectual approach on a non-intellectual person. It won't work. Instead, go shopping with her and start a discussion on how hard it is to find shirts with long sleeves. You could say, "I've always wondered if it is difficult for you to find shirts with long sleeves. I also think it's a huge hassle." Try to see where she's holding. If she gets defensive, you could say, "I'm just talking about why it's so hard. I'm not telling you what to do."

Your goal is to open her up with the intent to say at the end, "Let's find out what the halachah really is." Let her suggest a Rav and encourage her to discuss the issue with him further. If she's genuinely open to learn the truth, she'll be honest enough to want to change.

"MINHAG HAMAKOM"

Q *I live in an area where some women wear tights and some don't. How do I determine what the minhag hamakom is?*

A Your *makom* is the community that you are a part of. You have to ask yourself where you define yourself and where you really belong. You can then go by the customs of that community.

Another thing to consider is, "*Maalin ba'kodesh v'einam moridin* — We always want to ascend spiritually and not descend." If the *bnei aliyah* (the people who take halachah seriously and desire to grow) in your geographical area follow a certain path, then you should strive to model yourself after them.

DRESSING MODESTLY AND BEING CONSPICUOUS

Q *If the whole point of dressing in a tzniyus manner is not to attract attention, how can one dress modestly in a place where most people are not doing so, such as in Manhattan or in a small Jewish community? Won't this draw people's attention?*

The point of modesty is not only blending into the background but appearing dignified. Self-respect comes from within. *Tzniyus* means projecting a polished, gracious image, so that your inner self is your defined self.

In Manhattan you could dress quite modestly without being conspicuous. You won't be on the cutting edge, which is a lot shorter and tighter than *tzniyus* will allow, but will shorter and tighter make you look more dignified? Is that what the soul finds comfortable as its outer expression? Of course being fully clothed on a hot summer day in a non-Jewish city is conspicuous, but not more so than a yeshivah student sporting *tzitzis* on a plane or an observant Jew wearing a *kippah* at his secular workplace. This sort of sticking out is a statement of who you are and what you stand for, and it's okay.

In a small Jewish community, people expect a rebbetzin to look like one. If you're a Bais Yaakov graduate, even if you're 17, you're a rebbetzin in their eyes. As Rav Hirsch would put it, wherever you are you have to make a *kiddush Hashem*. See yourself as a lamplighter. You have the power to open up new possibilities for them without even saying a word. If it is what they need to see, they'll eventually want it on their own.

The key is really liking people, seeing their virtues, and realizing that if you had to fight their battles, you wouldn't necessarily win either.

DIFFICULT TRANSITION TO TZNIYUS

I've been adhering more and more to the strict standards of tzniyus, though I didn't grow up with these laws. Yet whenever I return to visit the people and places I grew up with, I tend to discard most of it. I don't want anyone to notice that I'm dressing differently, especially my friends and family, who equate tzniyus with some kind of strict religiosity that they resent. What can I do in order to make this transition easier for myself and those around me?

The real problem is within yourself. You don't value your *tzniyus*. You see it as a system you'd like to adhere to, but it isn't something that makes you proud.

I question your attitude toward the observant community. It seems somewhat ambivalent. You need to associate more with the people who are respected and admired in the community. You need role models. You must be able to say, "I'm on that team," and mean it and feel happy about it.

If you can do this experientially that is best, but if not, do it through reading. Develop your pride in *tzniyus* until you reach a point where you feel comfortable projecting yourself to others as a person who made a decision in life to be what you truly admire being.

If you are not self-conscious wearing *tzniyus* clothing, people will pick up on these vibes and feel the same way toward you.

Chapter 3

Raising Our Children

Questions of Chinuch

AT WHAT AGE SHOULD A CHILD DAVEN SHEMONEH ESREI?

Q *I have an 8-year-old son who enjoys learning and going to shul with his father on Shabbos. His reading skills are fine — not excellent, not too bad. He stands to daven Shemoneh Esrei, but certainly does not say every word. At what point should my husband start insisting that he pray properly?*

A simple answer would be at around age 10 or 11. However, it really depends. Although most 8-year-olds can reasonably be expected to daven *Shemoneh Esrei*, some may find saying the whole thing difficult and tedious. Since your son needs encouragement and not discouragement, you'll want to wait till his reading skills are really good so that he can read the words easily.

Another thing that might help is if every so often his father mentions something included in the *Shemoneh Esrei* that your son can relate to. For example, your husband can talk with him about the things your son likes about Shabbos — family time, good food, nice clothing, having friends over. He can then say, "You know, we didn't first find out about Shabbos when Hashem told us about it at *Matan Torah*. Moshe already knew about it beforehand. Picture the *nachas* Moshe must be having in Heaven when he sees so many thousands of people keeping Shabbos."

Before Shabbos, you can put a pencil mark next to the *berachah Yismach Moshe* and say, "Imagine how happy Hashem and Moshe are when we keep Shabbos."

Mini-lessons in *kavannah* can kindle that spark of inspiration within your son's heart to really want to daven.

TEACHING CHILDREN THE MEANING OF PRAYER

My young daughter recently informed me that while she learned how to bentch in preschool, she never learned the meaning of the words. Neither does she know what she's saying when she davens. This astounds me. I learned the meaning of all the prayers when I became religious, and I figured this was something Jewish children must know at an early age. Why aren't all Jewish children taught the language of their people — at the very least as it pertains to speaking with their Creator?

Young children don't daven with *kavannah* because they can't grasp abstract concepts. Their world is very concrete and self-oriented. They're mini *ta'avah-ga'avah* packages. It's unreasonable to expect them to understand what they're saying.

When I was a child, we had to say the "pledge of allegiance" in school. I recall being clueless about what some of the words meant and entirely uninterested in finding out. What mattered to me was that I could stand up, put my hand on my heart, and say the words right. That's basically where *frum* young kids are with *tefillah*. As long as they can say it the way they're supposed to, they feel okay. Don't worry about it.

At this stage, the most important idea to teach little children is *emunah*. Tell them about the Creator and how everything they touch, smell, or eat comes from Him. Teach them how Hashem gives us everything because He loves us and how He set up the world to benefit us. Explain to them how when they break the rules, there is punishment because Hashem wants us to keep the mitzvos. If they grasp *emunah*, they will eventually develop *kavannah*. The day will come when they realize that what they're saying has something to do with the invisible being called Hashem.

Be proactive in nurturing their *emunah*. Stories of *tzaddikim* are a wonderful way to impart faith to your children. In the Bais Yaakov system they do teach the explanations of prayers in the older elementary grades and in high school. Your girls will eventually learn what the prayers mean. However, whether that will translate into actual *kavannah* or not will very much depend on their foundation of *emunah*.

INSPIRING MY CHILD TO DAVEN

Q *My 10-year-old daughter finds davening boring. I can't think of ways to inspire her aside from telling her that Hashem is waiting for her tefillos and that she can ask for anything she wants (like new shoes or clothes). Can you help me with more ideas?*

A If, like most 10-year-olds, your daughter is not extraordinarily spiritual, she will not like davening. Accept this as realistic for her stage of development, just as her *chessed* is probably not completely *lishmah*, either. Babies start out completely materialistic and as their spirits grow, they become more spiritually attuned. Your daughter has a good two years before she'll become more sensitized.

All you can do during this time is make davening more appealing and inspiring by teaching her the tunes to some of the *tefillos* and helping her understand what the words mean. Sometimes communal davening helps too. Obviously she'll need a lot of affirmation and appreciation, but 10-year-olds in general don't daven with *kavannah*, so don't have unrealistic expectations.

MY CHILD IS BEING BULLIED

Q *Could you suggest what I should say to my child if another child tells her, "No one wants to play with you"?*

A This is a very "girl" kind of thing to say, so I suspect the child is a girl. You need to ascertain whether your child is socially deficient in any way or if the other child is just being nasty. There could be a number of reasons why your daughter is being ostracized. Is she clean, dressed well, "with it," and properly equipped when she comes to school? If there is a specific reason why the other children view her as different, then make it your business to fix it right away.

If it's just the usual picture of an insecure child zeroing in on another because of her own needs and insecurities, you need to respond in a different way. Make your house attractive for kids by providing good games and *nosh*, and invite other children to play with your child. This will tell your daughter that she is basically okay and will make you much more credible when you say, "That girl felt bad so she wanted to make herself feel good by putting you down. Poor girl, for some reason she doesn't feel like number one already. She'll grow out of it."

Teach your child to respond on a mature level by suggesting that she tell the nasty girl, "Why are you saying these things? Do you enjoy saying things like that?" Your child will realize it's not her problem but the other person's.

If there really is something wrong that you cannot fix, then you will need to toughen up your child. Tell her, "Look, the issue isn't you. This girl would like everyone to have exactly the same of everything. You're you. Hashem gave you what you needed. She just doesn't see it." In this way, you've created an attitude that says, "Poor her, her vision of life is limited. You're okay. Don't take it personally."

WHO ARE OUR HEROES?

Q *How do I convince my day-school students not to want to be sports or entertainment celebrities? How do I prevent my own future children from thinking this way?*

A There is a part within us that yearns for spiritual perfection. The way to access it is through stories. The more you can weave past and current tales of *tzaddikim* into your interaction with your students, the more the invisible ceiling of righteousness will move upward. Tell them about today's Torah heroes. Read to them about people who did things that were extraordinary. You can dial into *Kol HaLashon,* a free telephone *shiur* service, and listen to tales of *tzaddikim.* Learn them and tell them to your students.

Imagery is what binds the mind to the body. You can tell a story and it will inspire your child's heart. When you talk to your kids, tell them about the people you really admire. Let them feel your awe. Tell their stories with drama. This will move them and instill within them a sense of who our true heroes really are.

DEALING WITH ADHD

Does the Torah say anything about the proper way to raise a child with ADHD? I'm somewhat skeptical of the diagnosis that the school seems to have pushed on my son.

Find out if the child really has a problem by having him tested privately. ADHD is definitely over-diagnosed. Many parents think their children suffer from ADHD, when what they really lack is a sense of order in their lives. The first step is to institute set rules in the home. The child should be made to adhere to getting-up time, cleanup time, suppertime, and bedtime. Be sure he has all his school supplies and is dressed neatly and properly. The more order you introduce, the safer and more secure the child will feel. If the child feels externally equipped, it will give him enough control to contend with his inner world.

In the event that he does have an authentic case of ADHD, it needs to be addressed. *Chazal* believed strongly that all medical problems should be treated in accordance with normal medical treatment. The difference one sees in kids on medication in terms of their ability to succeed is huge. Don't be quick to dismiss that option. Sometimes the need for medication can be avoided by carefully watching the child's diet and eliminating sugar and food additives. This may or may not work. However you treat the problem, make sure it is dealt with properly so that your child can be successful and happy.

HELPING YOUNG CHILDREN UNDERSTAND HASHEM'S WAYS

Q *How do we give young children ages 4 to 7 a sense of security and reliance on Hashem? How do we explain on their level that sometimes Hashem will give us illness, pain, and financial difficulties?*

A At that age, children love stories. Virtually any *tzaddik* story you select is going to have a similar story line. In this regard, let's look at the story of Rabbi Akiva. He knew close to nothing. He had to go far away to learn so he could develop into a *talmid chacham*, and he did. He became one of the wisest people of his generation. How he got there wasn't easy, but a person on a holy mission won't find the process difficult, because he focuses on the reward.

Similarly, you can teach children the story of Hillel on the roof in the snow. Point out that in the middle of a story, you don't oftentimes see meaning, but in the end you always do.

DEVELOPING YIRAS SHAMAYIM IN CHILDREN

Q *My 10-year-old son attends an excellent cheder and, baruch Hashem, has nice friends from great families. Recently he confided to me that he and his friends like to talk about, in his words, "being bummy." He mentioned very subtle examples, such as speaking in a rough way, though they don't mention any bad words. I would tend to ignore this as a passing phase, but he feels torn between wanting to fit in and be macho, and following his conscience. How can I support and validate him while helping him preserve his yiras Shamayim and self-esteem?*

The fact that he confided in you tells you he wants validation very badly. He wants to know that it's natural to talk this way and that he is a good boy and not on the "other side." You have to address these unasked questions.

Tell him, "This kind of talk is for kids who are still figuring out who they are. Once they know, they don't have to show off to anyone anymore." Give him examples of people with secure identities whom he admires, such as his father or rebbi, who don't need to talk like that. Make all the rough talk sound ordinary and not evil. Explain to him that people talk like that when they don't know what to say. People who know how to communicate usually use words that give expression to their real feelings.

Show him the shallowness of the phenomenon while validating its normalness, encourage him to find his identity, and make him realize there are better alternatives and he is on the good side. This will support his self-esteem.

Developing your son's *yiras Shamayim* will take more than one conversation. There's a lot of cynicism in today's generation that filters down even to children. I'm not opposed to religious newspapers, but I would suggest you keep the news section away from your kids. Nurture your son's *temimus* and *emunas chachamim* by telling him true stories about the *gedolei Torah* of today. Tell him about their *hasmadah, yiras Shamayim,* and *ruach hakodesh*. These are qualities that can be verified. He has to see that the people he's meant to admire are real. He should recognize that Hashem put us in this world for a purpose and a *yerei Shamayim* lives up to that purpose.

HELP! MY DAUGHTER HATES READING

My daughter is a wonderful girl, does fine in school, and helps a lot around the house. The problem is that she hates reading. She'd rather sit on the couch and do nothing. She loves going shopping, which also concerns me. I try to explain that we go shopping only when there is something specific we need, but she isn't satisfied.

A Different people like different things. You need to learn to accept your daughter for who she is. If she is not a reader, that's okay. She is doing well in school, which means she is responsible enough to read when she has to. Let her be. Your role is not to figure out how to get her to enjoy reading, but to find out what speaks to her. Most nonreaders enjoy externals rather than focusing on their inner life. Shopping involves interacting with people. There is a lot of movement and excitement. Your daughter may be more of a people person than a book person.

See how you can channel her drives in a healthy way. Doing activities with other people will probably make her happy. Find out if there are *frum* drama or singing clubs in your area. Summer camp would be marvelous, if you can afford it. When she gets older, you can encourage her to run a day camp for younger kids. If her passion is clothes, see if you can find a designer course for girls her age.

If you don't see more than shopping on the "I like" list, then go shopping. Once in a while take a trip into town and devote the afternoon to looking around for things with her. Don't view it as a waste of time but as spending quality time with your daughter. If she sees you making an effort to make her happy, it will make all the difference in fostering a continued positive relationship with her.

STARTING A NEW SCHOOL FOR GIRLS

Q *Several mothers in my neighborhood are interested in starting a school for girls that will eventually go from preschool through high school. We want our students to thrive and emerge strong in their Jewish identity, values, and observance. Can you give us some pointers?*

A You need to formulate goals before you begin.
The construction of your *kodesh* program should be based on imparting Torah learning with the aim being to imbue *ahavah, yirah, deveikus, bitachon, emunah,* and good *middos.* Jewish studies should be set for the morning when your students' hearts are open and more receptive to learning. In this way, you also give them the unspoken message, "*Kodesh* is what it's really about." Your teachers should aim to achieve exactly what you describe, giving the girls a sense of Jewish dignity, pride, and identity.

Give the girls a solid grounding in *Chumash,* early prophets, Jewish history, the holidays and practices of Judaism, good *middos,* and Torah values. Teaching them Hebrew-language skills will only be to their benefit, as it will help them get ahead in high school.

Teachers should concentrate not only on textual learning, but also on what their students will take with them into their personal lives. For instance, if you're teaching about *bikkurim,* the first fruits, you can describe how people beautified the baskets carrying the fruit and how they made processions to bring the fruits to the *Beis HaMikdash* (Temple). You can then say, "There are people who love Hashem so much that they want to do more than they have to." Somewhere in the lesson it has to be there, the mirror message: "See how much Hashem loves us and wants us to draw close to Him. See how much He wants us to care for one another. See how precious every Jew is." There must be a bottom-line message in every class.

In later grades, when they study the prophets, make sure your lessons don't come through as adventure tales. They should look at themselves when they learn about David HaMelech, Shlomo HaMelech, and Yehoshua. Studying the way these *tzaddikim* relied on Hashem, the mistakes they made, and how they rectified them are all valuable lessons for life. Teaching Judaism has to be about the self and the community, and it should be accompanied by practical, hands-on lessons. Introduce *middos* campaigns periodically throughout the year. Take on a project and teach the children to identify with people through stories and songs.

When you hire a *kodesh* teacher, you have to ask yourself, "Does she have the skills to teach, and is she credible?" Nothing will turn off kids more than a teacher whose unspoken message is, "This is what we say but this is what we do."

For secular studies, there are two approaches on who should teach these subjects and how to teach them. One view posits that everything in the world has inherent beauty and reveals Hashem. Therefore, secular subjects should ideally be taught by someone who can show this to the girls. The teachers should be trained to lead everything back to the Torah, so that there's a seamless unity between the first and second halves of the day. Your girls must understand clearly that the Torah is the blueprint of the world, and everything they study, whether it's Torah or science, has Hashem's hand hidden beneath the surface, which leads us to the issue of *derech eretz*.

The other view of secular studies is that it's much better to hire non-Jewish teachers who are decent and can give over information, than to hire Jewish teachers with compromised values. If there will be a barrier between students and teachers, it is better that it be airtight so that nobody gets confused.

You should enforce respect for teachers, and there should be very little tolerance for lack of it. Students should stand up when a teacher enters the classroom, and teachers should be referred to only by their last name. The atmosphere should be one of mutual respect between teachers and students.

Tzniyus issues should be dealt with before high school. *Tzniyus* is a *middah* that comes along with halachah. The *middah* is internality, having a self, and not needing the outside world to define who you are. One successful way of teaching *tzniyus* is through clubs and groups in which the requirement for admission is a diary in which the girls themselves keep a record of their *tzniyus* and other *middos* they would like to improve, such as not speaking *lashon hara* or being honest. They are then eligible to enter a lottery and win prizes. Rewarding students not only for academic excellence but also for *middos* and *tzniyus* is important. What makes this work is that the girls have to account only to themselves and not to a parent or teacher.

My former principal, Rav Wolf, did not endorse uniforms, and I agree. Girls will wear the uniform to school and as soon as they graduate they'll drop it all, because *tzniyus* was never integrated into their lives. Giving them the freedom to choose in conformance with *tzniyus* standards set down by the school will train them hands-on in what *tzniyus* is all about.

IMPROVEMENTS IN BAIS YAAKOV EDUCATION

Q *I wonder if our Bais Yaakov schools need to change somewhat and provide more of what the home might have taught. Do you think any particular classes, programs, or activities should be added or removed? What is working now? What needs correction?*

A I think our schools are doing a wonderful job. I can recognize a woman who went to Bais Yaakov not by how she dresses, but by the way she responds to life. Basic *hashkafos* and fundamentals of *emunah* are deeply ingrained. There are certain things that are a given for Bais Yaakov graduates, such as doing *chessed* and being self-disciplined, which are foreign values in the secular world.

However, I still think our schools need to work hard toward training their teachers that every class needs to have relevance to the girls' lives. Ideally, after a class, students should be able to write down what they can now put into practice. Even technical topics like *korbanos* can be taught in a meaningful way.

I also think that if halachos were taught more thoroughly so that the girls had some idea of the complexity of the system, their keeping of these laws would be a lot different and more logically based. They would also be less likely to make mistakes.

Secular subjects can be taught in a purposeful way too.

I'd like to see schools address more of the girls' inner lives so that the girls develop more *penimiyus*. Our *gedolim* shouldn't have to reproach us about too much ostentation and emphasis on externalities. It should come from the inside, which means better *chinuch* for our girls in school.

ARE KIRUV-ORIENTED CLASSES SUITABLE FOR FRUM-FROM-BIRTH STUDENTS?

Q *Do you think we should expose our children to kiruv presentations, such as the Discovery program? Should we teach our children to know Hashem and to be committed to Judaism in the same manner outreach professionals bring Jews back to our heritage?*

A I find that many *frum* girls graduate seminary knowing very little about the basic building blocks of Judaism. Yes, they have solid *bitachon* and *emunah,* and I have seen almost no Bais Yaakov girl break under stress because of lack of faith. But there are gaps in their knowledge of how the Torah works, and their concept of *mesorah* is not very clear.

An educated woman I know was unsure whether covering one's hair was a mitzvah or not. She also couldn't differentiate between a *gezeirah* and a mitzvah *d'rabbanan*. Critical principles, such as the fact that doing mitzvos is supposed to be an enjoyable experience and that our first obligation is *l'hisaneig al Hashem,* to bask in the joy of Hashem's Presence, are not adequately taught in our school systems.

Many girls also have a very primitive idea of reward and punishment. Certainly real *kiruv* issues, where the girls are told exactly who they are, where they are going, and why, must be dealt with in a better manner than they are right now.

There should be a time and place for girls to ask these questions. If the open classroom isn't a good forum because it would make some of the girls who wouldn't normally have these questions suddenly develop them, or because the teachers themselves don't know the answers, then there may be great value in bringing someone from the outside who is trained and can answer questions to give a seminar on "What you've always wanted to know about Judaism but were afraid to ask." I think if the girls were made to feel safe about asking, it might prevent many problems in the future.

Our Lives as Mothers

DAVENING AND CHILDREARING

Q *Often when I daven in the morning, my 7-month-old baby gets cranky after being ignored for 30 minutes. So while I'm davening Shemoneh Esrei, I will turn around to smile at him periodically. Is this okay? Is it better chinuch to ignore him, or should I skip Pesukei DeZimrah so my davening will be shorter?*

A If you have an irritable 7-month-old, then 30 minutes is much too long for davening. Ideally, your child should see that when you daven, he can't interrupt you. You have to make davening sacred in his mind.

One of the things you will want to teach your children is *yiras Shamayim.* When you stand before Hashem and talk to Him as if you were conversing with a very important person, you give your child the message that Hashem is real. If you entertain your child in the middle of *Shemoneh Esrei,* you are indicating the opposite.

Daven the minimum and learn to talk to Hashem in your own words. When you're preparing lunch or when the baby is sleeping, tell Hashem what's in your heart and what's going on in your life. Ask Him for *deveikus, ahavah,* and *yirah.* Praise Him for all the good things you've experienced during the day.

You won't be able to do any extensive formal davening unless you're very organized. Daven *Birchos HaShachar* including *Birchos HaTorah.* If necessary, you can focus on your child between *berachos.* Try your best to say *Baruch She'amar, Ashrei, Yishtabach, Shema,* and *Shemoneh Esrei.* If you can't because your children need you, you may omit everything until *Shema.* And if even that is impossible because of your parental responsibilities, you can just say *Ahavah Rabbah,* since it includes the three elements of *tefillah:* praise, request, and thanks. But whatever you can say, do it with feeling and devotion, and let your child see this.

A CHILD IN A TROUBLED FAMILY SITUATION

Q. *My neighbor's child spends hours at our house. I think they are a troubled family. Although she is very sweet, she can be demanding and sometimes takes away time that I would otherwise give to my own children. Should I continue to welcome her?*

A. If the child is not a negative influence on your children, it would be a very positive example for you to unconditionally give her a safe place whenever she needs it.

I find it ironic when people ask, "If I give too much to others, isn't it detracting from my own children?" Helping a child in need is teaching your children to emulate Avraham Avinu, to be *amudei chessed,* and to cultivate a relationship with Hashem by imitating His ways of kindness.

CONVERSATIONS WITH CHILDREN AT BEDTIME

Q *Children need structure, but they also need parents they can talk to. My children seem to want to talk to me about their daily adventures only after bedtime. Conversations such as these cannot be scheduled; their whole beauty is their spontaneity. But my children must go to sleep on time. I can't let this become a way to manipulate me. Is there any advice you can offer?*

A Boy, are your kids smart! Of course they're trying to manipulate you. I suspect that you're trying to send them to bed too early, before they're really tired. It's very tempting to do this when you want some quiet time in the evening. Not all children need as much sleep as others. Sit in their room a bit and schmooze about the day. I've never heard anyone wax nostalgic about their childhood by saying, "Yes, we slept enough." Don't give up talking to them. It's the most crucial part of *chinuch*.

When Rav Shlomo Zalman Auerbach was young, his family lived in abject poverty, with barely enough food to go around. His father was very strict about bedtime, to keep their resistance to illness strong despite their lack of nutrition. Rav Shlomo Zalman would sneak out after his father left, go to the *beis midrash* and learn *b'chavrusa* with Rav Sholom Schwadron. When their eyelids drooped with fatigue, they would close their books and slip into the house to go to bed. When Rav Shlomo Zalman would reminisce about those days, he would say they were the sweetest years of his life. The message here is, don't sacrifice what's memorable and precious for sleep.

HANDLING CHUTZPAH IN THE PRETEEN YEARS

Q *Can you give me guidelines on how to handle chutzpah in my growing children ages 10 to 13? What should I say if my otherwise sweet daughter keeps saying to me, "I can do whatever I want"? Should I force her to comply or teach her negotiation skills?*

A You not only have to teach her negotiation skills, you also have to teach her the laws of *kibbud av va'eim*. Preferably your husband should show her these halachos in a *sefer* so that she sees that the same Hashem Who commanded us not to kill or steal commanded us to treat our parents with respect. She has to see that you and your husband take these laws seriously in your relationship with your own parents.

If a child says, "I can do what I want," you have to say, "Can you go to the store and take what you want without paying? Can you get on a bus and not pay the fare because you just feel like riding the bus?" Of course she will answer no, and you should ask her why. She will tell you that if she gets caught, she'll be in big trouble and that the Torah forbids it. You have to then explain, "My dear child, the Torah does not allow you to behave with chutzpah. And if I care about you, I can't allow you to continue acting this way, just like I can't allow you to do anything else that will harm you."

As children move toward adolescence they need greater autonomy. So while you can't tolerate chutzpah, you should foster opportunities for success by giving them more responsibilities. Let your child prepare a new salad for Shabbos or allow her to visit a friend without having a specific curfew. Inform her that you trust her to come back early enough to get a good night's sleep. Convey to your child that you have confidence in her and that you see her as an adult. This should not change the fact that she must see you as a parent, just as you see your own parents as parents.

Teaching your children negotiation skills is good because it is a respectful way of stating one's needs in a way that the other person doesn't lose out. But when it comes to your child dealing with you, this has to be presented as a way of fulfilling *kibbud av*, not as a way of manipulating a parent into doing what the child wants.

WHEN BROTHERS FIGHT

Q*My sons, aged 10 and 7, are very different in temperament and personality. They often get on each other's nerves and can be pretty awful to each other. This is really an issue, because they walk to school together. Should I try to keep them separate in order to avoid conflict, or should I insist that they continue to spend time together and resign myself to having to referee their arguments until they mature?*

A Obviously you can't totally separate your sons, because by Hashem's providence they are brothers. However, you don't have to discourage them from having outside friendships. You can schedule play dates with their friends and take each of them to different homes to spend time. This could mean a lot of chauffeuring about for you, but it will get you some peace of mind.

In any event, what you have to do is set down basic rules of behavior that you will enforce. This includes no hitting, no name calling, and no taking or breaking things that belong to the other. These rules may not make them the best of pals, but at least it will lead them to behave more civilly to each other.

In the beginning, you will probably have to do a lot of policing, lecturing, and punishing until they understand that your rules are non-negotiable. Things will get better, but until they do, it's worth putting your effort into educating your children that getting along is a must not only in school with friends, but even more so at home with siblings.

ENCOURAGING INDEPENDENCE AND RESPONSIBILITY IN CHILDREN

Q *How do you know when to guide children toward more independence and responsibility, for example, getting dressed on their own, making their bed, or doing chores around the house? I find that when I start out with star charts and small prizes, it goes well for a while and then the novelty wears off. How do I know when to put my foot down?*

A Everyone likes to feel successful. A prize is just a means of getting children to take on new responsibility. What will keep them going is the feeling of adequacy and achievement. So when your child makes his bed, be sure to compliment him profusely. Lay it on thick, more than you'd like to. This will encourage him to continue.

Another way to accomplish this is through having expectations. People consciously and subconsciously respond to expectations. There is what I call the "80 percent rule." Since we all have a *yetzer hara* and are all somewhat lazy, we tend to do 80 percent of what's expected of us. So train your children to take on responsibility as they mature, but don't get discouraged if they don't perform 100 percent.

BEING A SAFE PLACE FOR CHILDREN

Q *What is the balance between being a safe place for your children to confide in and not condoning wrong behavior?*

A You certainly have to be a safe place for your children to confide in. Your *chinuch* is more likely to succeed if you know what your children are up to. If you're going to make it impossible for them to tell you the truth, then you won't be able to guide them. Don't fly off the handle or make them feel small. This will shut them down. Listen, identify with them, and then make them visualize what it would be like to be the victim through a strong image, picture, or story.

Tell them, "Imagine what it's like for your rebbi. He probably stayed up late preparing for class and woke up early the next day to catch a morning *minyan*. He wants to make something of you guys. That's why he's teaching and not in business, where he could be earning a lot more money. If you were trying to help someone be something and he rejected you, how would you feel?"

Point out something real and painful that once happened to your children. Project it onto the incident that just occurred and say, "Don't you be the one to cause others anguish. It's okay to have a good time, but never at the expense of others."

FEELING LOVE FOR ONE'S CHILDREN

Q *I love my children very much, but I don't feel it when I'm taking care of them. I am worried that I am more like a teacher than a mother to them. How can I become a more loving mother?*

A Parenting is very unstructured in halachah. You have to write your own script. Love grows through giving. You are obviously giving enough, but emotional love can happen only if you learn to see the world through your children's eyes or work to find something beautiful about them.

Become a child again and force yourself to broaden your emotional spectrum. When you bathe your 3-year-old, share his delight

Our Lives as Mothers / 181

as he splashes around in the warm tub with his rubber ducks. When he cries because someone took his toy car away, feel his pain.

Try to find something unique and special in every child. Focus on their purity, cleverness, innocence, and beauty. If you are intellectual, it may help for you to journalize.

Work at connecting with your children in a deep way and in time you will sense that bond of love.

BAR MITZVAH — THE SPIRITUAL ASPECT

Q *What can I do before, during, and after my son's bar mitzvah to make this special day meaningful both for him and myself? How can I digress from the stress on shopping toward a more spiritual perspective?*

A It's important that you get across to your son that his bar mitzvah celebration is only part of a process. His goal should be to see himself as someone whose life will have meaning.

It depends on your son. Most boys don't enjoy long, profound conversations with their mothers. When he's in a good mood, maybe after a shopping trip, you could say, "Those shirts look incredible. You're going to look so good, like a man. Let's flash forward. What do you think you'll be doing by the time you're 19 or 20 and engaged to be married? We'll be shopping then too. How would you imagine yourself then?"

He may say, "I don't know." Let it go, but the next time you have a conversation, try to pull an answer out of him. Get him to indicate that he'd like to be like someone he admires, preferably someone you admire too. You could then say, "I bet he also didn't know at the beginning what he would become, but look what he made of himself. People turn out all different ways. It doesn't just happen. I wonder how he became what he did. What do you think?"

Listen carefully, because a lot of what you will hear won't really have much to do with the person he admires, but with what he thinks he has to do to reach a goal. He may not say much, but whatever he does say, keep it in your heart, and find the right time and place to encourage him to take the steps to be the person he wants to be.

Try to fit some visits to *gedolim* into your schedule. Get the wheels turning so he sees the kind of people we all look up to. Make him think, *I want to be like this gadol one day.* If you know anything about the early lives of these *gedolim*, it is important for you to tell him. It is very moving to have someone you placed on a throne suddenly step off the throne and become a kid just like everyone else.

Make him understand that nobody starts out life as they end it. This is true for evil people too. Get him to see that there are choices, and start him thinking about purpose and where it will all lead to. Be careful not to substitute your voice for his. Your role is to get him to listen to himself. You can elicit the questions and create a vision, but don't overshadow your dreams for his.

His picture of what he could be and how he'll get there may be totally unrealistic. He may or may not have what it takes to realize these aspirations. This could be a very serious problem, so another one of your roles is to break down the steps of your son's goals into smaller steps. Your first objective should be to make sure the learning frame he's in fits his abilities and aims. If his gifts aren't expressed and he comes to feel that his dreams aren't important, it could be tragic.

If his goals are far beyond him, it can lead to one of two responses: "Yes, the *gedolei Yisrael* did it that way, but I'll be me and do the best I can." This is not all that awful, but it would be better if he had more realistic goals that would enable him to feel successful. What's worse is if he says, "Forget it. This is boring. I don't feel like anything here." This could steer him to the wrong friends and activities, which however harmful, give him a sense of success, and could eventually lead him off the *derech.*

Give your son an exciting and realistic picture of what he could be, break it down into manageable steps, and infuse him with enough love, warmth, and encouragement to make it happen.

QUANTITY VERSUS QUALITY TIME

Q *In one of your classes, you mentioned that children don't need a lot of time with their parents. They just need their love and attention when they do spend time together. Do you mean that quantity is inconsequential as long as there is some quality time every day?*

A Children need focused time in order to feel beloved. There are women who are home all day who give their children very little time. I've seen some sad situations. I know a family where the mother is so busy cooking and cleaning that she virtually pays no attention to her children. The children are on their own most of the time.

Quantity time is not inconsequential, but that alone is not enough. If you fail to give your child quality time, he will get the message that you are uninterested in him and that he is not all that important to you. I know parents who have relatively little time, but when they're with their children, they're fully there and their children feel cherished.

Of course, if a mother can give her children both quality and quantity time, that is ideal. However, quality time is still the most critical factor.

REWARDING CHILDREN FOR HELPING

Q *Is it wrong for me to give my 10-year-old prizes for helping around the house and watching the baby? Am I raising her level of* *expectation in gashmiyus that way? If so, what alternatives do you recommend?*

It's a marvelous idea to reward your daughter for helping — much better than having to spend money on a counselor to find out what to do with a child who is not cooperating. Certainly you shouldn't expect a 10-year-old to do things for purely altruistic reasons. However, be careful not to reward her consistently. From time to time, ask her to do small chores or errands and don't offer anything. This way, when you do get her something, she will see it as a prize or reward and not as payment. As she gets older, at around 12 or 13, begin rewarding her less frequently and instead praise her for her help. Eventually she'll reach a point where she herself will realize that it's foolish to expect a reward all the time, especially for chores that she would be expected to do on her own.

HOW TO MANAGE MY REBELLIOUS DAUGHTER

I have a daughter who has a streak of rebellion in her. She is a very intense, responsible, and caring girl. I know that if channeled properly, her talents will serve her well. However, the problem is that her personality often clashes with mine. She likes to be in control and so do I. She also has a hard time speaking respectfully to me and will accuse and blame me for things. How shall I manage this 11-year-old who is going on 15?

First, consider yourself lucky. You have a daughter with leadership qualities who will make a great mother and be a wonderful asset to *Klal Yisrael*. You do, however, need to consider how to guide her properly.

Give her responsibilities. If you like her taste, have her choose the clothes for the younger children for the next day. This will give her something to do and take the chore off your head. If your preferences clash, tell her, "I'm preparing the clothes for tomorrow. Would you like to get the shoes and book bags ready?" Be clear about the areas you would like her to take responsibility for, and then don't talk unless something gets radically out of hand.

You should not tolerate any insolence. Listen to what she tells you and affirm her words by rephrasing what she said. Tell her she can suggest possibilities, but be very firm that the way you run the house is the way she will have to deal with it.

When she wants to offer helpful advice, she will need to say things differently. You can tell her, "Let's not hear complaints; let's hear positive ideas. If you want to have a constructive role in the house you need to learn how to talk to me." Repeat this many times. Be very clear that she cannot criticize or blame you. She can make suggestions or ask questions. You will listen, and if she's right, you will consider it seriously. Have your husband back you up on this.

Be firm but friendly, keep her parameters defined, and hopefully things will work out.

CONNECTING WITH TEENAGE DAUGHTERS

How can we build a close connection with our daughters? What can we do to help them grow to be fine Jewish women?

There is an excellent *sefer* by the Slonimer Rebbe called *Nesivei Chinuch*. It may be the best book on *chinuch* that I have ever read. He writes that as a child grows older, a parent must switch roles to become almost like an older friend. Include your daughter in your life. Ask her opinions. Share practical suggestions, intellectual ideas, and emotional experiences. The more you give of yourself, the more she'll want to give of herself.

Realize, though, that there is a critical difference between you and your daughter. While you're comfortable sharing with her, a teenager doesn't always find such exchanges emotionally safe. You already know exactly who you are. Teenagers are more fragile. They are not sure where the borders separating them from you begin and end. Sharing with you may feel emotionally risky. Therefore, the response you will initially get may not be exactly what you want. Be patient. Build the relationship slowly by giving and receiving in a way that is loving and close. As she matures, she will begin to open up more to you and the relationship will deepen.

A daughter who becomes more religiously observant than her mother can become distant from her. A mother who values her daughter's friendship and respect should endeavor to stress the areas they have in common, rather than their differences. Be a good role model for your daughter and project a happy disposition. If you are *b'simchah* she'll want to follow in your footsteps. A tragic thing that woman do is project a verbal "poor me" to the world in order to get validation. If you need to *kvetch*, talk to Hashem, not your kids. Ask Him for help.

A secondary problem arises when a child is exposed to negative influences. I know a woman whose daughter had to choose between her mother's and her school friends' approval. She chose the latter. Her mother should have never allowed her to attend that school. If indeed there were no other options, the mother should have warned her daughter not to mingle with the other girls. She should have then tried to create for her an after-school life that would be engaging and interesting, with good friends her age and grown women who could be her role models. This could have replaced the negative influence of her school environment.

Make the most of your daughter's growing-up years. Build an intimate relationship with her, let her look up to you, and provide her with enough emotional and positive reinforcement to become everything she can be.

LISTENING TO TEENAGERS: IS IT LASHON HARA?

Q *Please help me understand how to balance listening to lashon hara with developing a deep and meaningful relationship with my teenage daughter. Are there different rules when dealing with teenagers, who need to be able to talk freely in order to understand themselves and their circle of friends? How far does the dispensation to listen to such lashon hara go?*

A If you care about someone, you want to give them what's best for them. If you had a brilliant child who desperately wanted to become a doctor, I'm sure you'd do whatever you could to get him through medical school. If you had a special-needs child who required extra intervention, you'd surmount all obstacles to help him progress. Your daughter desperately needs to learn the skill of differentiating between actual *lashon hara, lashon hara l'toeles*, and developing a positive eye. As her mother, you are responsible for teaching her.

The first step is to gently get her to focus on what is unique, special, and precious in every person. The next step would be to steer her to look for constructive solutions to her social problems. The final stage would be to have her come to these conclusions on her own. This will change your relationship with her in a very pivotal way. It will now be based on the common goal of finding resolutions and developing positivity rather than speaking negatively and putting others down.

Some people have the illusion that if they confide in their spouse about what they think of others, they are drawing closer. In fact, they are doing quite the opposite, notes the Chofetz Chaim, because their relationship is now based on the common desire to tear people down.

If you don't set your daughter straight and she continues analyzing and discussing people endlessly, the day may come when you'll be the bull's-eye. She'll be talking about you in a way she's been talking with you all along about others.

TEACHING A NON-RELIGIOUS GIRL ABOUT MITZVOS

Q *I'm starting to teach an 11-year-old girl as she approaches her bas mitzvah. Her newly religious father divorced her mother, who is still not observant. What should my focus be and what kind of relationship should I try to develop with the girl?*

A You can plant the seeds of Judaism in your student's heart and lay the groundwork for her to grow into a fine *bas Yisrael*, but in her particular life circumstances, she will not be able to practice many mitzvos externally. Your role is to give her a framework, a picture of *emunah*, and the desire to see herself as having a purposeful life in which Hashem plays a major role. True faith is believing that everything comes from Hashem, is an act of His compassion, and is there for the sake of *tikkun*.

You should show her how mitzvos make things better for us since Hashem, Who runs the world and wants only the best for us, is the One Who commanded us to observe them.

Your goal is not to have her keep kosher in the palace like Esther. It may not happen. Your objective should rather be to get her to eventually *want* to keep kosher. Your goal at the moment is not to get her into Bais Yaakov, but to make her want to learn Torah in the future.

Give her stimulating and inspiring Jewish books. Show her that Judaism is alive and vibrant and full of joy. When she is old enough to make her own choices, she'll have the head-start you've given her to launch her on the path of return.

ENCOURAGING MY HUSBAND'S CAREER IN CHINUCH

Q *Should I encourage my husband to pursue a career in chinuch just because he thinks he has something to contribute to the klal? I know it's difficult to find a position in this field, which seems to be overflowing with overqualified people.*

A *Chovos HaLevavos* by Rabbeinu Bachya gives us a series of questions to ask ourselves as we contemplate what career path to choose. The first question is, "What can I do?" Does your husband want to contribute to the *klal* specifically through teaching? Does he enjoy reaching out to people verbally? Does he have presence, so that when he walks into a room, people notice him? A person can force himself to do any job he has to, but Hashem gives people talent and abilities so that they can be used constructively. Try to step back a bit from your husband and ask yourself, "Is he really a teacher?" If the answer is yes, then your next question should be, "What's out there?"

I have observed that because *chinuch* is a field that many unqualified people enter, they leave relatively soon. Therefore, there are usually positions open. If there aren't any opportunities where you live, consider whether you really need to stay where you are. There may be other places that are desperately seeking teachers with your husband's talent. The *klal's* needs are huge. If teaching is what your husband could do best, then he can certainly find his niche.

The next question to ask is, "What kind of an influence will your husband's career choice have on him? What kind of a person will he become?" In this sense, *chinuch* does have an edge over many professions. The senior *mechanchim* who have been teaching for years are exceptionally fine people.

The final consideration is whether the career pays well. We all know *chinuch* doesn't, but you should weigh that against the other considerations. It's certainly not the only priority to consider, but it is nonetheless a priority.

Still, the number one question should really be, "Is he a teacher?" And if he is, you should encourage him to go for it.

LEARNING TO TAKE THE HEAT IN KLAL WORK

Q *I'm a teacher, and sometimes I have to discipline students who aren't behaving properly. This can create ill will between myself and some parents, especially if they back the child and not the school. Sometimes seeing these parents or my students at functions in the community can be awkward and uncomfortable. My Rav thinks I'm making a valuable and important contribution and that Klal Yisrael desperately needs good teachers. How do you take the heat without letting it get you down?*

A Everybody encounters opposition and conflict at some point. No one is perfect in everyone's eyes. You have to see yourself in terms of what Hashem wants of you and not in terms of what other people tell you about yourself. When you hear negative messages, you have to ask yourself, "Is it true?" If it is, you should set yourself on the path to improve. If it's not, you have to accept that you aren't meant to have a *gaavah* problem and that Hashem is sparing you the superfluous praise that could lead to haughtiness. Thank Hashem for it.

It sounds like the parent body at your school needs *chizuk* in giving their children a Torah education. Maybe the parents need to learn to be more appreciative, not only of you, but of what their children are receiving in school. They are fortunate that their children are getting a Torah education, and they should be made to understand that. You might want to discuss this with your Rav or the principal of your school.

We are only human and imperfect. Sometimes in the course of disciplining children, a child will feel embarrassed and will suffer. I would suggest you sit down with a teacher who is skilled at classroom management and discuss your methodology with her. See whether you can improve your methods so that you maintain a level of discipline without compromising on your emotional relationship with your students.

Raising Happy Kids

MAKING KIDS HAPPY

Q *My four children, all under the age of 10, are very unhappy. They complain and argue and are thoroughly miserable. I buy them gifts, play with them and read to them for hours, and take them on trips almost every Sunday. They are content only when things are just right. What am I doing wrong, and what does it take to make kids happy?*

A I'll suggest a radical solution. Stop trying to make them happy. Although you can offer someone the opportunity to be content, you can't force them. It sounds as if your children feel under pressure to be happy. Don't play with them all afternoon. Don't take them on trips so often. Let them come and ask you for a game or a story and even then, don't agree right away. Tell them you'd like to first finish cooking dinner, or whatever else you're doing at the moment, and invite them to help you.

If they come and tell you that they're bored, counter with, "What would you like to do?" Not, "What would you like me to do?" Let them see that you are doing these special things for them and that you don't need it for yourself. Let them feel that you are giving them what they want when they need it. If children sense that their mother is there for them and understands them and allows them freedom to be themselves, it will build their sense of security and in turn help them become more joyful children.

TEACHING KIDS NOT TO COMPLAIN

Q *I have a child who complains a lot. How can I get him to improve?*

A You have to teach your child to recognize what a complaint is. Sometimes children don't realize that they are complaining. They think they are just stating their feelings. There are kids that are more acutely aware of what is negative, rather than what is positive. You have to make your child realize that he is not making himself happy by focusing on what he thinks he is lacking.

If he is old enough, make a gratitude journal together. Sit with the child at the end of each day and ask him to tell you three good things that happened that day. If the child is young, you can draw pictures of what happened and talk about his feelings. Ask the child what he enjoyed most that day. Ask him where it came from. Trace the gift together on its journey back to its ultimate Source — Hashem.

If the child is not only complaining, but degrading everything, it is a sign that he's unfulfilled. Get him involved in constructive activities such as cooking or baking with you, encourage him to pick some hobbies, or give him outlets to help out others. If he is old enough, let him find a small side job where he could earn some pocket money.

This will not only build his self-esteem, but give him a chance to use his strengths in a positive way.

TEACHING MY IMPULSIVE DAUGHTER SENSITIVITY

Q I have a sweet 7-year-old daughter who is very impulsive. For some reason, she thinks she can insult people and call them names with abandon. I have explained numerous times that it is not nice but she doesn't seem to care. She is also rude to her sibling's friend. How can I deal with this situation?

A The wisdom of seven years hasn't taught your daughter the art of sensitivity. She probably doesn't understand how people feel when she calls them names or speaks unkindly. She understands her own feelings, but not those of others. Try to find several good children's books in which the theme is getting beneath another person's skin. It could be in the genre of "The Ugly Duckling," where the one who was despised and in pain ultimately turns into the swan. Get her to identify with the hero and feel his pain. Then ask her, "If you would have been there with all the others, would you have made fun of the duckling?" Better yet, tell her about Rabbi Akiva's experiences learning in "*cheder*" as an adult, and ask her, "Had you been one of the kids in the class with Rabbi Akiva, learning *aleph-beis*, would you have laughed at him?"

Try to find as many opportunities as you can to tell her stories such as those, either at bedtime or on Shabbos. Stories are good because they create enough emotional distance so that she won't be defensive. It might take at least a month or so to open her heart a little.

When you see visible signs that she's starting to understand, you can talk to her more, not about why it's wrong to mistreat guests, but how to make them feel good. Invite someone she likes and have her serve. Then move the conversation on to how one should treat a visitor. Ask her, "Do you want our guests to feel bad? Of course not. Even if you don't like them, you'll try your best to make them feel comfortable." As time progresses, you can make her aware that nobody enjoys being called names. It hurts people's feelings. Teach her different ways to express herself. Have her discover new words that are positive and encouraging. With the right guidance and the resilience of youth, she's bound to change for the better.

REBUKING A CHILD WHILE MAINTAINING HIS SELF-ESTEEM

Q My 8-year-old son sometimes stumbles into ona'as devarim. How do I balance giving rebuke and elevating his self-esteem? I know he's clearly acting out when he's feeling bad about himself.

A There are a few concrete things you can do. Don't talk to him when he's stumbling, but before or after. Pick a time when he's available to you emotionally and tell him a story about the animals in the barnyard who exclude the weak horse. Talk about the new boy in *cheder* who came from Russia or the wonderful rebbi who adopted an orphan. You should get across the point that the good guy is the one who saves the persecuted ones.

Once he's identifying with the good guy, then you can say, "I wish sometimes that I was like that. Many times when I read about heroes in the Holocaust who saved hundreds of people, I wish I could be like them, but of course we can only do what we can. At least we should never hurt anyone or tell someone he's stupid or clumsy." Then list the kind of words he uses without him knowing that you are referring to him. It may not work right away, but it's sure to enter his heart, even if he doesn't give you any signs.

If you catch him using those words again, you can tell him, "There are things we don't say. They hurt people's feelings." Now he already knows from your stories that that's what the bad guys do. He may say, "Yes, but he really is stupid and fat." You could then answer, "That may be true, but how do your words make him feel? You can be his friend and make him feel good about himself. These words break him and make him feel bad."

If you've done the preliminary work, your son will get the message.

TALKING TO CHILDREN ABOUT JEALOUSY

Q *My 10-year-old daughter is very aware of how big her friends' homes are, how nice their cars are, and how luxurious their lifestyle is, compared to our simple one. How can I deal with her jealousy and feelings of inferiority?*

A You need to teach your daughter that *gashmiyus* isn't what's important. Books where harmony and good relations are what matter and material possessions clearly don't are excellent tools for teaching this lesson. Take a good look through the kids' section in your local Judaica store and find the stories that will inspire your daughter to be happy with what Hashem has given her.

There are many stories of *tzaddikim* who lived humble lifestyles. The recurring theme that runs through them is how the *tzaddik* who had so little still gave *tzedakah* and shared whatever meager resources he had with others. More often than not, the ones the *tzaddik* rescued from trouble were the people who owned the big, fancy homes.

Of course, at the same time, every child needs to know that she is heard. After you speak about the *tzaddikim*, you may tell her that it is normal for people like us to enjoy nice things. Point out some things that she knows you like (such as a new outfit), but make it clear that there is a difference between enjoying something and loving it. Ask her which of her friends she likes the best. When she tells you, you can point out that she would do almost anything to save her friend's life (say *Tehillim*, run for a doctor, maybe even donate a kidney or bone marrow, etc). That is love. The outfit you enjoy the most will one day end up in the trash without your shedding a tear, because it isn't something you love, only something you enjoy.

TEACHING CHILDREN CONSIDERATION

Q *How can I teach my children to have more consideration? Sometimes, especially when I am very tired, I feel as if they should be offering to help me more.*

A It's okay to ask your kids for help. With a young child, express your needs, state your request, and make him feel good about it. Don't *kvetch*. With an older child, you can use the same method with more mature vocabulary. "Honey, I'm bushed," you can say. "What do you think about making some supper? You get the cookbooks and we can decide together what's good." Try to avoid projecting the "poor me" image onto your children. It doesn't provide for a healthy atmosphere in the home. Asking for help, making it fun, and including yourself in the picture is fine.

In school, your kids should be getting the message that helping outside the home isn't a greater mitzvah than helping inside the home. If your husband is the type, enlist his help in this endeavor. Encouraging kids to be kind to parents and to each other is good *chinuch*. Complaining isn't good for anything.

TRAINING CHILDREN TO BE TOLERANT

Q *My children label as "goyim" anyone less religious than we are. How do I teach them what we must do without their making assumptions about people who are different from us?*

A You have to teach your kids a new vocabulary. A friend of mine who is a convert faced a problem far more extreme than yours. Her family members are actually non-Jews. Before they came for a visit, she decided to have a talk with her 4-year-old precocious son. She didn't want him putting his foot in his mouth and calling his grandfather "goy" in a disparaging way.

So she said, "Remember Yitzchak from the *parashah*? He had a son Yaakov, whose name was later changed to Yisrael. All Jews are called *bnei Yisrael* because we come from Yaakov. Hashem chose us to accept the Torah and keep the mitzvos. Everyone else is here to make the world work. They can be good people, but they are not sons of Yaakov."

He got the message so she decided to take it further. "There are people who are really *bnei Yisrael* but they never went to *cheder* and therefore they don't know much about the mitzvos. They are Jews, but it's like they're still in preschool, only they're big. It's not their fault."

He understood, so she took it even further. "There are also people who are *bnei Yisrael* and know the mitzvos, but they don't keep them because their *yetzer hara* got them." He understood that too. Her parents' visit went smoothly and beautifully.

Her husband is a *baal teshuvah*. His brother, who wasn't *frum*, once came for a Shabbos visit. He was very respectful during the meal and didn't do anything wrong. In the afternoon, when everyone went to lie down, he lit a cigarette and sat down in the living room to read the paper. The 4-year-old wandered in and asked, "So which one are you? Are you not Yaakov's child, are you in preschool, or are you just bad?" Needless to say it didn't go over very well. However, *baruch Hashem*, the end of the story turned out well, and the boy's uncle eventually even became a *baal teshuvah*.

You have to make it very clear to your children that every Jew is a Jew no matter what his level of observance is. A non-Jew is someone who doesn't come from Yaakov. For Jews who really don't know, the preschool example works.

For Jews who are less *frum*, introduce a new concept called growth or, in kid language, "getting better and better." Explain to your child that there are some things people can do better than others. Ask him, "Who runs faster, you or Chezky?" If he answers, "Me," tell him, "That's because you're particularly good at running." Now tell him, "There are some Jews who are big *tzaddikim* and are used to doing many mitzvos." Show him a picture of a *gadol* and tell him, "We're not as holy as this *tzaddik* but we're trying. Maybe one day we'll get there." Explain to him that some people do more *chessed*, some are greater in *tzniyus*, and some are better in *middos*. Whatever level we're at, we are all working hard toward the goal.

DEVELOPING TALENTS IN AREAS OF MUSIC, ART, AND DRAMA

Q *Should I encourage my children to develop their talents in the arts if it will invariably lead to frustration when they are frum adults?*

A Before you get on a bus you should know what the last stop will be. Let your kids have art, music, or drama lessons, but don't let them take it too seriously. Your children can enjoy these outlets, but it shouldn't take over their lives.

The problem in secular society is that art, music, and drama are spelled in capital letters in most people's minds. Don't let that happen. Treat it as if they were baking or swimming lessons. If you have a child who is exceptionally talented, let her develop her gifts. But be sure to guide her in using them in a way that expresses her entire being, which includes her *ruchniyus*.

Music is easier than art or drama. Playing music as a way of expressing one's love for Hashem comes naturally. It's our addiction to audiences that turns it into a challenge.

One Friday, I was at the *kever* of Shimon HaTzaddik and there was a man sitting in the corner playing original melodies on his guitar set to the words of *Tehillim*. This is where music is supposed to take a person.

If your child understands that music is a gift to be developed and is not contingent on an audience, it will not pose a problem for the future. If the child is outstandingly gifted and may eventually use his talents to make a *parnasah*, tread carefully there. There are many considerations to take into account. For a girl, there is very little she can do if she needs an audience. She can produce cassettes or CDs for women only, but they won't be best sellers as they will not sell in the secular market. If she can handle it, encourage her. If not, don't.

If you have a talented son, consult his rebbis. Is he likely or unlikely to stay in learning? Can he by nature turn away from the temptations of such a career? Ask advice and think carefully before making any decisions.

Art is a different question. If the child sees it as something fun and thinks that maybe one day she'll be an art teacher, that's fine. She should not come to a point where she visualizes herself as a major artist. The social environment and method of study at reputable secular art schools are so destructive that you would not want your child going anywhere near there. Artists at these schools are dedicated to portraying their deepest feelings and their takes on the world through color and form. Since they have no inner discipline or values to speak of, all moral barriers disintegrate. This is not what you want to expose your children to. Let them see art as a means of personal expression, but don't let it go any further.

With art, the instrument is your painting. With music, people listen to your melodies, but in drama what you are projecting is yourself. Should a child sell herself on stage, be the focus of everyone's attention, and become filled with arrogance? I think drama is good as an outlet, but it should never develop into anything more serious than that.

EXPLAINING TRAGEDY TO CHILDREN

After the shocking murder of the Fogel family of the yishuv Itamar [a horrific terror attack in which Rabbi Udi Fogel, his wife, and three children were stabbed to death], I'm not sure how much to tell my children. On the one hand, I feel that they should know when a tragedy happens in Klal Yisrael and in Eretz Yisrael. On the other hand, I'm afraid to traumatize them, especially since we also live in Eretz Yisrael.

The Rambam says that a person who doesn't feel the suffering of others isn't evil or insensitive, he's cruel. When we empathize with the pain of our fellow Jew, it's because Hashem wants us to move forward and change. Suffering awakens us. We have to ask ourselves, "What does this say to me, how does it speak to the *klal*, how can I become a better Jew?"

Your children should know about the tragedies that *Klal Yisrael* undergoes. They must come to the realization that life is frail and transient.

If you listen to the *hespedim* of the surviving daughter and the father of Mrs. Fogel *o"h*, you'll find courage, faith, and acceptance. These are the paths we need to traverse before Mashiach comes.

Point out to your child how Avraham was rescued from the fiery furnace but Rabbi Akiva was not saved from his Roman executioners.

He was a hero in *Olam Haba*. Sometimes *kiddush Hashem* is part of the picture. It's not dreadful for the person who suffers; it's sad for the world in which such cruelty exists.

Your child should understand that life is fleeting and that there's nothing to be afraid of in death *al kiddush Hashem*. The fear should be of having wasted one's life or, worse still, leading a bad life. We are part of something greater than ourselves, and when Mashiach comes there will be *techiyas hameisim*.

Stories are a good medium to get these concepts across to children. Just as a seed must disintegrate before a flower can blossom, there are things we must go through before Mashiach comes. In the end all the puzzle pieces will come together and we will understand that it was all good.

RAISING JEWISH DAUGHTERS TO BE HAPPY WITH THEIR ROLE

Q *How do we ensure that our daughters grow up happy with their role as women?*

A I will describe to you the happiest woman I know. She comes from a Chassidic, rabbinic family. Her parents are more modern than her ancestral family, but certainly still mainstream Orthodox. They are Hungarian. Hungarians are known for their love of fine food, chic clothing, and beautiful decor. Her mother revels in being a woman and creating a nurturing, warm atmosphere in their home. Her daughter picked this up and enjoys cooking gourmet meals, maintaining an elegant home, and making people feel comfortable. She loves receiving guests with grace and warmth. She enjoys the process of building.

The real issue in the *frum* community is contentment with a woman's role. The problem is not about being barred from *krias haTorah* or learning Gemara. The more you can provide your daughter with a living example of happiness and fulfillment, the more joyful she'll be as a woman. You can create a beautiful meal, build people, learn and expand your knowledge if that is what you want, interact with others, have a career, and be happy. The key is *simchah*. I have not yet met a woman within the *frum* community who had problems with "Shelo asani ishah," or sitting behind the *mechitzah*. The real issue is not about women's roles, it's about being happy. Some women complain a lot, don't develop themselves enough, don't demand as much from themselves as they should, and don't look for role models of women who live vital, happy, and fulfilling lives.

Tell your daughters how much you do for them, without making it sound like a complaint. Let them picture what Shabbos would be like without tasty food and a beautiful, clean home. Make them aware that the cornerstones of Judaism very much depend on women. Their place is providing the framework, the spiritual infrastructure, and the very foundation of serving Hashem. Their role is special, irreplaceable, and maybe in some ways even greater than that of men.

If your daughter is an intellectual, be sure that she has access to books that deal deeply with issues of *hashkafah* and that get them across in appealing language. It is also important for her to recognize that Hashem gave her abilities so that she can use them in both her self-development and in making a meaningful contribution to *Klal Yisrael* through teaching. This doesn't conflict with her role as a woman any more than it did for Miriam, who spent the years in the desert teaching the women (as Moshe did the men).

MY DAUGHTER'S FRIENDS SEEM TOO SUPERFICIAL

My daughter's friends spend an awful amount of time talking about trivialities such as hair, clothing, and makeup. Should I be concerned that my daughter will get influenced and become more like her friends? Should I encourage them to speak about more significant issues? How relevant to frum girls should appearances be?

Welcome to the great big world of teenage girls. There's nothing unusual about your daughter's friends. Teenagers don't have much of an identity yet. Therefore, they tend to harp on externals. Wanting to exude a sharp, with-it impression filters down to appearance.

Don't discourage your teenagers. When girls are involved in worthy projects, their time and energy gets redirected constructively. This is a great age for volunteer work and *chessed*. However, in order to motivate them, these activities have to be presented in an exciting way. Speak to the staff at your daughter's school and see what they can come up with. Volunteer tutoring or organizing a fund-raiser for a nonprofit organization, such as a carnival or an entertainment evening, are great ways to involve your teenagers in good things. In Israel, many girls volunteer at hospitals and distribute candles for Shabbos. Some go to entertain sick and elderly women in convalescent homes or old-age homes.

Teenagers don't like being lectured to. Rather, they need to absorb good *hashkafah* in a subtle way. In Israel, teenage girls enjoy *sichot nefesh*, deep conversations about feelings and beliefs. American girls call them "DMCs"— deep, meaningful conversations. This is an emotionally healthy way to spend time. A candlelit *kumzitz* or a *melaveh malkah*, accompanied by soul-stirring music and a moving speaker, can create the right mood. Give them the chance to connect with inspiring people.

I don't know if girls have to be so serious as to feel pressure to regard shopping as trivial or frivolous. It is antithetical to their nature. I think being happy and balanced is more important.

Chapter 4

Understanding the World

Tough Questions About Judaism

WHY DID HASHEM CREATE US?

Q *I am confused about why Hashem created us. I don't understand the concept that He wanted to do good or that He wanted to give to others. Nonexistent creatures don't need kindness. I also don't know how to relate to a Being Who created us to do good when things don't always seem so good. I am perplexed about why I am here altogether. Where did my soul begin and what is the point of it all?*

A I would strongly recommend that you first read the Ramchal's *Derech Hashem* and then compare it to the introduction and the first chapter in *Mesillas Yesharim*. This will answer many of your questions.

Of course nonexistent creatures have no use for kindness. Hashem created people with needs in order to give them the gift of pleasure. The highest level of joy is *deveikus baHashem*, cleaving to Hashem, which can never be experienced through nonexistence. That is why, barring French existentialists, most people don't envy the dead. We cling to life tenaciously because we desire growth, change, achievement, and connection. This is the good that Hashem wanted to bestow on us.

What you will observe when you read *Derech Hashem* is that if you look at life and think that Hashem created you for one specific reason, it is as if you are observing a workshop where everyone is working at building one part of a car without ever seeing the finished product. Our lives are so brief, our vision so myopic, our world so limited, that until we get to the era of Mashiach and *techias hameisim* we will never really understand the full picture. The true *simchah* of achievement will come when we see the fruits of our labor.

Imagine what joy our forefather Avraham would have experienced had he seen the great sages who would eventually emerge from him, among them Hillel HaZaken, the Rambam, and Rabban Yochanan ben Zakkai.

When Rabbi Akiva stood at the funeral of his last student, he didn't know about the five outstanding new *talmidim* he would later teach or the *Torah She'be'al Peh* that would emerge from them. It's easier to see this when you look at other people's lives or watch their development, because when you look at your own life you don't see the whole picture.

Your soul is the essential part of you. It's the self that you remember being when you let yourself travel back to your earliest memories. It's your inner core, the part of you that longs for approval, desires to give, and strives for achievement. Use your spiritual capacities to broaden your Torah knowledge, pray to Hashem for guidance and assistance, and with His help you'll reach your destined purpose.

TRUSTING HASHEM AND PERSONAL RESPONSIBILITY

What is the proper balance between trusting in Hashem and being responsible? According to the book "The Seven Habits of Highly Effective People," most things are preventable and can be controlled, as long as you are smart, think ahead, and prepare for different situations. I trust Hashem, but I have so much to work on when it comes to my own actions that I can't write off everything that happens as His decision because I really could have done better. Is this correct?

You can do everything right. You can plan ahead, define what your goals are, take steps to work toward them, and consult experts, but you will not necessarily get the results you anticipated. You can follow the "seven habits," but unlike what the book espouses, it doesn't guarantee a positive outcome.

On the flip side, if you do everything wrong, your results will most likely be influenced by your misguided decisions. Hashem created the world in a way where He gives us what we need if our hands are outstretched to receive. The balance of *hishtadlus* and *bitachon* is doing what you can and trusting Hashem. It means opening your hands to receive, but realizing that ultimately Hashem will give you what's good for you. However, no outside force can change anything except Hashem Himself.

DOES JUDAISM STIFLE CREATIVITY?

Is creativity in and of itself somehow wrong or not conducive to Judaism?

In Judaism, there is no idealization of creativity as an end in itself. Words are meant to express what you think and feel; however, writing is not an art for its own sake. If you take a look at Jewish classical writers, even those who wrote religious poetry, you will see that they did not idealize conveying emotions in words as an end in itself. In fact, the Rambam, who was an exceptionally gifted writer, in his collected letters strongly warned against using writing and music as a means to ride on the emotions of foreign cultures.

Creativity is a gift. Certainly in the Chassidic world, music is very much a part of *avodas Hashem*. In *Likkutei Moharan*, the chapters on *neginah* explain that one's heart should be full of song and that one can discern Hashem through the melody in one's soul. One can find enormous creativity in the works of the *mussar* masters, including contemporaries such as Rav Shlomo Wolbe, but it's reality oriented.

My daughter's father-in-law, Elya Sukot, is an accomplished artist. He does evocative, beautiful, impressionistic art, but it's not separate from his life. He's a Breslover chassid. He gets up at midnight, recites *tikkun chatzos*, and then proceeds to paint whatever his mind shows him. So whereas secular society views art as separate from life, Judaism views it as an expression of life.

TRAGEDIES AND IMPROVING OUR ACHDUS

Why do we need horrific tragedies to make us aware that we need to strengthen our achdus? What can we do as individuals or as a community to rectify this?

I have seen *chessed* break down barriers in a tremendous way. The people who do *bikur cholim*, those who serve lunch at soup kitchens, and the families that open their homes on

Shabbos, are all people who do not have big barriers separating them from other Jews. The more *chessed* you do, the more you identify and empathize with others. Many times people are afraid that associating with people at a lower level of observance will have a negative impact on their own or their children's spiritual development. There really is no consensus on where to draw the limits. However, you can start by refusing to speak evil about any Jew under any circumstances. You don't have to become the other person to do this. Make an effort to broaden and deepen your perception of others. If you are strong in your religious beliefs and your children sense that you are guiding them and not the other way around, then only good can come of reaching out to others.

BAD DREAMS IN JUDAISM

Q *What is Judaism's view on bad dreams? Can they just be disregarded or do they have some credibility?*

A dream may sometimes be a message from Hashem coming via the emotions rather than the mind. When a person's intellect isn't sufficiently pure to receive *ruach hakodesh*, Divine communication may come in a dream in the subconscious state. *Orchos Tzaddikim* explains that speaking the truth is only the beginning — thinking the truth is where we have to take ourselves. One who can distance himself from his own inner life so that he can objectively look at his thoughts and ask himself, "Is this true?" will have dreams that are genuine, because the filter of self-interest and fantasy that would make dreams false isn't part of his thinking process.

I will assume that this is not your level. Nevertheless, if you have a recurring bad dream, most Rabbanim will advise you to take it seriously. You can recite the prayer of the amelioration of dreams, preferably in front of three people, and request that everything negative in your dream be turned around for the good. The *Shulchan Aruch* notes that one should fast after a frightening dream. This is generally no longer practiced, but the *Igros Moshe* writes that one should "redeem the fast" by giving charity equal to the sum of money one would spend on food in one day.

What a dream says to you depends very much on how you interpret it. Try to see the dream as an indication of something good. If you have a reason to think that your bad dream is true, consult with a knowledgeable Rav, making him aware beforehand that you will be asking about a dream. If you will suggest a negative interpretation, he will interrupt you and attempt to change it to something positive.

Our Sages say that dreams are indicative of our inner workings. It is like receiving your own uncensored script. The Gemara says that seeing oneself dying in a dream is a good sign. If you can envision your own physical death, it means your essential identity is your soul. Let your dreams talk to you and tell you where you truly are.

THE TORAH VIEW OF MENTAL DISORDERS AND FREE CHOICE

Q *What is the Torah perspective on mental disorders? Do people who are mentally ill have free choice? Are they accountable for their deeds?*

A Everyone's *bechirah*, free will, is limited. No one can make all the choices there are to be made. If you weren't gifted with extraordinary intellectual capacities or fiery passion or language skills, you will not be expected to become the next Vilna Gaon, Sfas Emes, or Rav Hirsch. Every individual has his own point of choice, based on his natural capacities and environment. The point at which a person experiences conflict is where he exercises free choice. Someone who goes beyond his individual comfort zone to do what is right is utilizing *bechirah* in a significant way.

Mental disorders create limitations. A depressed person will not have full *bitachon*. It is not within his area of choice. What is within his choice level is choosing to get out of bed even though he desperately wants to stay there. Mentally ill people are rewarded in the areas of life in which they have free choice. They can still reach unbelievably high levels, because Hashem judges people by how far they've traveled relative to where they've started. Anyone with mental illness who is making the best choices he can, given his limitations, is a *tzaddik*.

The Torah relates to mental illnesses that are physiological just as it does to physical illnesses. The same way we don't expect someone without arms to put on *tefillin*, we do not expect a mentally ill person to do things that are beyond his point of choice. However, there are some mental illnesses that are self-developed. People get tangled in crooked methods of thinking that lead to disorders. There is far more responsibility in neurosis than in psychosis. A person like that needs to ask himself: What are my real choices? Do I have to think this way? Is this the truth? Seeking therapeutic help may be the key. This too is a choice and one that can eventually lead to healing and recovery.

EMUNAS CHACHAMIM

Q *Can you explain the concept of emunas chachamim in our day and age? Recently, a friend of mine gave birth to a very sick baby who remained alive for only thirty-six hours. Prior to the birth, she went to two great gedolim who told her, "Yiheyeh b'seder, bari v'shaleim." (It will be okay, the child will be healthy and well.) How are we supposed to view the words of the gedolim in this context and in any similar situations that occur?*

Nowadays we are so bent on having everything quick and easy that when troubles come, we want a Rabbi to bless us with instant salvation, instead of thinking things through and searching out Hashem. That is certainly not what *emunas chachamim* is. Simple *emunah* means that everything comes from Hashem, all His actions are compassionate, and all things in this world exist for *tikkun*.

What role do *chachamim* play in *emunah*? The *Chovos HaLevavos* tells a parable about a philanthropist who took a strong interest in helping the blind. He built a special home for them where everything was tactile and nothing required vision. Simultaneously, a staff of medical experts worked tirelessly to heal each patient. Indeed, their efforts paid off and they were ultimately able to find a cure for everyone.

Hashem put us in this world, where we are basically blind. We don't see the consequences of our deeds or the meaning of our choices. The role of our *chachamim* is to advise us through the lens of halachah and by explaining the Torah's viewpoint on specific situations.

There's another aspect to *emunas chachamim*. When a person learns and lives Torah with a great deal of consistency, he becomes Torah. The *chachamim* see reality through the eyes of the Torah and become like the doctors in the parable, with one critical difference. These *chachamim* can cure many, but they cannot cure everyone, because the ultimate master is Hashem. If He decrees that we should suffer a certain amount of chaos, confusion, and difficulty, it will happen, because that is His will. Of course one should go to a *gadol* for advice and *berachos*. If we are in a position where we honestly don't know, we have to ask ourselves if we want to hear the Torah's view through the mouth of a sage or if we want to go it alone. Your friend acted correctly by going to *gedolim* for *chizuk* and a blessing, but ultimately it is Hashem Who determines people's fate.

FIXING THE WORLD

Q *What is a Jewish woman's responsibility regarding everything that needs fixing in this world? So many people around me are struggling with problems, and I feel that as much as I try to help, not always do I succeed. I know there are difficulties that I can't rectify, not to mention all the troubles that I don't even know about going on everywhere. What should be my approach?*

A We were not placed in this world to change things; rather, we are here for the sake of the journey. Only Hashem sustains the world and is *"konei ha'kol."* Your responsibility is to become more similar to Hashem by assisting and supporting what is in your reach, but not more. This indeed is why our great leaders never get tired of constantly giving. They have *bitachon* in Hashem's capacity to bring about the ultimate *tikkun*, and they content themselves with doing whatever they can.

I remember that before the terrible turnover of Gush Katif, my friend asked the Amshinover Rebbe what to do. He answered that everyone should do what he is capable of, and that his way would be *tefillah*. He didn't necessarily say, "Here's what you can do and it'll work out." He said to try according to one's strengths and capacities. Not standing by with folded hands and at the same time not thinking that one has to complete the task fully is where perfecting oneself and *tikkun olam* fit together.

HASHKAFIC DIFFICULTIES WITH MENTAL HEALTH CAREER

Q *I am considering going into the mental health profession, but I have a few hashkafic difficulties. I have heard that you cannot study psychology without being exposed to a lot of kefirah and strange ideas about societal norms. I also do not feel comfortable about building a parnasah around other people's problems, especially mental health patients, who are usually not well-off and need to scrimp to meet the high fees generally charged by therapists. I want to go into a lucrative profession that will fit in with my other responsibilities and suit my kochos hanefesh, but I cannot resolve these doubts.*

A Today there are mental health programs that are run under the aegis of Bais Yaakov. In Israel, Maalot is a good choice. I know the rabbi in charge. He had the non-Jewish professor teach him the entire course before the professor was allowed to teach it to the girls. This rabbi sat through hours of lectures, and anything that had any negative connotations or that was related to *kefirah* was automatically deleted from the syllabus. The non-Jewish professor had no difficulty building a program around kosher ideas. I would assume this is the case with other *frum* programs.

However, if you choose to go to a non-Jewish school or to a Jewish school that has no supervision, you will definitely encounter problems. You must develop a sifting mechanism. If you walk in the street and live in the world, you need to be able to say, "This is true and this is false." However, I've seen many people with sifters that had holes in them. It is not for everyone. If you are the kind of person who is easily affected by your environment, both academically and socially, I would recommend that you attend a supervised program.

Don't feel guilty about earning money from people's pain. Medical doctors do the same. However, ethical doctors charge moderate fees, and many give *maaser* from their time and *tzedakah* from their profits. There is a need for *frum* therapists in the Jewish community.

Therapy is different from the medical world in that you will probably be getting a disproportionate amount of clients who aren't coping due to financial difficulties. This makes the *nisayon* harder but not impossible. See that you do not exploit people, offer a sliding-scale rate for clients who cannot afford to pay, and give *maaser* of your time. As long as you see beyond your immediate desire for money, pursuing a profession in the mental health field can give you a lot of satisfaction and opportunities to help people.

WHEN SOMEONE SAYS THE MITZVOS ARE OLD FASHIONED

Q *I meet people who aren't religious who tell me that mitzvos are old fashioned. Something similar happens when I talk with off-the-derech teens. I wish I knew what to say that would make a positive difference.*

A First echo their question so they feel heard and understood. Then try to find the truth in what they said. After that, ask them if they really want an answer. If they say yes, you're obligated to provide them with one.

Talk to them about Hashem. Explain that there's an intelligent higher Force behind this world Who gave us rules to make our lives meaningful. We have kept these laws for thousands of years, not because we were forced to, but because they have profound meaning.

They may not be prepared to hear about the religious significance of mitzvos, so discuss how they help us. Shabbos compels us to let go of our creative forces and recognize that we are not in control. It makes us step back from the picture so that we can really see the picture. It is a day to enjoy the fruits of our labor and to thank Hashem for His endless kindness. Kashrus is not just a meaningless set of archaic laws, but a system that reflects that there is a mind-body connection. What we eat has a spiritual as well as a physical influence. We do Hashem's Will and thereby create a certain refinement within us. People will usually accept these explanations.

Disillusioned teens usually go off for one of two reasons: not feeling loved and understood or not having appropriate limits and discipline. If they aren't accepted, their pain is deep. If they lack discipline, they are sold out to their *taavos*. In both cases, their problem is emotional rather than rational. Therefore, giving rational answers will not help. Try to give these teens a sense of why you enjoy mitzvos. Describe how it makes you feel connected and how it gives you a sense of achievement. Involve them in acts of *chessed*. This will give them an enormous sense of being.

Off-the-*derech* teens usually dress in a way that offends religious people. However, don't go for the externals. The likely aspect that you can initially affect will be the inside. Talk to them about their *penimiyus*. Invite them to do *chessed*, which shows that you believe in their inherent goodness. Letting them sense the warm feeling of *ruchniyus* moves them toward acknowledging that they have a soul. Talk to them about Hashem's benevolence and about His grandeur hidden in nature. Let them feel the satisfying feeling that comes from self-restraint by telling them stories of heroism and self-sacrifice.

It will be a slow, gradual process, but with Hashem's help you'll see gratifying results.

GENUINELY ANTICIPATING MASHIACH

Q *The consistent theme of the times of Mashiach is one of fear, pain, destruction, and confusion. How do we genuinely anticipate his coming if it seems so frightening? Is there something practical we* *can take upon ourselves to ensure that we get through this turbulent period safely?*

A How it will be is really up to us. It depends on how much we are willing to make changes and how aware we are.

A friend of mine went to the Rachmastrivke Rebbetzin and asked her, "What should we be doing about all the tragedies happening in our time?" She answered, "Don't you trust Hashem? He is taking us to where we have to go. Things will happen soon and it will be good."

We need to realize that Hashem has far more compassion on us than we have on ourselves. If the price we'll have to pay to get to the *geulah* will be awesome, we should know that all our suffering is only to get us to a place that is far better than anything we can imagine. The financial calamities, the unbelievable *chutzpah,* the lack of respect for Torah are all events that were foretold.

Rav Elyashiv says that people are asleep. We need to arouse ourselves to the possibilities of every moment and to encourage others to do the same. Torah and *chessed* can save us from the birth pangs of Mashiach.

As women, we can be kind to others, offer support, and love our fellow Jews with all our hearts. We can study the parts of the Torah we find relevant and inspiring. We must yearn for Mashiach. It is the only solution to the terrible things happening around us.

Don't confuse the answer with the problem. The problem is *galus;* the symptoms are all the horrific things happening to awaken us. The solution is Mashiach leading us to the time of enlightenment. We have to point our hearts in that direction. In our minds we should hope for the redemption. With our actions, we should endeavor to move forward day by day, so that when Mashiach finally arrives, we will be ready to greet him.

WHY SUCH HARSH PUNISHMENTS?

Q *I learned two pieces of Torah recently and I am not sure how to apply them to my life. One was about the daughter of Rav Chanina ben Tradyon, who was punished severely for walking gracefully before several Roman officers. The other was about the mother of Acher, who listened to secular music.*

A The rule is that Hashem judges great people with a different yardstick. Just as it is much harder to get into Harvard than it is to get into Dwight D. Eisenhower Community College, it is a lot more difficult to live up to the standards of a *tzaddik*. *Tzaddikim* strive for perfection. When they fail, it is analogous to a wine stain on a beautiful chiffon wedding dress. While such a stain on a worn T-shirt won't make much of a difference, it will stand out starkly on a pristine gown.

The daughter of Rav Chanina would have wanted her stain to be erased. Her punishment did just that. The suffering she experienced earned her eternal perfection. In fact, *tzaddikim* see their death as their highest, most perfect moment.

The story of Acher's mother is complex. When his mother listened to Greek poetry and songs, she created a potential for evil within her child. Still, Acher could have chosen differently. However, understanding where his roots came from is important. It tells us concretely that Grecian philosophy, which placed humans at the center of life and consciousness and made Hashem a minor side note, was corrupt at its core.

THE SPIRITUAL LEVEL OF THE JEWS IN EGYPT

Q *How do we understand the low spiritual level of the Jews in Egypt? Wasn't Egypt supposed to be the kur habarzel (the smelting furnace) that would refine them?*

A The Arizal teaches that the generation of *Mitzrayim* was a reincarnation of the *dor hamabul* and the *dor haflagah*. The *dor haflagah* created a human-centered world. They equated themselves with Hashem. Therefore, they needed to go through the torment of exile in order to subjugate their physical selves and acknowledge that ultimately Hashem was in control.

Suffering serves as an atonement. It uproots the core of sin, but not necessarily the sin itself. It is true that the Jews in Egypt worshiped idols. They did not know why they were in exile. However, the experience served to loosen the roots of sin, which ultimately prepared them to receive the Torah.

WOMEN IN JUDAISM

Q *I have never resolved the issue of women in Judaism to my satisfaction. Here are two questions that have bothered me: The Mishnah tells us that if a male and female are both drowning, one should save the male. Sforno in Bereishis says that men and women are somewhat equal but not totally equal, for if they were totally equal, "It would not be fitting that one should work for and serve the other." Do I have to choose between Judaism and my self-respect, or am I missing something?*

Suppose you did have to choose between your self-respect and Judaism. What would you choose? Suppose you were a *mamzer* or a *metzora*. What would that do for your self-esteem? As a *mamzer*, your future marriage choices would be limited. As a *metzora*, you would be shunned and excluded.

We are all in this world to reveal Hashem's glory. The Torah is the blueprint of the world. It comes from a higher place than the collective soul of the Jewish nation. One of the most distinctive traits of a Jew is our yearning for a state of *bitul* (submission) before Hashem. We seek to negate our ego and build an authentic relationship with the Source of all things, rather than have an autonomous relationship in which the Torah is meant to fulfill our emotional need for esteem.

Where was Rabbi Akiva's ego when he sat with the little children to learn *aleph-beis*? His self-esteem must have been very high, because he was aware that he was doing Hashem's Will. The same would be true for someone who would accept his illegitimacy or leprosy with *emunah* by proclaiming, "I'm here to do Hashem's Will."

As to your question about saving a man first from drowning, the actual halachah is equivocal, as you can see when you turn the page of the Mishnah at the end of *Horayos*. It is not as simple as it seems. Men have more mitzvos. Therefore, all other things being equal, we would save the man first.

The world was created to put light into a dark place. Men are in the world of *divrei halachah;* they are obligated to do the mitzvos. Women are in the world of *divrei reshus;* for the most part they are permitted but not obligated. A mitzvah has inherent superiority over anything that is *reshus*.

The *middah* of *malchus*, which has a female element, means following, negating the self, serving, having fewer mitzvos. It is is in some way superior to *chochmah*, the male element, which is giving forth light. A man's role is to take Torah from its place above and bring it down to this world. A woman's role is to take *emunah* — this world, with all its concealment — and elevate it for Hashem without necessarily having an exact framework.

There's no halachah advising a woman on how much food to buy or how many stories to tell her child, but all of it is critical to ensure her family's well-being. A woman's role is invisible. You can see the skill of a surgeon only by the health of his patient. What women have achieved will be seen more clearly *b'acharis hayamim*, at the end of days. In the world as it is now, the male element is viewed as superior. In the future there will be a different level of appreciation for the female element, which is why the *Navi* says that at the end of time, "The light of the moon will be as great as that of the sun."

As to your question about the *Sforno*, if you look at the previous *Sforno* on the verse "*E'eseh lo eizer kenegdo*," you'll understand. "*Kenegdo*" means they are of equal weight, yet a woman is still an *eizer*. This means that their relationship to each other is not equal, because one is serving the other, but their inherent value is still the same. A woman is dependent on a man in a way that a man is not dependent on a woman. A woman must receive Torah from a man and build with it. He draws down, she elevates, but if he draws nothing down she cannot elevate.

There is a famous Gemara that says that a woman turns linen into a garment, wheat into bread; she stands her husband on his feet, and brings light to his eyes. A man has no use for something unless a woman can refine it and turn it into something meaningful. You cannot build without components. Women do have a level of dependency on men that should be acknowledged. When it is not, it can be disastrous, as proven by the feminist movement. The ideal relationship requires women to work in the area of elevation and *reshus*, rather than taking on the male role of exclusive provider.

Women have great emotional, spiritual energy, but without Torah as its direction there is no place for it. You can be a woman in the Torah community and have enormous self-esteem by building people, cultivating *emunah,* and inspiring others. There are certainly things that need improvement, but by and large, the recognition that a woman is a valued, essential segment of creation is alive and well in the Torah community.

THE AUTHENTICITY OF THE ORAL TORAH

I am learning with a Jewish woman who is not observant. She has questioned me about the authenticity of the Oral Law. How do we know that the Oral Torah isn't just one big game of broken telephone? How can we be sure that the mesorah was transmitted properly through the generations?

I would recommend you read Rambam's Introduction to the Mishnah, where he traces the transmittal of the Oral Torah.

There are many proofs in the Torah that Hashem presented the Oral Torah along with the Written Torah. For instance, the Torah commands us to place *"totafos bein eineichem."* What are *"totafos"* and where is *"bein eineichem"*? It is obvious from the text that there is an accompanying interpretation, which is the Oral Law.

How was the Oral Torah transmitted? Moshe received it from Hashem. He gave it to Yehoshua, who gave it to the elders. Each group who received it had to repeat it to the giver. Moshe gave Yehoshua *semichah*. This process of responsible transmission continued until the dissolution of the Sanhedrin. Every village of twenty-five people had to have a *beis din*, but it had limited authority. Anything more serious was brought to the city *beis din*. Something even bigger went to a tribal *beis din* of twenty-three *dayanim*. A case of major import went to the Sanhedrin, where the scholars had to be fluent in the entire Torah. It would not have been possible for someone to stand up one fine day and make up his own halachah. If he tried to do so, he would be caught and immediately discredited.

The Torah we have is constantly growing. Whenever someone develops a legitimate new Torah insight, it becomes part of the continuity of Torah. Just as a geologist uncovers new layers of rock, we too are constantly uncovering more layers of the Torah through the course of time. Yet everything can be traced to the original text and *mesorah*. It is all contained in the Torah we received at Sinai.

WHAT ARE KIDDUSH HASHEM AND CHILLUL HASHEM

Q *What do the concepts of kiddush Hashem and chillul Hashem mean? Most explanations of them are about fostering awareness of and respect for Hashem in another person. On occasion I've heard that even if nobody sees you sinning, it's still a chillul Hashem. What does this mean? Does kiddush Hashem have to do with being a tangible ambassador of Hashem or is it the mystical revelation of spiritual good in the world? Does every mitzvah or aveirah that we do affect this, or only when people are present?*

A *Kiddush Hashem* means bringing Hashem's focused Presence and holiness into the world. This can happen in two ways. The Torah tells us, "*V'nikdashti b'soch Bnei Yisrael* — I will be sanctified in the midst of Bnei Yisrael."

On an intrinsic level, *kiddush Hashem* means that there are choices. We can choose to do Hashem's Will rather than follow other people's will or even our own will, if they are contrary to His Will. There is an internalized dimension and an externalized dimension of *kiddush Hashem*. On an external level, *kiddush Hashem* is publicly performing any mitzvah that will subsequently change the consciousness and awareness of the world. The actual halachah relates to the externalized dimension, but in terms of our progress and *deveikus* with Hashem we also need the inner dimension, which means the degree to which we maintain mindfulness of Hashem's Presence moment by moment. Your awareness, love, and awe are also dimensions of *kiddush Hashem*. In fact, being a visible ambassador of

Hashem and initiating the mystic revelation of spiritual good are really two sides of the same coin.

The same holds true for *chillul Hashem*. When evil behavior makes Hashem an invisible presence, when we conceal Hashem rather than reveal Him, it's *chillul Hashem* on an external level. When we are alone and act as if Hashem doesn't see us, that's *chillul Hashem* on an intrinsic level. Rav Dessler adds that in some ways this is worse than external *chillul Hashem*.

MEN AND WOMEN — IS ONE IN CHARGE?

Q *In Bereishis, where we read about how man should "conquer" the earth, the word "v'kivshuhah" is written without a vav. The commentaries say that this also hints to man "conquering" a woman so that she should not be a "yatzanis." This was before Chavah's sin. Does this mean that a woman was created with certain negative behavioral characteristics and tendencies that need to be subdued by a man? Were women created inherently inferior to men?*

A If you examine the *Eishes Chayil* poem in *Mishlei*, you'll see that there is enormous potential open to a woman. However, it won't come naturally to her, just as it won't come naturally to a man. It needs to be developed. In that sense, both men and women are equal. Women are not born more or less spiritual than men. Neither of them is complete without the other. The Gemara writes, "Rav Chanilai said: A man who has no wife lives without joy, without blessing, and without goodness."

What a woman desires most is to take what her husband provides and build with it. Therefore, a woman feels a certain dependency on man — spiritually, intellectually, and materially — which makes her reliant on her husband and not on Hashem. Because of this, there is a spiritual difference. *Bitachon* is an even greater challenge for women, because they seem to lift their eyes up to their husbands to provide everything.

"*V'kivshuhah*" means that in order to actualize the ideal relationship of giving and receiving, the wife must be willing to take from her husband. She is dependent on him emotionally and must look up to him, which is not an easy role. He too has to gain her respect and "conquer" her so that she will focus on using what he provides to build.

The worst thing is for a woman to be a *yatzanis* and receive from no one. She is on the go, unconnected, and what we erroneously call "free."

Women's higher dependency is not a result of Chavah's sin but of a Divine plan that came forth out of her sin. However, it is worthwhile to note that the division of man and woman happened before the sin, which means there is purposefulness in it rather than simple punishment.

WHAT LACK DID CHAVAH FILL?

Chazal say that Adam HaRishon's vision reached from one end of the universe to the other and that his consciousness was so expanded that it included almost the entire creation, aside from the nachash. If this was the case, why did Adam need Chavah? What was he lacking? What caused this lack and how did she fill the void?

When the word "Adam" is used, it is often meant to include Chavah. As it says, "Male and female I created them and I called them Adam." Adam is the universal term for humankind.

The first human had this level of expanded consciousness. When the two aspects of Adam are separated into *Ish* and *Isha*, Chavah is described as being an *"eizer kenegdo,"* a helpmate parallel to Adam, not less than him. The need that she filled was his need to give and her need to receive, his need for interaction and expression, and her need for creativity and building. Adam needed his expression of wisdom to be taken in by someone who could then bring it forth into the real world. Both parties needed to have the same vision and level of clarity. The production of something new would come through the combined efforts of both. That is why Hashem said, "It is not good for man to be alone."

WAS LEAH REALLY THE HATED WIFE?

Q *Why wasn't the spiritual goal of building Klal Yisrael adequate to bond Leah to Yaakov in the same way it bonded him to Rachel?*

A By definition, special love is unique and focused and cannot be for two people. Therefore, Yaakov's love for Leah could not be like the love he had for Rachel. Had the world been on a higher level, Yaakov would have had one wife. Rachel would have had within her both her own attributes and the spiritual attributes of Leah. Yaakov would have had within him the spiritual forces of both Yaakov and Yisrael.

Rachel was the more practical of the two sisters, the one who could address the revealed physical world. Since the world was created in a physical manner, the physical deeds themselves are the most important, which is why Rachel is called the *akeres habayis,* the mainstay of the house of Israel. Our function is to bring the idealism of Leah into the world of Rachel, the *akeres habayis.*

PHYSICAL BEAUTY IN THE TORAH

Q *Why does the Torah mention the physical beauty of our Matriarchs and other Jewish women?*

The Torah tells us about the beauty of these women in order to give us a picture of who they were and what challenges they faced. Our foremothers were extraordinarily beautiful, and it was a trial for them. Their greatness shines through precisely because of their beauty. Sarah, who was strikingly beautiful, chose a spiritual life with Avraham instead of becoming a famed beauty like Cleopatra. Yael did not fall into a trap or get carried away with the role she was playing. This too was an enormous choice. Rachav, whose beauty was misused the first part of her life, made a definitive turnaround, which was a tremendous achievement in and of itself. Rivkah was a beauty in an immoral society, yet she was exceedingly modest, and when she encountered Yitzchak she immediately covered herself with a shawl. This is related to self-development. Rachel's beauty, however, had to do with her persona. She elevated this world as opposed to the world of the spirit.

Kohanim with physical deformities were forbidden to serve in the *Beis HaMikdash*. The human body is meant to express the soul, and therefore a body that is perfect and beautiful reflects a certain dimension in creation. However, there is purpose in having another sort of body too. When the emperor's daughter asked Rav Yehoshua ben Chananya, who was known to be very unsightly, "Why did Hashem put such wisdom into such an unattractive vessel?" he replied, "Why does your father store his fine wine in such ugly earthen jugs?" When she replaced her father's jugs with gold ones, the wine soured. Rav Yehoshua explained, "Just like wine ages well in ugly vessels, so too Torah is better preserved in unappealing people."

The emperor countered, "But there are beautiful people who are very wise." To which Rav Yehoshua replied, "If they would have been less handsome, they would have learned more."

Perhaps the outside isn't always meant to reflect the inside.

RAIN AND HASHGACHAH PRATIS

What is the difference between rain in Israel and rain outside the Land of Israel in terms of hashgachah pratis? Is rain dependent on our actions and prayers? When rain falls, can it be taken as a sign that we are repenting, and when rain is held back are we meant to understand the opposite?

First we need to understand what *hashgachah pratis* actually means. People mistakenly think that Hashem is either entirely involved or completely not there. In truth, there is *hashgachah pratis* and *hashgachah klalis*, general and individualized providence.

Hashem created the cat for a reason. Yet there is no such thing as a righteous cat, because they have no free choice. Humans are the only ones to whom Hashem responds directly and individually.

There is a rule that the more open a person is to Hashem, the more open Hashem's response will be to him. It's as though they are reflecting each other. Therefore, the more righteous a Jew is, the closer he will be to Hashem's Presence. The Land of Israel is under the *hashgachic* microscope. Hashem's vision is bound to the Land eternally. Just being there puts you on a different plane.

There is a degree of *hashgachah* outside the Land of Israel as well, but it is not necessarily tied down to anything that can be clearly seen. (For example, every man and woman who marry find each other through Hashem's Providence, though they may not realize it.)

This is why it says in *Hallel*, "Ram al kol goyim Hashem … — Hashem is exalted above the nations and His glory is in heaven." The non-Jews see Hashem as a Higher Being, but they don't see Him as so involved in human life, because for them there is, in fact, less involvement. They do not have the covenant through which Hashem promised the profound and intimate level of involvement that is part of His relationship with His Chosen People.

You can see Hashem's *hashgachah* clearly with rain. We say this every day in the second paragraph of *Shema*. Rain is the source of life, which Hashem uses as an instrument in the *hashgachah* involvement. Surely, if you are in Israel during a drought, you should be praying and doing *teshuvah*.

So yes, there is unique *hashgachah* in Israel, especially as it pertains to rain, and the closer you are to Hashem, the more openly you'll discern it.

THE ATONEMENT RITUAL OF THE AZAZEL

Q *I am not an animal activist, and I have no problem with korbanos or shechitah, but I find it difficult to understand the concept of the Azazel goat on Yom Kippur. I learned that one should not inflict unnecessary pain on animals for our own soul's sensitivity, and this atonement seems barbaric.*

A I think your real issue here is not that you think animals and humans are on the same plane, but rather that this particular sacrifice seems horrific. It was meant to be so. *Korban* comes from the root word *karov*, to come near. A sacrifice is supposed to take the animal aspect of the human personality and elevate it for Hashem. The *Azazel korban* is somewhat different. It is not atonement for an individual sin, but a sacrifice for the collective animal soul of the Jewish people.

Two goats of identical nature were chosen. A goat signifies desire, which can be good or bad. One goat was offered as a sacrifice to Hashem, which symbolizes that desire can be a means of elevation. The other goat, the *Azazel,* was sent out of Jerusalem to the barren wilderness and hurled from a cliff. This sacrifice was meant to show us the consequences of desires expressed in a negative way.

It is a mistake to think that if we haven't uplifted desire, we've just missed an opportunity. If desire isn't dedicated to Hashem, it takes its owner down the slope of desolation. The Ramchal notes that a desert is a place where evil resides. It is barren, with no people to make it a place of Torah and mitzvos. When a person pursues desire, he thinks he is filling his life with meaning. In reality, his life is just getting progressively emptier.

The Mishnah writes that the *Azazel* goat was reduced to pieces before it hit the ground, which meant that the animal's suffering was of very brief duration. The *Azazel* ritual was not meant to torture the goat but to leave a visually dreadful impression on the witnesses. It was designed to make people understand that sin is horrific. The core source of evil is departure from Hashem's Will. Desire that is unconnected to holiness is destructive.

The *Azazel* sacrifice was specifically brought on Yom Kippur, the Day of Atonement. This is because the weakest of the three links of *teshuvah* is regret. We willingly confess our wrongs and commit not to transgress again, but there is still the syrupy taste of sin left in our mouths. Sins don't seem that awful to us. The *Azazel* goat was meant to uproot the saccharin sweetness of sin and replace it with a powerful horrific picture of the destruction evil can bring.

Part 2:

Bringing Torah to Life: Essays on Deepening Our Children's Jewish Experience

Chapter 5
Shabbos, Yom Tov, and Kids

Making Shabbos Come Alive for Our Children

How do we impart the special meaning and sanctity of Shabbos to our children? The Chofetz Chaim gives us a parable. Shabbos is like an engagement ring. An engaged couple may occasionally have minor spats, but if the bride throws the engagement ring at the groom and he picks it up and leaves, we know the engagement is over. Shabbos is the ring that binds us to Hashem.

We can understand Shabbos through *zachor* and *shamor*. The negative commandments move us away from our own desire to control and create. We then take the empty space and fill it with *Elokus* — consciousness of Hashem's creativity and His *kedushah*.

How do we explain this to very young children? Start with the creation of the world. Open a package of soup nuts and count out 100 pieces. Make ten piles to illustrate the concept of 1,000. This will give the children a sense of what big numbers mean. If the children "get it" you can give them a deeper perspective on time, and how long "long ago" means. If they grasp what 1,000 means, explain that more than 5,000 years ago there was nothing and Hashem made it all start.

Discuss what Hashem created each day of the week. Explain the idea that humans are meant to accomplish and that there is free will to choose good or bad. Talk about how once a week on Shabbos we tell Hashem by what we do, "I know how to use Your world."

Go through some of the common foods your children eat and trace them back to the source so that they understand how it all comes from Hashem and how thankful we should be. Emphasize that Shabbos is a day of expressing gratitude to our Creator for all His kindness.

Explain *kavod* and *oneg Shabbos* and how we make special efforts to honor the Shabbos with bright candles and fragrant *challah*. Get the children involved in preparing for Shabbos. Take them shopping for treats. Give them simple tasks, such as setting the table or making the beds.

Discuss the concept of the thirty-nine *melachos* and that Hashem meant us to work during the week but gave us one day to rest and connect with Him.

Young children are impulsive and lack self-control. Therefore, when teaching them about specific *melachos*, choose carefully and discuss those they will actually keep.

It can be confusing and even damaging to children to invite non-*frum* relatives who will violate Shabbos. Tell your guests that you want consistency in your children's education and that they must keep Shabbos in your home. Otherwise, limit visits exclusively to weekdays. If you invite a *baal teshuvah* and he makes a mistake, tell the children quietly, "Remember how you once also didn't know? He is going to school. He's still learning."

During long Shabbos afternoons, you must have activities planned for young children. Taking a nap and leaving kids to their own devices is a bad idea. Buy some good Shabbos games, put *nosh* out on the table, and spend time together.

Youth groups are wonderful. Accompany your children there,

even if it means taking a long walk. If necessary, make your own group. Have the children recite selected Mishnayos from *Pirkei Avos* and reward them with goodies. Halachah quizzes with prizes are also great. Songs, *parashah* reviews, and treats are all wonderful ways to make Shabbos delightful for children.

When my children were young they had to be at the Shabbos table for *Kiddush*, the first course, *zemiros*, and *bentching*. Then I would act as if I didn't notice when they got up to play. Kids this age shouldn't be expected to sit for too long.

It's important for children to go to shul as long as they don't disturb the davening. It takes effort to balance both. Very young children should not go at all, or perhaps only for the end of Mussaf. It's good for them to feel the Shabbos aura and to see a multitude of Jews getting together for *tefillah*. As they get older you can take them for more of the davening. At around age 8 or 10, they can start going regularly.

Encourage your teenage girls to go to shul. Doing something spiritual instead of just wiling away the time with a novel, eating, and schmoozing, adds a special quality to the day. Emphasize to them that *tefillah b'tzibbur* has extra *kedushah*. Explain that shul is a place where one can draw down the *Shechinah*. Tell them that the *Zohar* says that the holiest point of Shabbos is during the *Kedushah* of Mussaf when the congregation says "*Ayei mekom kevodo*." When so many Jews express their desire for Hashem's honor, it's a glorious moment. If you can, accompany them.

Recently, the Belzer Rebbe had the women's section of his beautiful shul in Yerushalayim improved and expanded. He asked that the girls in his school be told that *Am Yisrael* needs their *tefillos* and that *tefillah b'rabim* has unique power.

If a teenage girl attends shul regularly on Shabbos, then later on, when she is married with little children and tied down with a lot of responsibilities, she will still make time to daven, having already integrated its importance.

Older children like being involved in the Shabbos cooking. They enjoy tasting the fruits of their labor. Send them shopping for the foods they like and involve them in creating special treats to enhance the *seudah*.

Being busy on Shabbos becomes a bigger issue for older kids from age 12 through the teen years. On long winter Friday nights, arrange a platter of nuts and chocolate and stay up with them to shmooze and share ideas. At this age, your goal should be to deepen your teen's concept of Shabbos. Discuss why the day is different and what makes it special.

Encourage them to invite their friends over. This way you have some control with regard to with whom they spend time. Have plenty of good books available for their reading pleasure. Some kids will enjoy question-and-answer games with prizes.

Becoming a youth group leader is a great experience for teens because it gives them the ability to influence others. Get them involved in *kiruv*. If you have a student who is committed but just starting out, suggest a simple *sefer* and set your teen up as a learning partner. This can be mutually beneficial.

I don't let my teens leave the Shabbos table. Teens don't like feeling excluded or listening to boring adult talk, so find a way to engage them. Encourage them to sing *zemiros*. Shabbos talk should be elevated — no politics or *lashon hara*. Work hard to find topics in which your kids will be interested. Talk about Jewish history in light of the *parashah*. Present interesting halachic scenarios and *shaylos*. Invite guests. Make the meal shorter if you have to, but make sure your children are there.

Your child's bond with Hashem is developed through Shabbos. Make it meaningful and everlasting.

Elul, Rosh Hashanah, and Yom Kippur

Creating Elul consciousness in the home really begins with your own understanding of what Elul means. The Sfas Emes explains that there is a place within Hashem's infinite reality where His love for us is so great that nothing can touch it. Similarly, there is a hidden spark of *ahavas Hashem* within each of us that can never be defiled. The theme of Elul is *"Ani l'Dodi v'Dodi li."* Discovering that place of pure love, *emunah*, and yearning for *deveikus* within ourselves draws down Hashem's unconditional love and forgiveness. For adults, Elul is a time to forget the trivialities of daily living and to get in touch with our deep inner selves through *teshuvah* and *cheshbon hanefesh*.

A good way to explain Elul to young children is through a parable. We can tell what something really is by looking at the end product. Following the directions exactly while baking a cake will usually yield good-tasting results. Similarly, who we were during the year is clearly evident in Elul.

Ask the children to pretend that you've invited an important guest to come visit. You bake a delicious cake but it comes out a flop. It's too late to go out and buy new ingredients. Imagine that you could sprinkle a magic potion on the ruined cake and transform it to its original raw ingredients. You could then bake the cake again and it would come out perfect. That's the wonderful gift of *teshuvah*. We can go back as if we hadn't made the mistake, change it, and make it better once again.

In Elul, Hashem gives us a whole month to reflect on our wrongdoings and correct them. Teach your children that if they hurt someone, they have to apologize. Show them how to do this sincerely. Go through their possessions with them. If they took something without permission, direct them to return it

Rosh Hashanah is about accepting Hashem's Kingship. Explain that Hashem, our loving King, comes down to us once a year and that we prepare to greet Him with joy and awe. Children should understand that there is accountability for our behavior. Although they most probably will have learned in school of the three books that are opened on Rosh Hashanah, point out that every person writes his own story through his speech, actions, and thoughts.

Very young children should not be taken to shul. If they are forced to sit quietly for long periods of time, they may subsequently come to resent going to shul. Letting them run wild in shul is *anti-chinuch*. If feasible, take them for shofar-blowing and for some of the serious parts of the davening such as *U'Nesaneh Tokef*. This will serve to increase their *yiras Shamayim*.

During the *Aseres Yemei Teshuvah*, encourage children to do additional mitzvos. Give them extra coins to give to *tzedakah* and recite short chapters of *Tehillim* together.

Introducing the highlights of the *Yamim Noraim* to older children, from age 10 to early adolescence, can be more complex. Take time to speak with them during Elul. Begin a conversation such as, "What would you desire more, a fancy camera or to be married to someone you respect?" Of course they'll answer the latter. Explain to them that the pleasure we derive from people stems from tapping into their *ruchniyus*. This is somewhat like the yearning we have for closeness to Hashem.

Get your children to identify all the gifts and talents Hashem has given them. Tell them that Hashem gives us these things as a form of *chessed* and that He expects us to use them well. Explain to them that Elul is the time to redefine ourselves, a period of great *chessed* where we can once again resolve to do things properly. Let them see what you're making of Elul, how you are trying harder and working on yourself.

Tell your children stories of people who completely changed themselves. Ask them for *mechilah* and encourage them when they express any signs of regret for past misdeeds. Visualize what you would want to be like, and make a sincere effort to change. The real message of Elul should come through clearly through you.

Rosh Hashanah is a time when we renew our relationship with Hashem by recognizing Hashem's *Malchus*. This should awaken a certain desire for *penimiyus*. Children can get very distracted by the externals of the day, such as new clothing and the *simanim*. Stories are a good medium to explain *Ol Malchus Shamayim*. Tell your kids to aim for absolute acceptance of Hashem's Kingship. They should understand that our only desire is to do Hashem's Will. In a sense we are telling Him, "Wherever You take me, this is where I want to go."

Older teens don't like being talked down to. Share some inspiring ideas or stories you have read. The more indirect you are, the more directly they'll listen to you. Children in this age group will also see through you more clearly, so be sure that you're "walking your talk." Ask yourself honestly if you are at the level you want your children to be.

Think ahead and plan things out carefully. Ask Hashem to give you the right words, clarity of mind, *siyata d'Shmaya*, and credibility to make Elul and Rosh Hashanah an inspiring and lasting experience.

Succos and Simchas Torah

Succos is a colorful holiday filled with meaning for children. The whirlwind of activity can very easily take on an energy of its own. Therefore, it's important to take time to explain to your kids that the *succah* is holy, we are decorating it for the *Shechinah*, and we are working hard to make everything beautiful in honor of Yom Tov.

Very young children won't understand the deeper concepts behind the four species. Try to bring some ideas down to their level by talking about how the species are different. Compare this to how Hashem created all kinds of people who make up the Jewish nation and how He uses various means to help us in all kinds of situations.

Older children can already grasp the concept of *kedushah* related to the *arba minim* and the *succah*. Listen to *shiurim* that explain the depth of the holiday. You can then simplify them for your children. Succos is about *bitachon* and about Hashem's love and care for us. Hashem is like a *succah*, constantly enveloping us in His protective embrace. Emphasize the intimacy between the Jewish people and Hashem, the encompassing nature of the *Shechinah,* and the concept of *Hashem Hu HaElokim,* that He is with us in every way.

Chol HaMoed looms with the big question of what to do with the children. Spend quality time reading stories to your kids about *bitachon.* Visit friends and relatives. If you live in Israel or close to Yerushalayim, tour the holy sites such as the Old City and the *Kosel* with the children, and share your knowledge of *Tanach* and Jewish history with them. If you don't live in Israel, you can take them to a nature reserve, botanical gardens, or a zoo and point out the wonders of Hashem's creation.

Entertaining teenagers takes a little more thought. Prepare before Succos and plan how you will keep them busy and happy. Make sure that whatever they do is in keeping with the extra *kedushah* inherent in Chol HaMoed.

Succos is a time of *ahavah.* Do everything you can to make your teenagers feel beloved and important. Give them freedom and let them choose what they would like to do. If you don't feel you can trust them, make the effort and accompany them, even to places that may not interest you all that much, just to be sure they stay in line.

Let the motif of Succos flow through whatever you do. Let your children sense the special aura of the holiday. Let them tap into the *kedushah* and revel in the joy of *simchah shel mitzvah.*

The Beauty of Chanukah

As its name suggests, Chanukah is all about *chinuch*. There are several main concepts we should convey to our children. The first concept is that the battle of Chanukah was a war between the Jewish perspective of the spirit and the physically oriented Greek worldview. The second is that there is light and there is darkness. There are obstacles that seem insurmountable, battles that appear daunting, but if we do what is right, Hashem helps us in the end. The third is the significance of *taharah* and *zerizus*. When the Maccabees entered the Temple, they refused to light the *Menorah* until they found pure oil. They could have waited, yet they chose to act immediately. They searched for a sealed cruse of oil, and Hashem rewarded their efforts.

Young children love the idea of heroism. The main point of the Chanukah story is that heroism is about sacrificing for Torah and mitzvos as opposed to succumbing to what's easy and convenient. Tell your kids on a simple level how the Jews once lived in Eretz

Yisrael with the *Beis HaMikdash*. Hashem's Presence was more readily felt there, and the Jews knew that He was looking out for them. Today we are in exile even in Eretz Yisrael, and we don't always sense Hashem because He wants us to learn to trust Him.

It's important that your young children understand the nature of the war. Tell them stories about Jewish heroes, not the kind who displayed their physical prowess, but the ones who fought for Torah and Judaism. Talk to them about the Maccabees. They were many, we were few, but Hashem saved us because we desired to do His will.

Tell them stories of the *Avos*. Avraham grew up in a house of idol worship, yet he didn't give up. He broke the idols and proclaimed his faith in Hashem, and he was saved. Yaakov served Hashem even in Lavan's home surrounded by evil. Similarly, during the Chanukah story, the Jews couldn't keep Shabbos, Rosh Chodesh, or *bris milah*, yet they put their lives on the line to do Hashem's Will and He saved them.

Children can understand the aesthetic aspect of purity. Explain that it relates to not only physicality, but also spirituality. Something used for sin is ugly in Hashem's eyes. In contrast, something designated *l'shem Shamayim* is beautiful. The Jews decided they would use only pure oil for the holy *Menorah* in the *Beis HaMikdash*. They wanted to fulfill the mitzvos in the best possible way.

Kids from 6 to 11 can comprehend far more. You can discuss with them how the Greeks left an impression on the world that's still felt today. Western mentality is patterned after the Greeks' mindset, which proclaims that anything the human mind can't grasp isn't relevant. Because of this they think religion is nonsensical or evil.

In a sense we are still battling the Greeks today. They are the majority and we are the minority. You can ask your child what he thinks is the best way to fight the Greeks. In order to elicit the right answers, such as learning Torah, setting a good example, sharing what you have with others, you have to subtly introduce your child to what real heroism is. Tell stories about the Cantonists of Russia and about the Inquisition. Talk about the Jews under the Stalinist regime who lit Chanukah candles in secret and taught their children Torah in hiding.

What was the light they fought so hard to preserve? Where does it come from? What does it mean? Explain that Torah is light. Light helps you see what you wouldn't see otherwise. Tell contemporary stories of righteous people who were not born with great talents but applied themselves seriously and grew to become holy *tzaddikim*. If there are people in your own life who overcame obstacles, discuss that too.

Talk to them about the beauty of purity. Sensitize them to avoid things that may narrowly be permitted within halachah but are inherently unattractive, such as listening to secular rock music. Tell them about the *avodah* in the *Beis HaMikdash*. There are beautiful presentations with pictures and books available nowadays. Show them what the *Menorah* looked like and tell them about the amount of work that went into it. When people take art or music and let the *Elokus* flow through it, it is a beautiful experience. Yet sometimes people take these very forces of purity and distort them. This is an important concept for them to grasp.

Older kids from age 11 through the teen years generally do not appreciate stories as much. When Chanukah comes, they may just want to light and go. Try to make spending family time together attractive. Engage them in a debate after candle-lighting. We are told that the four exiles are contained in the Roman exile, which means the Greeks are still here. Where are they? Who would the Hellenists be today?

Kids this age may hear, talk, or read about the news. You can say, "All this can change. It depends on our sincerity." Talk openly about the terrible effects of *chillul Hashem* and how we can affect things positively through *kiddush Hashem*. Discuss different approaches to purity. What does purity mean today? What would the Maccabees reject in today's society? What are ways to reach higher levels of purity?

Enjoy the flickering Chanukah lights, the sizzling *latkes*, the stirring songs and stories, and the special family time together!

Teaching Our Children the Essence of Purim

Purim is the perfect holiday for children. They love everything about it. The main message you'll want to impart to youngsters between the ages of 3 and 6 is the importance of following Hashem's Will. Although the Jews sinned, Hashem gave them a chance to repent. He saved us because He loves us.

Purim is a delightful day. Be careful not to give your children any negative associations. Thoughtless comments such as, "Let's see if our *shalach manos* will be better than everyone else's this year," or, "Oh, no, another *meshulach* at the door, I can't take it anymore," are counterproductive.

Don't take your young children to the *Megillah* reading unless you're absolutely sure they'll sit through it quietly. Be realistic and find a solution. Take turns with another woman so she can hear the reading while you're watching the kids and you can go later and leave your kids with her. You could also ask your husband to read for you. Young children have no obligation to hear the *Megillah,* but adults do. I've been to places where parents brought their little kids to the reading and the adults present did not fulfill the mitzvah of hearing *Megillah*. It's bad enough that the adults who knew they weren't *yotzei* had to hear it again; what's worse is that there were those who didn't know or weren't that careful who surely weren't *yotzei*, because they couldn't possibly have heard everything.

If your husband and his friends get drunk, the *seudah* can be frightening for young children. Be careful about exposing them to too much. Have a plan of action if things get out of hand. Ask a friend or neighbor before Purim whether it would be okay if you dropped in with the kids in the late afternoon, or get an older teenage babysitter to take them out for a while.

Discuss the story of the *Megillah* with your children. Focus on the hidden hand of Hashem and the heroism of Mordechai and Esther. Tell them that the Jews lived in Persia and that there was an evil king named Achashveirosh who wanted to make himself as if he were Shlomo HaMelech. But it was really Hashem Who elevated him to the throne. Tell them that Achashveirosh was very haughty and liked to show off. At this point, you can ask your kids for examples of arrogant behavior. Be sure to steer clear of speaking *lashon hara*. Explain that haughtiness is making other people feel bad that you have something that they don't.

You can then tell them the following: Achashveirosh said, "I'm gonna make a party that's much better than anyone else's party, because I'm much better than everyone." And he did. Not because he cared about other people, but because he wanted everyone to think how great and wonderful he was. A lot of Jews, because they weren't learning enough Torah and keeping all the mitzvos, said, "Hey, maybe Achashveirosh is really great." So they went to his party. But there was one righteous Jew, Mordechai, who warned them, "Don't go to the feast. Achashveirosh is evil. He's profaning the holy vessels and the garments of the Kohen Gadol." They didn't listen.

Although we sinned, Hashem still loved us, and He conceived a plan to save us through Mordechai and Esther. Esther was the niece of Mordechai. She was righteous, modest, refined, and caring. She was like a queen even before she became one.

Achashveirosh did something really foolish. He ordered his wife Vashti to appear before him immodestly. He wanted to display her as if she were a couch or a picture. She didn't come, not because she was clever or modest, but because she wanted to make her own party and show off even more than he did. So he killed her.

Achashveirosh needed a new queen now. Esther was dragged to the king. She had no choice. She knew that if Hashem was putting her in this situation, it was for a reason. Although she lived in the palace and could have had almost everything she desired, she never stopped being righteous. She was nice to people, she only ate kosher food, and she dressed modestly.

In the first part of the *Megillah,* notice the points you've gotten across. Hashem is directing the scenario. He put Mordechai in the picture, and He made Achashveirosh choose Esther. Make these ideas very clear to the kids before you continue on to the second part of the *Megillah*:

Achashveirosh had an evil adviser, Haman. He came from Amalek, who was evil. Depending on how familiar your kids are with the *parashah,* you can discuss the Amalek story. Otherwise it will be far too confusing to introduce another account in an already complicated story.

Haman said, "Kill all the Jews." He was jealous. He wanted to be all-powerful. He commanded everyone to bow down to him as if *chas v'shalom* he were greater than Hashem. Everyone was afraid of him.

But there was one person, Mordechai, who wasn't fazed. He said, "Now the Jews will see that Haman doesn't bode any good and they'll repent and come back to Hashem." Mordechai guided people to do *teshuvah.* They fasted and returned to Hashem. This is what *teshuvah* is — transforming yourself and becoming better.

Ask your kids, "What are some ways we can improve? People lie and hurt other people and don't always do what they're supposed to.

You can do *teshuvah* and Hashem won't say, 'I don't care. You didn't do what was right.' Instead, He'll welcome us back with open arms." And that's what Hashem did. He saved us through Mordechai and Esther.

Esther realized that Hashem put her in the palace to help the Jews. She fasted and prayed and invited Achashveirosh and Haman to a party. Then she made another one. When Achashveirosh was in a good mood, she cried, "Someone wants to kill me and my nation." Achashveirosh became furious and asked, "Who would do something like that?" That spelled the end for Haman.

In the third and final part of the *Megillah*, Achashveirosh had Haman killed and Mordechai and Esther were elevated to positions of power. We read how Mordechai went out *b'levush malchus*. You could put a lot of *simchah* into that part with a rousing song or jig. Esther HaMalkah continued to rule and everyone lived happily ever after. That's how you would tell the story to very young kids.

I would not mention the incident of Achashveirosh's difficulty sleeping and the Bigsan and Teresh plot. I think it's too hard for them to get these subplots within the story. If you think your kids can handle it, tell them, but if not leave it out because it could easily cause them to lose the thread of the main story.

Of course they've already heard the Purim tale in whatever educational framework they are in. Your purpose in telling it over is to make sure they get the main message, that the heroes are Hashem, Mordechai, and Esther, and that *teshuvah* played a significant part. Emphasize that this is how Hashem always saves us. He gives us righteous people we can trust and follow, and He waits for us to repent.

Show your kids a picture of a *gadol* and tell them, "This is like Mordechai today. This is who we listen to." They'll probably ask about Esther too, which is of course more complex. Explain that Esther was modest. She wouldn't have wanted photos of herself all over the place. You can give them examples of righteous women in your own life or of people they know. In the days before Purim, if you have some time, take them to visit a *tzaddik* or *tzaddekes* so they can see who our true role models are.

Shalach manos provide a great opportunity for self-expression, but for some people it has become a way to show off their creativity and artistic talents. *Shalach manos* were meant to be for the recipient. Wanting to make them beautiful, so they'll make someone else happy is one thing, but doing it so people will say, "Look at these unbelievable *shalach manos*. They are so creative," is not where it is supposed to go. You have to be careful that your kids don't get swept up with the *ruach ha'z'man* that will tell them to make the best, biggest, or most extravagant baskets.

Try to think in terms of what people would want. Tell your kids, "We can't have everyone at the *seudah*, so we send *shalach manos*. It is as if Hashem is telling us, 'Make it as if you are inviting a lot of people to share in your feast.'" Send *shalach manos* to at least two needy people. Involve your kids in thinking of others. Who would be happy to receive a package? Who doesn't get a lot of *shalach manos*? Who may not have cooked food for the *seudah*? A single friend of mine went years on end without receiving *shalach manos* from even one person.

Even if you will be making a generic *shalach manos* for everyone, try to consider your kids' *shalach manos*. Sit with your children and ask them specifically what they think their friends would like. Even though it may be a bit of a hassle, it's good to train them to think about the needs of others.

Depending on where you live and what the generally accepted practice is, try to keep the *shalach manos* down to a reasonable level. Ask the children, "Guess what's more important than *shalach manos*?" Chances are they've already learned about this in school, so "*matanos l'evyonim*," will probably be their automatic response. Show your kids the *tzedakah* letters. Let them stuff the envelopes with the checks. Have them visualize how happy the poor people will be to receive the money. Tell, them, "Now this needy person will have food for the *seudah*, because people cared about him."

At the *seudah*, the message should be one of rejoicing with everything Hashem has given us. You can say, "Drinking on Purim is somewhat like what Achashveirosh's *seudah* was, but for Hashem, not for Achashaveirosh."

Explain the idea behind the costumes. Everyone thought Haman would kill the Jews, but it turned out exactly the opposite. Instead of being sad, everyone rejoiced. This shows that Hashem can make something that looked one way turn out completely the other way. If you have any personal stories of deliverance, whether involving family members or other people you know, who were saved from distress, recovered from a serious illness, or lost their money and ended up regaining it, here's a good time to discuss it.

On Purim you can show that things aren't always as they look. Children get dressed up to appear different from how they really are. So really you're Suri, but on Purim you can be Queen Esther. With little kids, imagery plays a key part in their development. Try to move them toward costumes that are positive. With boys it's a lot easier. Among the popular get-ups are Mordechai HaTzaddik, a Kohen Gadol, and a *Sefer Torah.* For girls there isn't as much to choose from. I've seen *kallah* and *Shabbos HaMalkah* costumes. Try to move your girls in that direction. Stay away from the dancers or Japanese lady costumes. Although they may be modest, these outfits don't channel their imagination toward something elevated.

In middle childhood, from 7 to 11, children will probably know a lot more about the *Megillah* story, but you can still enrich their knowledge. There are some charming books with the Midrashim woven into the story line. If your kids like to hear stories, this is the time for you to open a Torah anthology or *Me'am Loez* or whatever books you enjoy. Delve into the Midrashim and tell them over to your children. There are delightful stories you can find in old issues of *Olomeinu* and *Talks and Tales* about different communities around the world that were saved and celebrated their own mini-Purims. There are also inspiring stories of heroism in the concentration camps, how people kept up their *bitachon,* and how Hashem ultimately saved them.

The main ideas you want to get across are *bitachon* in Hashem and *emunas tzaddikim*. You can also emphasize that when the Jews sinned, it wasn't so obvious. The *seudah* was kosher for whoever wanted kosher. The issue was that they were following Achashveirosh instead of Mordechai.

There are games you can play on or before Purim. Memory games are fun. So are "Guess Who" games. You can say, "Guess who I am?" and mention something in the Midrash or, "I did —," and describe an occurrence in the *Megillah*.

Involve them directly in the mitzvah of *matanos l'evyonim*. Discuss *tzedakah* stories with them. Help them visualize what it would be like to be poor. What are the *nisyonos* of a poor person and a rich person? What is the best way to give *tzedakah*? What's the worst way? If you are giving away significant sums on Purim, you can set aside a small amount for your children to decide where to distribute. If they have their own allowance money, let them give some of it away with *simchah* and empathy. Make the mitzvah as endearing to them as possible.

Shalach manos has a lot of social value at this age. Whatever you can still say to little kids, you can't say to kids this age. If they need to show off a bit and express themselves creatively, let them do it. If the social pressure at this age is that you have to give all of the girls in your class, then your child has to conform. In most schools, everyone in the class comes to school with one nice *shalach manos* and then the teacher randomly picks out names, so that each child receives a *shalach manos*. In other schools, there's a cash limit on how much can be spent. However it's done, do your best to avoid a situation in which your kids feel different, because at this age it's important for them to be accepted.

Be organized and do the shopping a week or two before Purim so that you have time to do craft activities with your kids. Get creative. Look through crafts books and how-to articles. Have your kids' *shalach manos* ready in a box early so they can decorate it at their leisure.

At this age, going to shul for *Megillah* is important. Try to get them to sit through the reading. Set limits on what they will do when

Haman's name is said. You can't and shouldn't tell them not to bang. It's part of tradition. But you should let them know that it's important for the people in shul to hear every word and that they have to stop in time.

Kids this age may actually enjoy watching the drinking at the *seudah* if you prepare them for it. Tell them, "It's *same'ach, v'nahafoch hu*. We're not getting drunk on Achashveirosh's wine; we're celebrating with Hashem." There should be lively, upbeat music in the background.

If the revelry causes material damage, remember: it's Purim. Don't ruin it because of your personal frustration, regardless of what you think. If something expensive is broken, getting angry won't undo the damage. It'll just spoil the joy of the day. You can feel upset, but keep a grip on yourself and hold it inside. Of course there's no choice about cleaning up the mess, but you do have a choice on how you will react.

With preteens and teenagers, talk about the miracle as much as you can before Purim. Try to engage them at the table. Ask them stimulating questions such as, "Why would anyone want to be Achashveirosh? Do you think Haman's evil nature would have been easily recognizable before he issued his decrees?" Discuss what happened to Queen Esther at the end and how Daryevesh, her descendant, gave the Jews permission to build the second *Beis HaMikdash*. Talk to them about Hashem's hidden ways and how Purim is relevant to us in exile because we constantly find hidden miracles in our lives if we only look for them. Kids can understand these ideas if you simplify them.

Be sure to make it clear before Purim that doing things that are dangerous is really listening to the voice of Achashveirosh and the voice of *gaavah*. This includes drunk driving, handling anything explosive or sharp, or giving people hard liquor when they think they are drinking something soft.

Boys will be going around collecting for their respective yeshivos. They should understand that their role is to bring *simchah* to the homes they visit. They should be making their hosts feel good about the *tzedakah* they are giving, not terrorizing them. This year some *bachurim* from Brisk called my daughter, who volunteers for a *chessed* organization that helps widows and orphans. They asked her to give them some names of orphan children who would appreciate some extra *simchah*. And on Purim they came and danced with them.

With older kids you need to plan the day beforehand. Don't let your boys wander around drunk. If there's a rabbi in the neighborhood who is willing to make a *mesibah* for them, that's great. If not, give your husband the job.

Give your teenage girls a day plan, too. Otherwise Purim becomes a drag for them as they watch the boys get drunk while they're stuck cleaning up the mess. Purim is a day for *tefillah*. In the morning, take them with you to daven. If you are in Israel, take them to the *Kosel* so they feel the sanctity of the day. Let them deliver *shalach manos* to their friends. When you arrive home for the *seudah*, everyone should be in a good mood. Fill the empty spaces in the afternoon with reading and discussing stimulating topics about the *Megillah* or the special qualities of the day.

Purim is *"kiyemu v'kiblu."* It's a holiday of reciprocal love. May we treasure that closeness and take it with us into the year.

The Seder Night: Inspiring and Involving Our Children

Pesach is the one night in the year when there's no excuse to exclude children from the dinner-table talk. In fact, the opposite is true. The Seder was actually meant for children, as it says,"*Vehigadta l'vincha* — And you shall tell your children ..."

Very young children up to age 3 will sense the pre-Pesach rush in the air. There is a flurry of scrubbing, cleaning, shopping, and setting up. You can bring them into the holiday spirit emotionally even if they are too young to understand it intellectually, by cleaning in a way that's joyous and energized.

The best way to get ready for Pesach is to plan it backward. This way you can make a realistic week-by-week schedule of what to do. Check off what day Pesach falls on and leave Erev Pesach free to rest so you can be your best at the Seder. You may want to get in some pre-Yom Tov cooking, which means the kitchen has to be cleaned and *kashered* a few days beforehand. It's very nice and in tune with the feeling of renewal to clean thoroughly and to buy new things, but separate that from what really needs to get done according to halachah. Don't clean because it's noble to feel exhausted or because everyone is doing it. If you'll get stressed out, just do what needs to be done, which is not all that much.

At this young age, children can't grasp much of what the Haggadah is about except the basic story line, but they can understand feelings. So it's up to you to keep the pre-Pesach mood positive in the home. Try to keep your children's schedule intact as much as possible, including meals, clean clothes, and bedtime, so their world isn't turned upside down more than it has to be.

Children from age 3 to 6 can begin to understand the Pesach story. This is really where *chinuch* starts. You can encourage them to memorize the *Simanim* and the *Mah Nishtanah*. There are many beautiful illustrated Haggados with Midrashim for children. There are also CDs with songs that are great for young kids. The repetition of listening over and over will make these stories sink into their minds. Try to connect the story of Pesach with the four questions. This will give your children extra satisfaction when asking the *Mah Nishtanah*.

If you will be a guest at the Seder, call your hosts immediately after Purim and tell them tactfully that you hope your kids will be included at the Seder. There are hosts who are not keen about involving children. Be insistent about this. You can compromise by having all the children say the *Mah Nishtanah* in unison, as long as each one gets recognition afterward.

Do whatever you can as a guest to make things easier for your host. Make sure your kids nap before the Seder so they won't be cranky. Prepare nuts and goodies on the table for them. After *Mah Nishtanah*, it's a good idea to dress your younger kids in pajamas so they can go to sleep without disturbing your hosts.

If you will be going to a hotel, I strongly recommend that you ask for a private Seder room, even if it will be more expensive. The mitzvah of the evening is engaging the children, and a communal Seder doesn't lend itself to kids' participation. People are more interested in the *chazzan* or the Rabbi and not in a bunch of youngsters. If you have no choice but to attend a communal Seder, speak to the person in charge before Pesach to find out how your children can participate.

Children from ages 7 to 11 are fully capable of joining in the pre-Pesach preparations. Maintain a positive atmosphere, give them the option to choose which chores they would like to do, and be sure to compliment them on a job well done. Sometimes you'll have to assign them tasks that they don't really want to do, such as pairing socks or watching the baby while you clean the kitchen. Be sure to have small rewards ready beforehand so they'll be cooperative.

In our home, we begin cleaning after Purim. Using the system mentioned above, we plan backward week by week with a list of what needs to get done. We then talk about who should do what. Some jobs are suitable for younger kids and others for older kids. I let each child choose what he or she would like to do. If you've done a good job of selling them Pesach, it's unlikely that you'll get, "I don't want to do anything."

Don't trust kids with serious cleaning in the kitchen. An adult needs to supervise, because even a speck of *chametz* in your food is a serious transgression. They can do a lot of other jobs, like vacuuming, polishing the furniture, and running errands. Make a reasonable schedule that fits theirs. Use markers so they can see exactly what they're supposed to do and when. After you've assigned them their jobs, don't renegotiate and add new jobs, as this can elicit feelings of betrayal. Be sure to compliment and reward them when they're done.

Try to do the pre-Pesach shopping early so that you can avoid the last-minute rush and tears of frustration and weariness.

If you have bright and interested kids, get them stimulating Haggados so they'll have what to present at the Seder. To prevent the Seder from becoming tedious, figure out how much time *Maggid* should take, keeping *chatzos* in mind, and divide up the different sections of the Haggadah between your kids so you don't have ten kids speaking about the *makkos* and no one speaking about *Mah Nishtanah*. Plan it so each kid has time to say a piece and the adults are attuned to listening. Kids look forward to the attention, so be sure to play it up, because this is their night.

Some parents are naturally dramatic and can act out the story of *Yetzias Mitzrayim*. Others are not. If you belong to the latter category, make things come alive by investing in some good illustrated Haggados so your kids can visualize what it was like.

It's wise to make your children understand that they can ask only for something reasonable for *Afikoman*. Talk to them before Pesach about what they would like. Try to move them away from foolish, transient things to more meaningful gifts.

If you will be at a hotel, ask the Rabbi to prepare some songs and stories for the kids. Arrange this before you finalize reservations. Hotels are usually eager to please guests, and you should insist on these accommodations for your children.

Kids from ages 11 to 14 should actively be involved in the pre-Pesach cleaning. Let them decide who will do what and when. It's good to arrange some fun days during their vacation where they can have some time off after they've completed their tasks. Girls are capable of spending their whole vacation shopping, so make sure their work plan is ready beforehand.

You can hold an older child's attention at the Seder by telling *hashgachah* stories from your own life or having your guests tell theirs. Inclusion in the actual Seder is crucial at this age. For boys, this means singing and *divrei Torah*. If you have many guests, you can make the Seder move faster by preparing seating cards and pre-measuring all the *shiurim* and packaging them individually. You can serve the meal more efficiently by skipping the soup, serving out portions right away, and preparing a quick dessert that doesn't require new plates. The focus of the Seder should really be *Maggid*, not *Shulchan Orech*.

Taking older kids to a hotel can easily turn into a nightmare. You have to be very vigilant about what they see and pick up, as you have no control over who the guests will be. At the Seder, be watchful about who your kids sit next to. Make sure your children's days are planned out so they have something to do all the time. You'll be less aggravated if they're busy.

If you will be guests at someone's home, it is good *chinuch* and a courtesy to have your teenager call up your host at the beginning of Adar and ask when they can come over to help. Tell your host beforehand to expect the call.

At home, you might be liberal about your kids leaving the table in the middle of the meal when they get bored. However, your teenagers should know that this is not courteous behavior at a host's Seder. If you will be guests at the Seder of *frum* people who are not into *divrei Torah*, but would rather discuss the news or tell jokes, it is crucial that you speak to your hosts beforehand and let them know that your kids will need to sing and say *divrei Torah*. You can't force your hosts to behave your way, but you can ask them at least to accommodate your kids so they can experience the true spirit of the Seder.

The Seder night is a magical time of joy, freedom, and light. May we create deep and lasting memories for our children.

Making Pesach Meaningful

We've looked at the practical side of Pesach — the cleaning, the preparation, and ways to maximize the Seder night with your kids. Now let's examine the essence of Pesach — *sippur yetzias Mitzrayim*.

With younger children age 3 to 6, it's very easy to be distracted with the drama of the story. It's important to emphasize three main ideas: Hashem is constantly watching over us, He has the ability to transcend nature, and in the end, justice prevails. The wicked ultimately pay for their actions.

The story of the Exodus is rich and complex. Although younger children have surely learned all about the plagues in school, they don't always get the whole picture.

I once overheard one of my grandchildren talking about Avraham Avinu and his tent, which had four doors. "I know why it had so many doors. If guests came and you didn't like them, you could make them leave right away from any room in the house." Apparently the teacher got across the idea of the four doors, but she didn't quite make the connection about *hachnasas orchim*.

Tell your children that Yaakov and his children went down to Egypt. Slowly they forgot that they were different from the *Mitzriyim*. Discuss how we are not like the non-Jews. We know about Hashem and we follow His Will. The *Mitzriyim* forgot how much Yosef had done for them. You can elaborate on how a *tzaddik* is careful to show gratitude, while someone who isn't righteous doesn't care to remember too much.

The evil *Mitzriyim* made the Jews work for them. Pharaoh fooled them into thinking it was a mitzvah. He lied to them and said it was a *chessed*.

Bring down the concept of slavery to your child's level: "Imagine what life was like for a little boy your age. He would get up in the morning from his bed of straw on the floor. He'd put on his old tattered clothes. He didn't go to *cheder*. He had to work, and even when he got tired he had to keep on going and sometimes he would get beaten. He'd stop only at night when he'd go home to rest and eat a bit.

"The *Mitzriyim* enslaved us because they saw that the Jews had so many children and they were afraid that soon there would be only Jews and no *Mitzriyim* left. We'd be stronger than them. But the real reason they tormented us was because they were evil."

You can be dramatic about the suffering, but save the horrific pictures in the Haggadah for older children. It may frighten the younger set.

"Pharaoh got worse. He ordered the babies boys thrown into the sea." At this age, not all kids will understand what death is. You want them to know that killing someone is cruel and that it's sad for the family. But you can't be too graphic, so you'll have to walk a fine line.

"Hashem saw how cruel Pharaoh was to the Jews. He heard the Jews' cries, and he selected Moshe to lead them out of Egypt. Moshe was special. When he was born the whole room was full of light. His mother saw that he was righteous, and she attempted to save him."

Talk about some of the *tzaddikim* and *tzidkaniyos* of the generation. It's important to tell them about Miriam, Yocheved, and Batya. This teaches them that no matter what happens, a person's innate greatness and nobility can still shine through.

"Batya didn't say, 'I don't care.' She said, 'The baby is crying. I must help him.' She stretched out her hand and Hashem enabled her to reach Moshe." Don't talk about how Her arm got really long. It's confusing at this age to think that Batya did something good and ended up looking weird. Talk about how *tzaddikim* do the right thing even when it's hard. Give them examples from their own life, such as sharing their toys with their cousins, letting others sleep in their bed, and offering some of their snack to a friend.

The story of Dasan and Aviram is important. Don't elaborate too much, because it could get confusing, but emphasize that they spoke *lashon hara* and Moshe said, "*Achein noda hadavar* — Now I know why the Jews are suffering so much." It is because of the sin of evil speech. Give them examples of what *lashon hara* is.

Then discuss how Moshe had to run away to Midyan. He found Yisro and married Yisro's daughter. Yisro was a hero. He didn't know the *Avos*, but Moshe helped him discover Hashem. Tell them the story of Moshe finding the sheep, the point being that Hashem makes good things happen to good people.

Describe how happy Aharon was to greet Moshe upon his return. Ask your children, "Would you like it if you were in charge and then someone new came and took over?" They'll probably get quiet and think it over. Then say, "Aharon was happy because this is what Hashem wanted." If there are sibling rivalry or jealousy issues, this is a great time to discuss them.

You don't have to talk too much about the plagues because they probably already learned about them well in school, but do mention that Hashem sent the *makkos* because he loved the Jews and the Egyptians had to suffer for their evil deeds.

The concept of *korban pesach* is often not given enough attention. The whole concept of *korbanos* is very difficult for kids to understand.

Explain that Hashem wanted to give the Jews mitzvos so they would merit to leave Egypt. The *Mitzriyim* believed that their sheep were like Hashem. Therefore, Hashem ordered the Jews to sacrifice sheep to show that they didn't believe in the Egyptian idols.

Conclude with how the Jews packed up quickly and left Egypt with faith and joy.

In mid-childhood, children still enjoy a good story, so embellish the Exodus account with Midrashim to make it tangible and real. Start at the beginning, with how the *Mitzriyim* forgot Yosef and how the Jews forgot themselves. Talk about the idea of how easy it is to forget who we are. Tell them how hard it was for the Jews to retain their identity and how heroic they were for not changing their clothing, language, and names.

Then discuss the enslavement. This is the age for a vividly illustrated and exciting Haggadah. You could begin by asking, "Why is the *Mitzri* happy that he's beating a Jew?" You'll have to explain about *taavas hanitzachon* on a child's level. You can say, "Some people only feel big when they can make somebody else feel small." Talk about where cruelty comes from. Ask them, "What do you think it was like in *Mitzrayim*?"

Trace Hashem's hand in the story. They are not quite old enough to get the idea that the first step toward *geulah* is *galus*, but you could say, "Hashem was with them all along and they had to go through this."

Tell them about *Bris Bein HaBesarim* and how Avraham asked Hashem, "How will I know if my children will walk my path?" You can say that Hashem answered, "They'll be strangers in a foreign land and they'll suffer and they'll say about the *Mitzri*, 'This isn't who I want to be.' They'll turn to Me and they'll transform themselves." You could tell them, "The worst thing a person could do is become like a *Mitzri*."

The next segment, which is usually underplayed in school, is Moshe's humility. Talk about how Hashem propels people to greatness. Some stories are well known from the *Chumash*, such as the story of the *Akeidah*, where Avraham and Yitzchak reached unbelievable levels, and the story of Yehoshua, who was chosen to lead after

Moshe. Give them real-life examples of humble people who scaled unimaginable heights because the situation required it.

The last segment is the plagues. Show them the pictures in the Hagaddah. Talk to them about what happened and help them visualize it in their minds. Emphasize the concept of *middah k'neged middah*. When you get to *makkos bechoros*, point out the concept of *beni bechori Yisrael*. We relate to Hashem the way a firstborn child relates to his parents. He turns his parents — two people who have not yet experienced parenthood — into parents. We bring Hashem into the world. Make it clear that the plagues came from Hashem and that He transcended nature.

With older children and teens, it depends on whether they are willing to listen to you. At the Seder, they may be more open to discussion, but then there is the pressure of *chatzos*. So as you are cleaning and preparing for Pesach, try to give them a sense of the *simchah* of the holiday. Find a few quiet moments as you are preparing for Yom Tov together to talk to them.

Explain that true joy is being part of something larger than yourself. You can say, "The *simchah* of getting married is moving on to something better and bigger and building something greater. When the Jews left *Mitzrayim* they grew spiritually. They became a people for whom *hashgachah* and *nissim* are the stuff of everyday life. *Chametz* is *gaavah*. It works the same way in marriage. Happiness in marriage is thinking about the other person. If you are only thinking about yourself, you cannot build."

Older children might ask, "If Hashem got us into *Mitzrayim*, what's the big deal that He took us out?" At this point, it's good to explain about the continuum of *galus* and *geulah*. You can talk about people who survived the Holocaust and rebuilt their families. Explain that the way to build yourself is by eradicating your limitations. You have to experience firsthand what you don't want to be in order to know what you do want to be.

Talk about *geulah*. You can say, "If you were in Egypt and Moshe came, would you start packing, or would you think it wasn't going

Making Pesach Meaningful / 269

to happen? If someone told you Mashiach had arrived, would you believe him?" Oftentimes they may answer that they wouldn't believe. Then you have to say, "Life is full of unexpected curves and Hashem can do anything." Share with them surprising occurrences in your own life. Teach your children that all possibilities are in Hashem's hands.

When you talk about the plagues, emphasize how Hashem demonstrates His love through *hashgachah pratis*. Hashem won't perform open miracles like He did in *Mitzrayim* because He wants us to attain our sense of faith on our own. Your goal is not just to get them to understand that Hashem is there, that He cares and can do anything, but to sense real *simchah* in being part of His nation.

Create an aura of *simchah* at the Seder. Think about what would make your family happy. Encourage your husband to tell over stories of the Exodus. Invite the children to sing.

Now that we've looked at ways to make your Seder more meaningful, let's think about what you can do to enhance Chol HaMoed. I find that Chol HaMoed can easily disintegrate to externals. Let the Pesach spirit flow into the week. At least when you are eating together, mention something about *yetzias Mitzrayim*, infuse a bit of *simchah*, sing, help your kids feel Hashem's goodness. Talk about His *Malchus* and try to impart a sense of the *chashivus* of Chol HaMoed to your children. Older kids need this desperately.

Throughout the year, the feeling of being a link to something bigger than oneself is hard to latch onto. Pesach can be a big *tikkun* in connecting us to the joy and majesty of being a part of the *am hanivchar*.

Sefiras HaOmer and Lag BaOmer

Sefiras ha'omer and Lag BaOmer are days of spiritual ascension. How can we help our children tap into the mystical energy of these weeks?

Most kids learn in school about the death of Rabbi Akiva's students and the story of Rabbi Shimon Bar Yochai, but these events aren't usually discussed in depth, nor are they told how it has anything to do with them at all.

Children between the ages of 3 and 6 should be given some background information. You can tell them about *sefirah*. Make it visual by showing them a chart with forty-nine days. They should understand that we are counting and getting closer to *Matan Torah*. All the days of *sefirah* are a preparation stage to make us worthy to receive Hashem's greatest gift.

There's no reason to get into the deep spiritual aspects of the period with little kids because they won't understand it. It's enough for them to know that this is a time when we strive to become better.

Our goal is to become *k'ish echad b'lev echad* and to say *na'aseh v'nishma* with complete faith and a trusting heart.

As children get older, talk to them about the seven *sefiros* in a simple way. During the week of *chessed*, teach them about kindness. *Chessed* is going the extra mile. When you go to the store to buy milk, you pay for it, but if you are extra nice you'll also say, "Good morning," and smile at the cashier. Discuss with your children various little acts of *chessed* they can do, like visiting a lonely shut-in, collecting food for a charitable organization, or watching the younger children so Mommy can rest.

You can mention that *chessed* is sometimes hard, which makes the mitzvah much greater. Talk about Avraham, who was a pillar of *chessed*. "Remember how Avraham was not feeling good after his *bris milah*? Still he went out into the hot sun to look for guests. That's *tzidkus*."

The next week talk about *gevurah*. *Gevurah* is overcoming the *yetzer hara* in order to do what's right. Then tell a story. "Once there was a girl who lost her wallet. She lived too far to walk home, so she thought, 'I'll get on the bus with a group of girls and sit down quickly so the driver won't notice.' But then she told herself, 'No, I'll be strong and do what Hashem wants.' She told the driver what happened and he said, 'Ask someone to pay for you.' And she did. That's a hero. She did the right thing although it was hard." You can give more examples of children who overcame their evil inclination and emerged victorious.

Tiferes is harmony, which is more abstract. It's something that will be experienced fully in the next world. *Tiferes* is the source of *emes*. Truth is when you can see the whole picture. It's a perfect balance between all factors. The most beautiful thing in the world is to use what Hashem gives us for the good. Hashem gave us the power of speech so we would always tell the truth. He gave us the ability to walk so we would go only to good places. *Tiferes* is using all our gifts in a perfectly balanced way.

Stories are great to illustrate this *middah*. Tell your children about the *savta* who sold her special Shabbos scarf so her son could have wine for *Kiddush*. What a beautiful *Kiddush* it was. She created *simchah* in Heaven because she gave away something precious for something greater.

Point out the pretty things in your home that are used for mitzvos. If you have the time and money, you can buy a new beautiful *cheifetz shel mitzvah*, such as a wine decanter or a *challah* cover.

Netzach means that Hashem's *ratzon* will ultimately prevail. This is a difficult idea for children to grasp. Try to phrase it in kid language. Emphasize that Hashem always wins. The Egyptians thought they were mighty and strong, but Hashem prevailed. Nimrod thought he'd finish off Avraham, and today nobody talks much about him, but everyone knows about Avraham.

If you have a child who is struggling with something, this is a very important week. A child with a social problem or an illness or one who suffered a loss should know that Hashem always comes out on top, and if we're good and make the best of our situation, we'll be happy in the end. Joyful people are those who do the Will of Hashem, and Hashem's Will always wins. Those who mock and hurt people are forgotten in the end.

Hod means being humble enough to see Hashem's splendor and greatness and feeling small because of it. This is a very esoteric *middah* even for adults. Use stories to explain it. You can say, "This week we say thank you to Hashem. We think it's all us, but really it's Hashem."

If you have the time and energy make something from scratch. Choose something that kids are used to seeing as a finished product. Go to the store to buy the ingredients. When you purchase the sugar, ask your children, "Where did this come from? How did it get into the bag?" Explain how Hashem makes sugarcane grow. Tell them that cocoa is extracted from beans, oil is pressed from olives, and flour is ground from wheat kernels. Trace everything back to its source, step by step, very patiently. Instead of saying, "Look at this great cake," say, "Look how nice it was of Hashem to give us all these ingredients. We only put it together." Get them to say a *berachah* with *kavannah* and then say, "Hashem is big, we are small."

Yesod is the capacity within us to be focused and devoted. It's taking everything you have and aiming it toward a goal. It's the source of loyalty, fidelity, and chastity. It's doing everything for Hashem. A *tzaddik* takes everything he has and directs it toward the Creator, the Foundation of the world. Discuss the Yosef story. Point out how he followed Hashem and didn't give in to his *yetzer hara*.

During the week of *malchus*, talk about how we can make Hashem king. No matter where we are and what we do, we should always ask ourselves, "What would Hashem want?" Tell stories about Dovid HaMelech. When he was a shepherd in the field with his flock and later, when he became king, he would always praise Hashem. If you are musical, teach your children a new *niggun*.

This should all lead up to *Matan Torah*. Somewhere at the end of the discussion, you have to say, "We have to learn to use all these *middos* right so we can reach a level of *na'aseh v'nishma*, of becoming one person with one heart. A long time ago the students of Rabbi Akiva didn't give *kavod* to one another. We are sad because they were so great, but tragically they fell short in this area. This is why we still mourn them today. We must do better."

Talk about Rabbi Shimon bar Yochai (Rashbi) and his righteousness. With young children it is enough to say that he was like Moshe who gave us the Torah. Rabbi Shimon helped us understand the Torah with new depth and profundity.

You can present *sefirah* to older children in a more sophisticated and personalized way. The first week, ask them to think of a *chessed* they can do. During the week of *gevurah*, challenge them to overcome something that's hard for them. In the week of *tiferes*, get them thinking about how they can beautify what they are already doing. *Tiferes* can also be a week to look at beautiful things and talk about their significance. If you have an artistic or musical child, you can encourage him to create something beautiful *l'shem Shamayim*. Showing your sensitive children evocative Jewish art could be a springboard for discussion.

During the week of *netzach*, talk about who our real heroes are. This is a very important aspect of *chinuch*. Children should hear about the heroes who held fast to the Torah through dark times and prevailed.

In the week of *hod*, start a gratitude journal with them. If they are too young for that, ask them at night to tell you what good things happened to them during the day, and together you can thank Hashem.

Yesod can take on meaning for kids if you explain it on their level. It is manifest through expressing loyalty and devotion to Hashem. It's taking all our *kochos* and elevating them. It's remembering that we are in the presence of Hashem and not looking for affirmation elsewhere. This is the age to discuss the Yosef story more in depth. You can talk about the *middah* of *tzniyus* in a refined way.

The week of *malchus* is a time to explore the idea of being a sovereign over oneself. This entails doing things for the sake of Hashem's honor, not being reactive to others, and standing up for one's principles. At this age children can appreciate the *mesirus nefesh* of Rabbi Shimon bar Yochai and how he brought Hashem's *malchus* into the world. Teach them some of the verses of the Bar Yochai song. Even if you talk about it on a simple level, your children will get some idea of what spiritual grandeur means and who Rashbi really was.

Discuss the relationship of Moshe and Rabbi Shimon bar Yochai. Moshe brought us the Torah, but Rabbi Shimon made us understand it in a whole different way by revealing its deeper meaning.

If you live in Eretz Yisrael, at this age, your children will probably be involved in building "*medurot*," giant bonfires. Remember to warn them about safety precautions. Help them understand the bonfire's deeper meaning: "The fires affirm the *yahrtzeit* of Rabbi Shimon bar Yochai. They're like giant *yahrtzeit* candles. It's his soul growing stronger and going higher."

If your teens are attuned, give them their own *sefirah* calendar with the *sefirot* explained. This will give your teenagers some idea of the potential for self-improvement and growth inherent in these weeks.

In Eretz Yisrael, the big issue is to go or not to go to Meron. It's become very political. There are some schools that encourage it and some that discourage it. Rabbi Shimon bar Yochai said that he is there for everyone on this day, and so it really is a huge opportunity for *tefillah*. He said to come, so I can't say it's a non-value. However, if you have boys in yeshivah who have opted to stay behind and learn, certainly you should make it clear that Rabbi Shimon's path was Torah.

I have found that the best time to go is in the afternoon when people are leaving. Then it's more possible to get into the *tziyun*. Arriving at night isn't easy, but the singing and the aura of holiness is so precious and so beautiful that if you're in Eretz Yisrael, why not go and grasp some of the glory of Bar Yochai and his *nitzchiyus* — *netzach she'b'netzach*?

Some people visit Rav Akiva's *kever* because he was Rabbi Shimon's rebbi and his life in many ways mirrored his student's.

For those not in Eretz Yisrael, you can tap into the light of this holy day through *tefillah* and *Tehillim*. May we soon witness the full revelation with the coming of Mashiach.

Shavuos

How do we make the holiday of *Matan Torah* real and relevant for our children?

For young children from the ages of 3 to 6, it's important that they not only know the story of the Giving of the Torah, but that they understand three main principles.

The first principle is that the Torah is from Hashem and that His rules are perfect. He gave us these laws to help us stay on the right path. Emphasize that Torah is always good, both for the person who keeps it and for the world. What's pretty or fun for one child isn't necessarily so for another child. But Hashem is different. He made rules that suit everyone. There are also laws that are only good for certain people, like Kohanim. Some rules are only for fathers and some are only for mothers. The Torah's laws are eternal, while a person's rules are transitory. Help your children understand that rules create order. Life without it would be awful.

The second point is that the only way to know the mitzvos is to learn them. This is especially important for boys to hear. To illustrate this, you can tell a parable: Once upon a time there was a king who had a son who lived far away. He missed him very much, so he wrote him a letter. The son couldn't read it, so he paid someone to read it to him because he loved his father very much and he wanted to know what he had written. Hashem is like the great king. He gave us the Torah, which is like the letter the king wrote his son. We have to learn how to read and understand it, and until we grasp it completely, we have to ask wiser people to help us. Your goal is to implant within your children respect for their teachers and a desire to learn.

At this point you could introduce the concept *havdalah bein kodesh l'chol*. The king's letter is more important than a story or a letter from a friend. Likewise, learning Torah is more significant than anything else. Children by nature prefer other subjects to Torah unless it's taught very well, because it's easier to simplify other studies. Therefore, getting across to them that the Torah is like a letter from the king gives it enormous importance.

The third point to talk about is how lucky we are to have the mitzvos. Explain that having fewer obligations, the way non-Jews do, isn't better. It means not fully knowing the king. The episode of Hashem offering the Torah to the various nations and them saying no is important for kids to hear so they realize that the nations lost out through their choice.

You can discuss humility as it relates to *Har Sinai* and to Moshe, who was the humblest of all men. Kids this age won't grasp the concept fully, so you can explain with a parable:

Chaim draws a picture. He's really proud of it. He buys fancy envelopes to send copies to all his friends and family, and he makes sure to write at the top, "Drawn by Chaim." Moshe wasn't like that. It was all from Hashem, not from him. Likewise, *Har Sinai* said, "I'm the smallest mountain." That's why Hashem chose Moshe and gave him the Torah on *Har Sinai*.

For middle-grade children, your goal is for them to appreciate the gift of Torah on a deeper level. You want them to understand that everyone has a portion in Torah and that Hashem and the Torah are one. Give them examples of great injustices. Invariably, the villains were those who didn't keep the Torah. They may say, "But he's *frum* and look what he did." Don't feel trapped. Ask them, "Did the Torah tell him to do this? His problem isn't that he listened to the Torah, but that he didn't." Tell them heroic stories about people who fought injustices perpetrated by people who didn't keep Torah.

This is also a good age to show them how the prophecies in the Torah came true. You can tell them that the Torah promises that if we keep *shemittah,* Hashem will provide for us from the sixth year onward. A human being couldn't make such a promise. Show them that the Torah not only creates structure and rules, but benefits us. Hashem, Who created all things, cares enough about us to give us laws that affect every aspect of our life. Emphasize that even if a mitzvah doesn't bring immediate blessing, it is not the end of the story. Hashem can see the whole picture, while we are limited. Bring examples of people who kept mitzvos and show how it worked out well.

Talk about the concept of everyone having his own portion in Torah. Most kids enjoy learning if it's on their level and they feel successful. Every so often there's a child whose abilities aren't the same as other kids his age. He may be sharper or faster and finds the learning at his grade level boring. This prevents him from appreciating Torah. Then you have to say, "Let's find something in Torah that you like." And you have to go to the trouble of figuring out what he does find challenging.

What's far more common is the kid who doesn't like learning because he finds it hard or abstract. Studying about the Kohen *hedyot* or Kohen Gadol doesn't grab him because he's never met one. You can say to this kind of child, "Torah creates an invisible fire that brings good and light into the world. The Torah has six million letters, and if one is missing the whole Torah is *pasul*. Every Jew is like a letter. If you don't learn, the light your letter should bring into the world doesn't shine, and what the Torah was supposed to bring forth doesn't come forth."

Every child should feel completely responsible for actualizing this light. Your role is to help him figure out his *cheilek*. Get your child to learn something on Friday night that will resonate with him. Then encourage him to share it at the table.

With girls you can talk about *chavivus haTorah*, the preciousness of Torah, and making it all happen. A woman is the foundation of her home. She's like the principal of a school who doesn't teach, but keeps the school running. She cooks the food, brings up the children, and supports her husband. She is a full partner in Torah. Point out that girls learn Torah too. Rashi says that Miriam taught the women while Moshe taught the men. A women's *cheilek* is expressed in the way she brings Torah into her own life. It's important for girls to hear stories about righteous women so that they see how a woman's strengths can be actualized.

Young girls should understand the gift of Torah and its *chashivus*, and that there are different ways of learning and expressing it. There were women whose righteousness stemmed from who they were for their husbands and sons. And there were women who achieved personal righteousness on their own. There were women who did both. It's essential to bring home the idea that a woman's role, though hidden, is significant, because in the world we live in today, the more public and observable something is, the more important it seems.

There are various views about learning all night and letting kids stay up. In my opinion, the drama of learning all night has the power to leave a lasting imprint on children. This can result in their learning more in the future. In addition, learning at night has its own value. If you do send your young boys out to learn at night, there should be an adult supervising. Otherwise it can easily turn into fun and *hefkeirus*. If your husband can fill the role, that's great. If not, try to find some framework of supervised learning for them. You can speak to the teachers at school and suggest they give the kids an assignment that's easy and fun and from which they can gain. You can sign a note to their rebbi saying that they completed the assignment, for which they can then earn a prize. If this isn't feasible, try to find books with Torah thoughts on their level that they can learn on their own and then tell over.

You can't really talk to teens about Torah the way you've spoken with your younger children, because they either already know the concepts or they are not interested in listening. They certainly understand the significance of Torah intellectually, but in terms of integrated knowledge it's not always that clear. Do teenagers think that more rules and regulations are good for them? Do they think their lives as Torah observant Jews are better and more fun than other people's lives? Many kids will say yes, while many will say no. Since you can't approach the subject frontally, try to put them in a position where they have to explain it to younger kids. Even if you have to reward your teen, get him to teach others.

With teenage girls, Shavuos can easily disintegrate into something very materialistic. Discussions tend to wander to who baked what and is it too much to have both blintzes and cheesecake at one meal. There's a place for this. We are supposed to prepare special foods for Yom Tov. But it shouldn't take over the essence of the holiday.

Try to plan ahead. Find interesting books for your girls to read. Get them to tell over stories to their younger siblings. Take them with you to a stimulating *shiur*.

If you're in Jerusalem, going to the *Kosel* for *netz* can be an inspiring experience, helping them feel the specialness of the holiday. Work out who they'll be walking with, how they'll get home, and where they'll hear *Kiddush*.

Teenage boys can easily join the learning programs for men on Shavuos night. Make it a badge of maturity so that they feel good about going.

Invest effort to make the Yom Tov significant and memorable. Buy a new *sefer*. Do something novel or promise a gift for learning well.

The only area of resistance I've seen with teenagers is keeping the Yom Tov spirit at the table. Plan with your husband beforehand to introduce *divrei Torah* and inspirational talk into discussions at the *seudah*.

May the light and goodness of Torah permeate Shavuos with your children.

Tishah B'Av

The three weeks and Tishah B'Av are one of the most challenging periods in the Jewish calendar to explain to children. Even for adults, the whole concept of the destruction of the *Beis HaMikdash* is very distant from reality. Of course, we have to do our best to convey a sense of this period to our children, but don't expect them to feel what you yourself might not be feeling either.

It's very hard to get kids to move into the abstract mode and, tragically, for most of us, the *Beis HaMikdash* remains an obscure concept. I remember a time when the children at a certain camp were assigned a project to build a model *Beis HaMikdash*. The kids poured all their talents and energy into the project, only to be told that it would soon be burned to simulate the destruction of the *Beis HaMikdash*. They certainly felt bad, not about the *Beis HaMikdash*, but about their wasted efforts.

Very young children from age 3 to 6 can't grasp much about this period. I once had a wonderful student with great *middos* from a small town in New Hampshire, who asked me, "What was so special about the Temple?" Kids think like that too.

You have to explain, "Hashem is an invisible Being. He wanted us to connect with Him." Bring it down to their level. "How do you know Shabbos is coming? Your senses pick up the signs. You smell the chicken soup and the *cholent* even before you enter the kitchen. When you see Abba's hat on the chair, you know he's home." Although their intellectual capacity is still limited, they'll catch on. Young children are spiritually sensitive. Continue to explain, "Hashem wanted us to know He was with us. He commanded us to build a special House so we would sense His presence, and He performed miracles for us."

If you live in Israel and can travel to the *Kosel,* take your kids there and show them the sights. Explain that the *Kosel* is part of the wall surrounding the mountain where the *Beis HaMikdash* once stood. It reminds us of the Holy Temple. It's like the front door of a house that leads to an inner door. You can take them to the inner area of the *ezras nashim,* which goes through the tunnels. Show them the models of *Har HaBayis* and the *Beis HaMikdash* if they're at the level to grasp the significance.

You can talk to your children about the miracles in the *Beis HaMikdash.* Don't list all ten; choose one or two. I would recommend telling them about the fire coming down from Heaven and consuming the sacrifices and about people bowing down with plenty of space to spare.

You can say, "When a Jew wanted to thank Hashem for all the good in his life, he would bring a gift in the form of a sacrifice. A fire would descend from the sky and burn the offering. This indicated that Hashem approved. The Jews were happy, and the whole world rejoiced with them. This was *simchas olam.*"

Talk about how everyone would come to the *Beis HaMikdash* and how great the crowd was. Show them how much room a person needs to stand and then how much more space is required to bow. Talk about the miracle of how all the people had plenty of room because Hashem wanted to show them how much He desired their prayers. These first two conversations should ideally take place before the Three Weeks commence or as soon as they begin.

As Tishah B'Av nears, help them understand the loss of the *Beis HaMikdash*. They won't comprehend much if they can't appreciate what it was. You can tell the following parable: "Once upon a time there was a king who had an errant son. He sent him far away from the palace to live with peasants. At first, the prince liked his new surroundings, but then he remembered that he wasn't like these people. The king missed his son terribly, so he sent a messenger to find his son.

"The messenger asked the prince, 'Are you the prince?'

"He answered, 'I don't know.'

"The messenger saw it really was the prince, so he gave him royal clothing and said, 'Come with me. Your father the king wants you back.'

"When the king saw that his son had repented, he beckoned him close and embraced him."

You can be dramatic and expand the story as much as you'd like, but be sure to get across that the father always loved his son. He sent his son away because he couldn't live in the palace anymore, but the father always hoped his son would return.

You can explain the destruction of the *Beis HaMikdash* by saying, "Hashem had a special house. We sinned, so Hashem allowed our enemies to destroy it." Your kids might ask, "What did we do that was so bad?" It's best to skip the reasons for the destruction of the First Temple. You could talk about *sinas chinam*, but save it for a later discussion.

Play house with your kids. Let them be the parents and you be the child. Tell them that parents really love their children and want them to be good to each other. Hashem saw the Jews fighting and making one another feel bad. Tell them the Kamtza story. Emphasize that this is what happens when people are cruel to one another, embarrass one another, and make others feel small. That's why the *Beis HaMikdash* was destroyed. But Hashem is waiting for us. He wants us to come back and be good to each other again. Then say,

"Let's think of something nice we can do for someone today, maybe even someone we don't even like so much."

Talk to your children about how the *minhagim* of mourning fit in with this period. Go back to the parable about the king. Tell them, "Every so often, the prince would remember the palace and his father the king and how much he loved his father, and he'd feel sad. We too must remember how much Hashem loves us, how good it was when we had the *Beis HaMikdash*, how there was *simchas olam*, and how everyone treated others with honor and respect. We feel sad because we've lost it all. The ache in our hearts makes us want these things back even more. This propels us to try to improve so that Hashem will want to welcome us back."

Young kids won't grasp what fasting has to do with self-rectification, so skip that.

Keep your children busy on Tishah B'Av morning with discussions about the *Beis HaMikdash*. If they are ready for it, tell them one or two stories about the suffering of exile and how people rose above their limitations and came back to Hashem. Don't tell them terrible *churban* tales or Holocaust stories or the details of the death of Rabbi Akiva. It's too overwhelming for young kids. Instead, talk about *mesirus nefesh* and how Jews sacrificed everything to keep Torah and mitzvos despite the travails of *galus*.

You'll have a much easier time talking to kids from age 6 to 11. You can be more practical, but at the same time deepen your approach. You can tell them the parable of the king and the prince, but embellish it. Your job is to give them the *penimiyus* of what the period is all about. Don't expect the schools to do it.

Ask your children, "What do you think is so difficult about this time? When you think how things could be and how things are now, doesn't it feel terrible?" Bring examples, such as a formerly wealthy person who remembers with sadness all the money he once had. Then say, "So too, in the Three Weeks we have to think about what we lost. We had a holy *Beis HaMikdash*. Hashem was close to us, and we could feel His Presence. Today we are so far away from this experience."

Talk about how much Hashem loves us. Tell them about the boy who came to the United States before the Holocaust and saved all his money so he could get his parents out of Europe. Hashem has saved us so many times, and He's still here with us, watching over us because He loves us. We don't feel this protection because we don't perceive Him.

In the *Beis HaMikdash* there were miracles that made us aware of how much Hashem cared for us. Children this age will enjoy going through the ten miracles with you. With older boys you can ask, "In Eretz Yisrael there's *Bircas Kohanim* every day, but in *chutz la'aretz* it's only on Yom Tov. Why? A person has real *simchah* in his heart when he feels that someone loves him. In Eretz Yisrael we can sense Hashem's love more. There's no *Beis HaMikdash*, so we don't see that love, but we feel it."

Tell your kids about *shemittah*, how Hashem makes things grow miraculously. Talk about Hashem's providence, how he brought people from all over the world to live in Eretz Yisrael, and how we feel so much more connected to Hashem in His holy Land.

Older kids won't be too keen on talking about awareness and remembering what love felt like. So tell the famous story of the young girl who was forced to convert and was sent to a monastery during the Inquisition. Her parents gave her the formula of *Shema* to remember them by. She kept it alive in her heart until she was saved.

Hashem gave us a foretaste of something holy so we could feel beloved. But we don't want it to stay like this. We want more. We want love between people; we want more focus on the inside; we want caring, connection, and empathy. We want to see only goodness within people. We want to feel Hashem's Presence. What we have now isn't adequate. We want to stretch higher.

Get kids excited about taking on a new *chessed* or *ahavas Yisrael* project. Match your children's interests up with suitable activities. Boys generally like stuffing envelopes and delivering food. Girls enjoy social projects. Get your kids to be nice to a new classmate or neighbor who needs an extra dose of attention, encourage them to do small acts of kindness, and teach them about *maaser* and giving charity.

At this age, you can talk about the first *Beis HaMikdash* and the three sins. Discuss the *asarah harugei malchus* and tell over stories from the Midrash. Talk to your children about the suffering of *galus*. This is the time to recount Holocaust stories and *galus* tales to which your kids can relate. For older kids, I would recommend some of the excellent stories at the back of *Me'am Loez, Sefer Devarim*.

Older kids from 11 to the teen years know most of the technical historical background of the Three Weeks. Your goal is to introduce them to the *penimiyus* of the period. Encourage them to start children's *ahavas Yisrael chaburos*. Of course you'll have to do most of the organization, but getting them to learn the three basic laws of *ahavas Yisrael* is worth it. They are: speaking well of people, giving them *kavod*, and being concerned about others.

Use stories and songs. If your children are intellectually inclined, this is a good age to delve more deeply into the symbolism of the *Beis HaMikdash*. Read up on it and learn more about it. There are some wonderful explanations by the Malbim that you can translate into kid language. Explain that we can build a *Beis HaMikdash*, but it's just a physical structure. The spirit has to come down from Above.

If you're in Eretz Yisrael, you can make the *Beis HaMikdash* more real by taking them to see the Old City walls, the *kosel hakatan*, and the Ohel Yitzchak Shul near Shaar Shechem, where excavations have uncovered remnants from the times of the *bayis sheni*. Try to give them a sense of the Temple's imminence. The *Shechinah*, the closeness, is missing because we are blocked. The way out is through yearning for that closeness deeply enough. Your goal is to get them to want to want.

Think beforehand about how you would like your teenagers to spend Tishah B'Av. At night, there's the *Eichah* reading and then there are *shiurim*. Perhaps there are some lectures in the morning. But the afternoon can be challenging, so have a plan ready. For older kids, *bein hazemanim* looms tantalizingly near. Try to have them keep all their vacation plans in their head so that they are not already into the next day while it's still Tishah B'Av. If they are willing to listen, discuss the symbolism of Tishah B'Av. Talk about Hashem's love for us, how He destroyed the *Beis HaMikdash* because He had mercy on us, how Tishah B'Av is the day of return, the birth of Mashiach, and that wanting to want can bring the redemption.

When you speak about Mashiach, ask them, "Who do you think Mashiach is? What will it be like when he comes?" Before Tishah B'Av, you can learn the Rambam on *Hilchos Melachim,* which discusses the period of Mashiach. Emphasize that Mashiach is a real person and that real people have been Hashem's emissaries and have gotten us out of exile before, like Moshe, Ezra, and Nechemia. Emphasize that things can change in an instant. Discuss which mitzvos can bring the *geulah* closer. This includes not speaking *lashon hara* and practicing *ahavas chinam.*

Ask your children, "What are you doing and what do you think we can all be doing to bring the redemption closer?" Open their minds to think of small deeds they can do to improve. Emphasize that each Jew's actions have an impact.

May we merit the final redemption speedily in our days.

Chapter 6
Teaching Our Children Middos

Teaching Children to Be Givers

By nature, children do not enjoy giving. In fact, babies know nothing about giving and everything about taking. This is because very young children only hear their animalistic souls. You as a parent must awaken their elevated voice.

We live in a materialistic society where giving is undervalued. What counts is physical reality. In the material sense, the more you give, the less you have, while in the spiritual sense, the more you give, the more you are. Therefore, the first step in educating your child to give is to question your own attitude toward giving.

Do a bit of introspection. How do you feel when someone asks you for a favor? What is your immediate reaction when someone asks you for a significant loan? If your attitude about giving is negative, don't be hard on yourself. It's normal not to want to give. However, be aware that the language of the soul is giving, and the language of the body is taking. By allowing yourself to be a taker, you commit yourself to your body. The body is journeying toward death, which is why it yearns for repose. Conversely, the soul is eternal and desires to give and do for others. If you have your own inner crisis about giving, you'll need to resolve it first before attempting to teach your children.

Ask yourself, "How can I come to enjoy giving?" There are various ways to do this. First, learn to identify with the recipient. Use imagery to cross a bridge that may be hard to cross otherwise. Suppose someone asks you for money to help pay for therapy. Picture someone who isn't coping with life, and imagine what will happen if you help out. Picture the person back on his feet, getting married, starting a family, and holding down a steady job. The more you see yourself in the recipient's shoes, the more you awaken empathy within yourself for others, and the more you'll love giving.

A child's desire to take and not give is much stronger than that of an adult. With very young children, don't expect much. They aren't mentally developed enough to understand spiritual pleasure. Therefore, laying down the law is the way to go. You have to say, "We share here. Look at the clock. You get 5 minutes and then he gets 5 minutes."

Starting at about the age of 5, children can begin to be taught empathetic understanding. This can be done through storytelling. Have the hero come from a different culture, or use animal characters. This takes pressure off the child. Your goal in storytelling is to have the child empathize with a hero who gives something to someone in need, after which they both end up feeling good. You can use this basic story line in endless variations with young children. The hero can offer emotional support, physical assistance, or practical help. It is essential that the hero be a winner and not a loser. Otherwise, the child will not connect with the story. Your aim should be to teach your children the joy of giving.

Give your child a sum of money and tell him about *maaser*. Initially, he won't want to give the money to *tzedakah*. Although he didn't work for it and does not as yet have a clear picture of what money can buy, he'll still be loathe to give away anything of his own. Open your child's heart by telling him stories of poor children who need help. Tell him how he can make a difference by donating his money.

Once he's experienced the pleasure of giving in theory, you can move up a notch. If you're in Yerushalayim, take your child to Geulah or the *Kosel*, where collectors abound. Give him money to drop into a cup or to place in the hand of one in need. Then say, "Look what a mitzvah you've done. Now this woman can go home and buy a cake for Shabbos."

Once you've laid the groundwork, you can then introduce the concept of giving into your child's personal life. A good place to begin is at home. Instead of saying, "You were so good. You brought the baby a cookie," create empathy by saying, "The baby was so happy when you brought her a cookie."

As your child grows older, raise your expectations. Teach him to do *chessed* for others. If someone left a small item in your house, have the child make the phone call to the owner to tell him where it is. The more your children learn to empathize, the more they'll want to give. Teach them to go the extra mile. Let them make fancy folded napkins or a complicated dessert for a *simchah*. Anything they can do in a beautiful way will implant the joy of giving in their hearts.

Dispense compliments generously, "Hashem must have such *nachas*. Look what stunning treats you created for the *simchah*"; or "What wonderful children I have. Look how much you love each other and want to give to one another." This makes them want to continue being givers.

Watch out for obstacles. There are always people who are happy to be recipients. Some children may question whether the deeper pleasure of giving is really as good as the immediate pleasure of taking. Therefore, you should sometimes back up your praise with material reward for giving. If your child gave his *maaser* to *tzedakah*, find a reason to buy the child a small gift that costs the same. This way he won't feel the loss as much. Watch your child carefully, though, and do this only if the need arises, because you can create a situation where every time he gives, he takes, which is anti-*chinuch*.

Some schools will send children around to sell raffles for *tzedakah* with the promise of rewards. Here the child immediately stops empathizing with the cause and focuses exclusively on the prize. Be careful with this, as this turns giving into taking. Sometimes you may be tempted to give your child the money so he can get the prize without having to collect. Don't do this unless you can build some compassion between the child and the cause. Without empathy, giving and taking become intertwined, which leads to internal corruption.

How do you get older kids to give? Interestingly, the harder it is for them to give, the more they enjoy it. The giving needs to be dramatic enough for it to hold them. Find opportunities for your children. It's easier with girls, who enjoy the social aspects of visiting old age homes and hospitals. Try to find projects to match your child's interests and talents. Otherwise it gets boring and they'll easily drop it. Use your skills and creativity to help them give in different ways. Have them do some necessary *chessed*, which may be uninteresting, but intersperse it with giving opportunities that are fun and exciting.

Create empathy through telling stories about *tzaddikim*. Often children feel that only nebs are givers, while smart guys are takers. This is because in the material sense, you only lose by giving, and there's immediate gratification in taking. You can make it worthwhile for them by using bribery, but don't make it too transparent. You can say, "Gosh, you girls went to the hospital every day of the first week of vacation. You deserve a treat. How about a trip up to the Galilee?" Rewarding for doing *chessed* takes the *lishmah* out of it, but less so if they first did the mitzvah and then got rewarded without knowing there would be a reward in the end.

Another idea that works is putting children in charge of something. Have them organize a day camp for kids with special needs under the guidance of adults. Let them be in charge, and let them feel important. For teens, feeling significant and giving has to be seen as one thing.

You can also slowly introduce to kids this age the idea of giving to people for whom you don't feel empathy. There are many stories of *tzaddikim* in the Gemara and of ordinary people who gave to others even though they knew they wouldn't receive any appreciation or love in return. Teach your teens that the ultimate gift isn't money or time, it's yourself. If you can give to someone who doesn't deserve it or to someone you don't like, that's self-transcendence.

Talk to your children about giving to their own family. It's much easier to give to needy strangers, because your family's needs are less dramatic and because you're not apt to receive as many effusive or appreciative thank-yous. There's not much honor involved. So how do you get kids to do *chessed* at home? Use empathy. You have to paint a picture that will make one sister feel for the other. "She's your sister. Look how it hurt her not to have the doll, let's share."

Use dramatic vocabulary to get your kids to help out at home. "I don't know how I'll get all these dishes done tonight. Shabbos ends so late and I have to be up at 6 tomorrow. If you'd help out, it would make a world of a difference."

Charts with duties for each child, even if you make them fair, don't foster *chessed* in the home, and often breed resentment. However, if you make your child aware that he is helping out by doing these chores, that's different. Telling a child, "Wow, this room looks great *l'kavod Shabbos*," is much better than, "It's your turn to make the beds today." Cultivate empathy and then aim higher.

Talk about heroic *chessed* and about giving even if it's sometimes difficult or tedious. At some point, responsibility will have to come into the picture too, but first incorporate the idea of kindness.

If we model *chessed* in our own personal lives, we can implant within our children's hearts a lifelong desire to give too.

Helping Children Feel Content

How do we instill a sense of *simchas hachaim* in our children?

Young children exude natural *joie de vivre.* What happens as the years progress? The travails of life wear people down. Age brings illness and a steady weakening of the body. But these are not the only reasons. Children see everything as *chiddush.* Genuine *simchah* is retaining that sense of fresh wonder.

Appalling statistics show that one in ten college students admits to entertaining thoughts of suicide. One in five high-school students reports the same. The problem is really twofold. We have no idea what contentment is, and we have very little gratitude. Our goal should be to help our children preserve their natural happiness and develop a sense of gratefulness. We must also teach them to appreciate the beauty of the moment.

With children age 3 to 6, show them how to differentiate between what is temporary and what is eternal. For example, you can say, "That was a great ice cream, but most likely you won't remember it by tomorrow. Look at what a beautiful card you made for Aunt Celia. I'm sure she'll cherish it forever."

Hashem created us with a feeling of lack. Nobody has *simchah* unless he feels grateful. Teach your children gratitude by pointing out the wonders and complexity of Hashem's creation. Talk about how rain is life giving. You can say, "Look how beautiful the rain is. Soon everything will be green again. Isn't it amazing?" Be sure to say this. Otherwise their natural reaction will probably be, "Oh it's raining again. It's so boring being stuck in the house."

Cleaning up for Shabbos shouldn't be drudgery. Be enthusiastic. Explain how it's all in honor of Shabbos. It's like making the *Beis HaMikdash* ready for the King. Help your children appreciate the wholesome goodness of life. Show them that you believe in them.

Fantasy is a good way to build up *simchas hachaim*. Play imagination games. Playing "House" and being the mommy with "tons of babies" will satisfy a very young child. Being a heroine or hero is the logical progression as children get older. Not all children will let you into their fantasy lives. If you are able to gain entrance into that magic kingdom, use it in a way in which they will grow. Nurture a feeling of gratitude for who they are and what they are part of.

In life, the more you have, the more you want. In order to be happy, you have to learn to roll with the punches and look for the positive aspects in all of life's experiences. Teach your child to see everything as a gift and as part of a larger, more significant picture. You can nurture happiness by praising common everyday things and making ordinary life attractive. Appreciating the love in a close relationship and sensing the good Hashem gives us is the core of *simchah*.

Feelings of achievement make children happy. Your responsibility as a parent is to find your child's point of excellence and provide opportunities for him to use his talents and abilities. Let your child express himself through song, art, and drama.

Set things up so your child can be a giver. Children love doing *chessed*. Let them be the ones to put the *tzedakah* in the *pushke*. Tell them where the money will go and how it will help poor families buy food and necessities. Toys and sweets will give them transient joy, but spiritual *simchah* is eternal.

Train your children to revel in doing mitzvos. People sometimes confuse *simchah shel mitzvah* with the mitzvah itself. You have to see that the actual mitzvah brings your children joy. Tell stories of *tzaddikim* that illustrate this point. Teach children to enjoy the experience of connection and spiritual bliss. They may not understand it intellectually, but they will sense it emotionally. Your child should feel happy to be a Jew.

Connection brings *simchah*. Children need to be held and spoken to. Today many women work out of the home and do not have as much time. However, at least when you are there with your children, be there fully for them. Give them your complete attention. Talk to them and really listen to what they say. Spend time with each child alone. Go for a walk or for coffee or an ice cream. Just the two of you being together will make your child feel special.

Children from age 6 to 10 can comprehend a lot more. Teach them gratitude by pointing out the details of things they receive both from Hashem and from people. For example, you can say, "Look what a beautiful wallet Aunt Ruthie bought you. It has such intricate stitching. She must have gone to several stores to find it, and it looks very expensive." This makes the wallet a lot more special.

There are good books about the glory of Hashem's world available. If you have a child who is curious, look at them together. You can admire the details of the pictures together with him and discuss the wonders of nature. You can then point out how much Hashem cares about us and how He tailor-made this world for us to enjoy.

Almost all children can appreciate the goodness of having when there's a possibility of not having. Tell stories of *tzaddikim* and discuss the hardships people had to endure years ago. Contrast the mode of travel once used and the smooth, comfortable transportation systems we have today. Talk about Rivkah at the well and how good it is to have running water in our homes.

Achievement brings *simchah*. At this age the pleasure of giving can be much more sophisticated. Depending on what the child enjoys doing, create opportunities for him or her to do *chessed*. Have them be your *shluchei mitzvah*. Let them stuff envelopes, deliver *tzedakah*, or pack food packages for the needy. Let them see how they made a difference by telling them what they did. For example, you can say, "It was so kind of you to bring our guest a glass of water." Don't tell them who they are. Talk about their actions, which is much more credible.

Encourage them to be part of something larger. Suggest that they join a *Tehillim* group or a *Kabbalas Shabbos* group, where they'll achieve that good feeling of social connection and achievement.

It's important for you to be happy. Children feed on the *simchah* you create in the home. If all the child hears is complaining and a litany of "poor me," it will make him feel like a burden. In addition, he will pick up the negativity in the air, and he won't want a family with many children. Don't complain to your children or husband. Don't even complain to your friends. Of course, there are times when you need a therapist or a Rav, but by and large address your litany of woes to Hashem. Ask Him for strength, mercy, and joy. He can give you anything.

Kids from ages 11 to 14 can grasp far more. This is a good age for challenging trips where they can see the depth, breadth, and beauty of nature and develop a sensitivity for the wonders of creation.

Help your child channel his talents and abilities so that he feels worthwhile and accomplished. Getting recognition for individuality is important. Give him opportunities to discover his own talents. Let your daughter be creative in the kitchen even if the mess makes it seem not worth it. Make her feel as if she accomplished something lasting and important.

As children approach the teen years, what they own and who they are become enmeshed. Buying them something significant will mean a lot more to them than buying a toy for a younger child.

Older children derive more happiness from shared social experiences. Spend time together.

It's important for your child to feel as if he is not just an appendage, but rather a part of a larger group. Belonging to a shul or a Chassidic or yeshivah community brings happiness.

Simchas hachaim stems from gratitude, achievement, inclusion, and nurturing close relationships. It's discovering the *tzaddik* within each of our children. May our homes be filled with the inner light of joy and true serenity.

Sibling Rivalry

Conflicts between siblings have been around since time immemorial. Kayin and Hevel, Yishmael and Yitzchak, and Yaakov and Esav all had differing personalities that ultimately clashed. Even those sibling relationships that weren't as disastrous, such as Shimon and Levi, and Yosef and his brothers, were still complex.

What are sibling relationships supposed to be like? What can we as parents do to foster positive connections? What should we be aiming for?

In *Shir HaShirim* the Jewish people are referred to many times as "*Achosi* — my sister." The perfect sibling relationship is one in which each sibling sees the other as a mirror. There's a certain level of balance and equality. Hashem calls us His sister because He desires to see His *middos* reflected in us. However, the fact remains that children are different in age, sex, personality, and life circumstances. They have different needs, and if you decide to give each child the same thing, there will be trouble. How can we give siblings a feeling of unity when they are not really one?

All children are born with an inherent, intuitive feeling that the world was created for them. This can be channeled toward responsibility, but at the same time it can easily be misdirected toward selfishness. It's very difficult for kids to understand why everything doesn't revolve around them and why other siblings seem to be more important than they are.

With very young children, sibling issues are much less complicated than with older children. If a one-and-a-half-year-old wakes up one morning to discover a new sibling, it becomes part of his reality very quickly. However, for an only child who was used to being the sole recipient of his parent's attention for several years, it can be challenging. An older child is far more vulnerable than a new baby, who has no expectations. The child has no way of understanding that the new baby isn't his replacement. Therefore, try to keep the older child central and introduce the baby slowly.

There are psychological theories that posit that a person's entire sense of self-value is formed by the end of the first year and that you therefore have to centralize the baby and not the older child. Still, I think that a baby's feelings of security and self-esteem develop with time after consistent warmth from his parents. The fact that his sibling is getting some of the pie won't make things all that terrible.

Some parents find a new baby more emotionally and physically attractive than an older child. Naturally, they will pay little attention to the older one. These feelings need to be checked. Your older child is just as precious and certainly shouldn't be neglected. When visitors come, have them talk to the older child first. The baby loses nothing, and your older child gains the attention he needs. Talk to your relatives beforehand about this so they are prepared to do this. Prepare a present that you bought that the relative can give to your child, before she shows you her present for the baby.

The intimacy, warmth, and closeness of nursing can awaken a primal instinct in your older child, who may regress back to babyish behavior, such as bedwetting or wanting a bottle or asking to nurse. Try not to make a big deal about it. He will not do this indefinitely.

Making a big fuss will just give him the negative attention he wants, which will encourage him to continue.

This does, however, tell you that he needs extra love. So when he is playing quietly, get down on the floor with him and give him the extra attention he needs. If he desires more than you can give him, try to get a babysitter to take him out for a while. This will give him quality time and will offer you some rest time with the new baby.

Children from ages 2 to 5 already have lives of their own. They can play, talk, and interact with others. The very intense feelings of jealousy you may sometimes encounter with younger children will be replaced with a kind of bookkeeping that these kids do. You may hear comments such as, "You only spent 5 minutes with me and then you spent 10 minutes with the baby. You love the baby. You don't love me," or, "You make me feel like only the baby belongs in this house and not me." It doesn't matter if the child is being irrational. The fact that there's no reason for him to be jealous doesn't mean that he isn't, and you have to deal with it. Be sure that your child's complaint doesn't have a basis.

Be careful too about not casting yourself in the role of martyr. This only gets worse and is not healthy for the kids.

Ask your older child to bring you a diaper or ointment for the baby. Then praise him effusively for helping. This tells him that he has a role called big brother and that he hasn't been displaced. Your goal should be to get your child to bond with the baby. The more you share the *simchah* of the new baby with his older siblings, the better things will be.

In today's society, children don't have that sense of appreciation of how good it is to be part of a large family. We've been affected by the general culture, and there is a lot of handwringing and "Where's me?" on the part of mothers. Unfortunately, children too have picked up this negative attitude.

As the baby grows, you will encounter the "I saw it first" problem. Whatever the baby wants, the older child wants first. This can happen at the park, during mealtime, and at playtime. You have to tackle this by making sure that each child gets enough attention. There's no real answer as to how much, because different children have different needs, but you do have to give each child some focused time with you. On a gut level, children this age already understand that the world is no longer focused on them. Instead of seeing the baby as a competitor, try to get your older child to treat him as his ally and playmate.

Babies tend to destroy their older siblings' possessions. If your child drew a picture and the baby spit on it and tore it up, your older child is bound to feel devastated and devalued. You can respond in several ways. "He doesn't know; he's only a baby. Here's another paper." Or, "It's only a picture. Don't make such a big deal about it." Or "That first picture was special. I don't know if you can make another one, but I like how you draw. Let's draw something together." If you choose the last option, you can distract the child from his feelings, which is good. I know that modern psychology theorizes that distraction is a form of manipulation and dishonesty. I would say it is neither. You are not trying to get anything from the child, and you are distracting him with something that's real.

Children from ages 7 to 12 can also become unsettled when a new baby arrives. You will probably be a lot busier and have far less time for them than you once did. Let go of the baby a bit and make sure the other kids are getting sufficient attention. This may require hiring a babysitter during some periods of the day, so that you can be accessible for homework and dinner. Although your older children will float into the role of helper much more readily than younger kids, your older children need you too. Your desire for assistance should not come at the expense of your older child's needs. Don't expect him or her to be your assistant. Your child is still a child and still needs what a mother can give both in terms of help and attention.

Children have different needs. How can you give one child what he requires without having to give the other child just as much? For instance, you have one child who needs a lot of help with homework, and you end up sitting with him and giving him a lot of attention. The other siblings see this and feel jealous. Children crave connection.

Therefore, you have to find time, at least once a week, to give each of your children some focused attention. Take your child out for an ice cream or a short walk. Spend a few intimate moments talking. You can say, "You're lucky you don't need help with homework. Isn't it more fun to go out for a drink than to do multiplication drills?"

Another problem that can arise is a jealous child who acts out. One child may be getting a lot of attention and the other child may feel left out. He will therefore try to get negative attention through unacceptable behavior, such as violence, yelling, or acting out in school. The only real solution is more connection. If you fall into the trap of giving your child attention when he acts inappropriately, his emotional self will make the equation that negative behavior equals more attention. Keep things low key and don't engage the child when he misbehaves. Instead, find a reason to spend time with the child later on. For example, you can say, "Hey, let's make that potato kugel together." This will reduce his need for getting attention negatively. If the child hits or shouts, you do have to correct him, but don't spend too much time on it. Try to find opportunities later to enter your child's world and build a relationship unconnected to his negative behavior. If the child overtly asks you about another child, "Why are you giving this to him?," you have to answer him openly, "Because that's what he needs. Thank Hashem that you don't need it." Then say, "What does a boy like you need? I want to be there for you too."

You don't have to notice every time your child acts out. If it's in-your-face behavior, you have to respond, because it's anti-*chinuch* not to, but if it's not, you can sometimes make believe you didn't see it. Of course this requires judgment and thought.

Another aspect that needs to be looked at is the source of jealousy. This is the mistaken idea that everyone should have the same things in life. Hashem's *hashgachah* tells us that everyone gets exactly what he needs to accomplish his individual mission in this world. You should get this idea across to your children through stories and conversation.

There are some kids who are easier to like than others. In fact, sometimes parents actually favor a specific child because they see him as the golden, special one. The first step is to be honest with yourself and admit that you think this way. The next step is to realize that you are putting your other children in an impossible situation. Even the holy *shevatim* could not understand what Yaakov had in mind when he favored Yosef. Yaakov saw that Yosef was superior, and he wanted the brothers to recognize this so that they would follow him and learn from his ways. However, it was a mistake, and it was more than the brothers could bear. Beware of falling into this trap.

In some instances parents will favor a child who is harder to love. This happens because they give a lot more of themselves to this child to try to fix his problems. In fact, this is one of the reasons why Yitzchak loved Esav. He saw who Esav was and tried to give of himself, which led to a certain bonding with him. Watch this feeling carefully, because it can sometimes lead to disaster.

Integrating the outlined principles will really take the edge off sibling rivalry. I've seen these ideas work even in large families where the children all had varying personalities and needs.

The growing-up years fly by swiftly. Help your children find joy in one another, teach them to be each other's best friend, and take time to treasure the precious souls with which Hashem entrusted you.

Helping Children Make the Right Choices

Guiding our children to make the right choices can be a formidable challenge. What are ways we can gear up our children to navigate the circuitous path of life with joy and confidence?

Very young children from ages 3 to 6 don't have free choice. They are prisoners of their fears, instincts, and desires. Therefore, don't expect too much from them. Give them opportunities to make good choices, and when they do, be sure to tell them what a wonderful thing they did.

Sometimes you will have to point out to your young children that they made a bad choice. They should be aware that their choices have consequences and that this is a power only human beings have. You can illustrate this by saying, "This flower is red whether it wanted to be that color or not, because flowers can't make choices." If your child is sophisticated enough, you can explain this concept with animals too: "This dog is barking because he is a dog. He can't choose not to bark."

Children from age 6 to 10 can comprehend far more. Show them that they have options. Make it clear to them that their good choices will bring positive results, while their bad choices will result in negative consequences.

When Yanky makes a loud *berachah* with *kavannah,* tell him, "What an incredible *berachah*. I bet all the *malachim* in heaven are answering *Amen.* That was a great choice."

Remind Chani, "Remember how you shared your toys so nicely yesterday with Chaim? That was a wonderful choice. Would you like to do it again now?"

The more you make your child aware that they have the choice to be good, the more empowered they'll feel and the less resentful they'll be. Show your child that bad choices have consequences and that they have the power to fight against making them. There's a huge difference, even for an adult, between being pressured or forced to make a good choice, and making the choice of one's own volition.

At this age it's not a good idea to make your child your buddy, but you can solicit his opinion on small matters. Asking your 10-year-old, "What do you think I should do?" makes him realize that there are choices and consequences and that you are making the effort to choose the best option.

Teach children negotiation techniques. It takes thought and effort to get both parties to feel that they got more or less what they wanted. Good communication skills are crucial for maintaining *shalom* in life. Many times, even with negotiation, there is a winner and a loser. In such a situation you can say, "This time we'll do it this way, and next time we'll do it that way." If the child persists and says, "No. I want it this way now," you should ask him why, and try to work out a compromise.

Tell children that they can choose how they want things to be. Use stories to drive this point home. Here's one example: "Estie was really looking forward to the family picnic. Every day she would pack more things into the picnic basket to take along. Finally, when the great day arrived, it rained. What are her choices now?" Draw scenarios. "Estie can say, 'Hashem didn't think it was a picnic day today. Maybe it can be a dollhouse, cutout, or painting day.' Or Estie can mope around the house and complain, 'I don't want to do anything. I just want a picnic.' Which choice will make her happiest?"

Teach your children to color in the outlines of life. Talk with them about the child who is willing to make choices and the child who chooses to ignore that other possibilities exist. Tell them that Hashem expects maximum *hishtadlus* from us, but the end results are always in His hands. If things don't turn out the way we want them, we can think of other options. Opening your children's mind to think this way can be life transforming.

Preteens and teens often feel they have no choices. How do you get a teenager to look at possibilities instead of getting autocratic about how things should be? Teenagers are much more sensitive to impositions. In situations where you limit their choices, their resentment level may rise to the point where they won't see any options. Even if you present them with other choices, if the options don't come from the teenager himself, he will probably not be receptive. Do what you can, while remaining firm, to make your child see that it's not you against him. Be willing to compromise and help your child explore other avenues of fulfillment.

Teenagers will often say, "It's not my fault. It's Hashem's fault," or "I can't help it. This is the way I am," or "Hashem knows how it will turn out. What's the point of trying?" Most of the time, it's not worth getting into deep philosophical arguments. Make him aware that his previous choices brought consequences. Illustrate this with examples from the child's own life.

As your teenager grows older, try to refine his choice-making skills beyond "What are your options? Let's choose one," to "On what basis do you choose one thing over another?" Teach him to select the options that are important and enduring. Help him evaluate choices based on what will bring him closer to what he wants to be as a person, as opposed to doing what will bring him immediate pleasure.

Find opportunities to tell your teens stories about people who made choices and about the good and bad consequences that resulted. Discuss with them what choices made the person into a hero and what other options were available. For example, you can tell your kids, "Look at the life of Rav Aharon Kotler. What are some ways he could have made bad choices and still lived with himself? He could have said, 'America is different. Torah won't grow here. I don't have the strength to start again.' What do you think made him choose differently?"

Having an intelligent discussion with your teenagers builds intimacy and develops their mind. Expect that your child's answers might not necessarily be your own. You can offer your opinions, but remember to respect his too. Sometimes your teenager might tell you a true story that he heard or witnessed. Every so often you should say, "Do you think he made the best choice? What were his other choices? What are his choices now?" Make him aware that there are options in life.

As teens mature and begin to make life-altering decisions, such as which seminary or yeshivah to attend or whom to marry, question how they are making their decision. Let them hear their own voice. For example, if your son comes home from a date and says he's not interested in the *shidduch,* you can explore with him why he decided that.

The final and most important component of all choice-making is to ask Hashem to open our hearts to make the right choices. Model this for your children. Pray to Hashem every day, "Show me Your way. Let me discern Your will, and let me not forget what my choices are really all about."

Teaching Children the Power of the Tongue

There's a famous idiom, "Sticks and stones may break my bones but words will never hurt me." It's not true. You can go to the clinic and get a cast on your broken arm and you'll be okay, but hurtful words can be devastating and leave long-lasting effects.

As an adult, you've probably mastered the art of sifting. You may hear things and take them to heart, or choose not to let them bother you all that much. A child won't make that differentiation. They will hear exactly what was said and believe it. Your son who gets top grades in school will think he's brainless if someone calls him stupid. Conversely, an adult who is content with where he is in life and has had the chance to develop a tough outer skin will not take disparaging comments to heart.

Children are insecure and vulnerable. Because of this, *ona'as devarim*, intentionally hurting a child with words, can be very serious. The Rambam gives us criteria as to what falls under this category.

Don't bring up issues that people usually try to conceal. For example, don't talk about a person's deficiencies, physical disabilities, negative appearance, or different ethnic or racial background.

Kids do a lot of *ona'as devarim*. They can be very cruel. Not that adults are any better, but they are more afraid of getting back the same treatment and more concerned with conforming to social standards. The first thing you have to do is make your own commitment not to hurt people with words. If you don't want your child to be brutal or verbally abusive, it's not enough to tell him. You have to teach him by example.

Show kids how to speak with sensitivity. Children from ages 4 to 6 usually blurt out whatever they think. Their cruelty may not always be intentional. Most of the time, they're just verbalizing what they see. Therefore, you have to tell them clearly, "Be careful not to make people sad with your words."

Children at this age learn concrete words easily. Abstract ideas such as emotions are more difficult for them to understand. There are excellent children's books that can help you explain them. Use words to describe feelings whenever you can. For example, if you get a present, express your joy by saying, "I'm so happy." Or you can say, "It's getting late. I'm so worried." This helps children synthesize different emotional states. Once they have an emotional vocabulary, you can teach them to avoid *ona'as devarim*. The idea is to refrain from hurtful comments and not to make people sad or afraid with words.

If you discover that your own child is bullying others, you have to address the problem. Take him back to a time when he was happy. Then have him remember the times he was down or afraid. Tell him that Hashem wants him to make sure that people will always be happy and content, not sad or miserable. Tell him that good people make others happy, while bad people make them sad, and that making others sad will end up making him sad. This may create some confusion, because sometimes the authority figures in his life will make him feel uncomfortable too. For this, you should explain that for the child's own benefit, he must sometimes be told no.

Teach children that hitting is unacceptable, not even to get back at someone. Parents and teachers are in charge of fixing things. If your child is the victim, you should emphasize that the fact that someone said something about him doesn't necessarily mean that it's true or important. Everyone shines at different things. Not being good at something doesn't make you bad. Bad is hurting others or making them feel sad or afraid. Emphasize that the major problem is the bully himself and minimize the child's deficiencies. Clarify to your child the difference between what is truly good and what is truly bad.

Storybooks are a great teaching medium. Many stories for children have the ugly duckling theme, where an animal or child didn't think he was smart or beautiful but was later recognized for his qualities. The child should come to identify with the one who stood up for the victim, the one who said, "No, she is a good duck."

During later childhood, from ages 7 to 11, *ona'as devarim* gets more sophisticated. In addition to talking to them about emotions, you have to explain to them what it feels like to be victimized. Ask them, "Do you think people enjoy inclusion or exclusion?" Make it clear to them from an adult perspective that what they are doing is cruel and juvenile.

Do what you can to make sure your children don't become the victims. Try to see that they fit in with their friends. If this isn't possible, either because the child has inborn limitations or because of circumstances that cannot be changed, you'll have to work hard to teach your child not to feel threatened when others put him down.

Talking to children about *shemiras halashon* is important. There are many games and books that can make it fun. Create a *shemiras halashon* group with contests and prizes. Make it socially cool to speak with refinement. List the various forms of *ona'as devarim*. The issue should not be, "Is it true," but "Will it make someone happy or sad." Let them think, "How will this make my friend feel when I talk about it?"

Having your child work with a special-needs child can do wonders for his emotional perception and sensitivity. You can then slowly move your child toward helping a shy friend adjust socially or standing up to a bully who is victimizing others.

If your child is the victim, you have to speak with the parents of the bully. However, make sure not to put them on the defensive. If the parents feel belittled or afraid it'll be hard to earn their cooperation.

Teenagers and adults often speak hurtfully to defend themselves against attack. Fear can generate *ona'as devarim*. The only tool we have against the enemy of defensiveness is *emunah*. Instead of thinking, "How can I cut this person down," think, "What is my role in this situation?" A short-term solution would be to stop the argument by apologizing and taking concrete steps to improve things. A long-term solution would involve speaking to the person at a moment when he is not angry. Say to him, "I cannot handle this kind of talk. Therefore, when things get out of hand between us, I will just not talk until they become more civil." Often, you may need to speak to someone else who can give the issue more time or see it more objectively.

Ultimately, working on our own negative *middos* and constantly striving to improve our own speech will impact our children so that they grow up to be refined, well-adjusted adults.

Emes and Sheker

The issue of *emes* and *sheker* is arguably the most central concern in *chinuch*. It is the only aspect of *chinuch* about which the Gra held that one must be strict and unrelenting.

Why is truth so important? We know Hashem through the world and our responses to it. Hashem's signature is on every situation, person, or thing we encounter, and it says, *"Ani Hashem."* When we use exaggerated speech to describe what we've experienced, we've lost Hashem's imprint.

Every deed carries with it positive or negative consequences. When we use words to avoid consequences, we create a fantasy world where Hashem's Presence cannot be found.

Emes is the whole picture, the way Hashem sees it. We often confuse truth with accuracy, which isn't always the same thing. Truth has a huge value. Lying is permitted only when it leads you to *emes*. At times we can change the truth, because keeping to it could conceal the picture rather than reveal it.

We see this in the story of Yaakov and the blessings. Yaakov said, *"Ani Esav b'chorecha* — I am Esav your *bechor."* Even though he meant, "I'm me and Esav is your *bechor,"* it still seems deceptive. Yet if one looks at the complete picture, Yaakov was the true spiritual heir and in essence was the rightful *bechor.*

This world is called *"alma d'shikra* — the false world," because our physical world is our way of knowing Hashem, yet it conceals Him. Our mission is to seek the truth and to discover the Divine imprint in everything. This should begin at a young age, which is why *chinuch* for *emes* is so enormously important.

Very young children are still experimenting with words. Oftentimes they imagine something and are unsure where the borders of reality begin and end. Correct them in a gentle way. Teach them the vocabulary of imagination, which starts with "Let's pretend." This will make it easier for your young children to separate emotional imagery from reality. Introduce them slowly to the idea that you can't say something is when it really isn't unless you include the words "Let's pretend."

Kids love pretend stories. Make it clear to them that they are just fun stories and not actual fact. Be sure that you're not taking your child to a place where he confuses truth with falsehood. A child who does that will easily make up stories about places he's never been to and things he's never done. He may not see the difference between a book that's innocent and fun to read and his story that's innocent and fun to hear. Make sure the difference is crystal clear.

Sometimes kids will lie to avoid blame or consequences. Respond to mishaps by correcting them and then going on to something else. It helps to reward children when they own up to the truth. This can be tricky. If you can pull off both consistent punishment for bad deeds and reward for telling the truth, that usually works best. Punishing for misdeeds and not rewarding for telling the truth will train kids to lie.

From age 5 to 8, a child's ability to differentiate between fantasy and reality becomes more developed. He is also morally discerning enough now to know that it's wrong to say something happened when it really didn't. Your job is to enforce *emes* by being scrupulously honest yourself.

At this age social acceptance becomes very important. Kids can fall prey to making up stories in order to gain prestige. They enjoy lying the way you and I enjoy fiction or a good play. You have to be firm and correct them. You can say, "It would be fun if it was 'Let's pretend,' but it is really not true." Be very strict with defensive lies. The Gra says you can even hit your child for lying and covering things up. Manipulative lies should not be tolerated either. (Some authorities maintain that the Gra was speaking to a generation that is a world away from present times, where corporal punishment doesn't work. It should be noted that today's more permissive methods have not necessarily produced children who feel more beloved or display greater security or compassion. The resolution isn't "Let's go back to giving a 'good potch.'" Rather, it means having greater control of your anger and ego when meting out any punishment, even a mild one such as "time out.")

If you don't discipline your child, he will learn very quickly that most of the time lies are believed, it's easy to get away with them, and life is much more painless if you're dishonest. If children come to associate lies with extreme negativity from the people they love, the balance is bound to shift.

At this age some kids have imaginary friends. Mocking this can be devastating. Accept them as your child's pretend friends, but make it clear that you don't consider them real.

Lying between the ages of 8 and 12 is much more like adult lying than the imaginative lying of very young children. The main reasons kids lie at this age is for social acceptance and to avoid trouble. Defensive lies should be dealt with severely. At this age, a child's self-esteem is still fragile. They want approval desperately, and if they come to associate your comments with a lack of appreciation and validation, they may stop talking to you. You have to cautiously and consistently correct them when they veer off the path of truth. Try to build up their self-esteem in other ways so they can feel accomplished without resorting to lying.

Adolescents will lie for social reasons. They want their friends to like them. They will say whatever they want to say. If your word still carries weight with them, you must correct them. Essentially, they have to see you as a model of truth. In addition, make a point of validating their efforts at honesty.

Teenagers lie to parents a lot and to teachers periodically. They may lie to anyone they feel they have to in order to get what they want. It's not just a problem, but a symptom of an additional problem. They don't see you as a safe place, so they will lie rather than be honest with you.

At this age, it's critical that you show them approval and validation. For example, your daughter lied and took money without permission to buy something you don't allow. The two issues are the lie and that she couldn't tell you honestly what she wanted. This can mean that she loves you so much that she couldn't bear to devastate you, or that she dreads the consequences, which is most probably the reason. Burying your head in the sand will just tell her you've given up on her.

Make yourself a safe person to talk to. Your first response should be acceptance. The next question you ask her should be, "Does this fit in with who you want to be?"

Build a relationship so that your children feel close to you. Spend time with them, discuss issues, and make decisions together. The more a teenager feels loved and included, the more likely he'll stay where he is and not search for validation elsewhere.

Kids will discover that adults treat other adults as potential liars. Teach them the concept of *"kabdeihu v'chasdeihu* — Be cordial but cautious," so that they don't perceive this erroneously as dishonesty.

At some point you will want to teach children the value of thinking honestly. Teach them about judging others favorably. You can look at people in different ways, but the more encompassing way would have to include a person's higher spiritual self. When children hear that, they become far more honest. Their need to demonize people is quelled.

May our children grow to be true *ovdei Hashem* and *anshei emes*.

Teaching Children Kibud Av Va'eim

Kibud av is not really about getting your kids to do what you want. It's about teaching them the importance of the mitzvah. The main thing a child has to understand is that *kibud av* is not a power play, but a mitzvah related to one's moral behavior and for which we will be held accountable. The more *ahavas Hashem* and *yiras Shamayim* a child has, the more *kibud av* will be easier to keep, especially when he hits the preteen and teenage years.

The main question most children have is, "If my parents aren't all that exciting or smart or good, why do I have to listen to them? My opinion is just as valid as theirs." The Torah teaches that if Hashem's providence made somebody the child of a specific set of parents, then there is something he will inevitably gain through his interaction with them that he will not gain from anyone else. A child should know that he owes his parents tremendous gratitude for bringing him into the world. The mitzvah of *kibud av* is about *hashgachah* and *hakaras hatov*, not about, "I'm big, you're small; you'd better listen to me."

Chazal say that *kibud av* is one of the hardest mitzvos. It has become especially difficult in our times because of the society we live in. In Europe, there are some higher moral standards. Children are expected to respect and care for their parents. But the United States has cut this value out of its moral fabric. A good child is considered someone who stays in contact with his parents. There are no expectations of taking care of elderly parents or supporting them financially. Unfortunately, this has rubbed off on us.

Very young children from age 3 to 5 are perfectly capable of understanding that they have to listen to their parents. They know very well that they are dependent on them for almost everything. Nonetheless, they don't always want what their parents want. The cardinal rule is, "Don't negotiate your authority." The only acceptable answer to what Mommy or Daddy asks is "Yes." If you're going to tell them to do something, make sure to carry through your request to the end.

If you make a mistake and you need to take back what you said, phrase it in a way that they recognize that the decision is still yours. Be humble enough to really listen to what they are saying. At the same time, be authoritative enough to leave the decision in your own hands.

Kids at this age want structure and authority. It gives them security and stability besides making your life a lot easier. Mealtime, bathtime, and bedtime should be non-negotiable. During the summer, you can be a bit more flexible, but try to stick to a schedule as much as possible.

Children from age 6 to 10 begin to develop more understanding and contact with the outside world. You can teach them the basic halachos of *kibud av va'eim*, such as not sitting in a parent's place or calling them by their first name. It's good for kids to learn about *kibud av* from a *sefer*. At the Shabbos table, when you get up to the relevant *parashah* in *Shemos*, have them read the mitzvah inside. It's important for them to see that this is an actual mitzvah in the Torah. The more you tell them, "This is how Hashem wants it," the more they won't feel belittled by honoring you. Teach your children to derive pleasure from doing small acts for their parents, and put it in the framework of a mitzvah. Tell them stories about *kibud av*, especially incidents in which the hero honored his parent because it was a mitzvah.

They should hear about the *Tanna* whose mentally ill mother yelled at him in front of his disciples and who nevertheless showed her great respect. Teach them about R' Tarfon, who made himself into a stepstool so his mother could climb into bed. These stories are great, but make sure they never come across in a self-serving way.

Children at this age learn by example. Always maintain proper respect between you and your husband. If you have differences of opinion, which you probably will, the time to iron things out is not in front of the children. When you show them that you don't respect your spouse's authority, they'll follow your lead. Back up your spouse in front of the kids, and discuss all issues later behind closed doors. Being grateful to your spouse teaches kids to express gratitude too.

In today's culture, parents are expected to help children and not vice versa. It is critical that you show your own parents proper respect, especially in front of your children. When they come to visit, greet them, give them a place to sit, and serve them. Your mother is not your unpaid maid. If she wants to take the burden off you, show her gratitude, but certainly don't make any demands. Your in-laws also deserve the same treatment.

Teach children how to verbalize their opinions and feelings in a respectful way. If your child yells that she won't do the dishes because she'd rather be outside with her friends, tell her calmly, "Screaming at Mommy is not acceptable. Tell me what you want nicely and we'll work it out for both of us." Listen to her, and then decide how to deal with it. But make sure the authority stays in your hands. If a child speaks disrespectfully, point it out and tell her that you will not respond to her request until it is rephrased correctly. It is important to listen to your children's emotions. Don't push them beyond their limitations. Weigh each crisis individually, and make the effort to accommodate their needs.

I don't believe children at this age should get an allowance. They haven't earned it, and you can't supervise how they'll spend it. Worse still is paying kids for doing household chores. A child should not be compensated for fulfilling his responsibility. He should learn about the idea of giving freely as opposed to giving with expectations. Children should know that giving is part of maintaining a harmonious home. Distribute rewards from time to time after a good deed, not before. The difference between a bribe and a reward is that a bribe is conditional, while a reward is a consequence of a good choice. When they do have spending money, teach children to give *tzedakah*.

Children from age 10 to 13 are maturing rapidly. You need to move the relationship from imitation to discipleship and friendship. This is achieved by showing the child how much you value his opinion and by sharing beliefs and ideas with him. Inviting a discussion with your child shows him that you think he is important, you recognize his unique value, and he's not an extension of you.

Rebellion is the consequence of feeling that one can't have a self. Build a relationship with your child. Nurture bonds of love. The more time you give your children, the more closeness and intimacy will develop, and the more they will have to lose by disobeying.

Show your child that you value him, but expect him to still treat you as a parent. Listen to him and be empathetic. When something about his behavior bothers you, explain your feelings in a nice way and show him that it's in his hands to correct the behavior. If he respects you enough, he will not want to disappoint you.

At this age, jealousy, lust, and honor are big forces in a child's life, and he will need you to teach him the skills needed to handle them before temptation overpowers him. Children can become envious and demand things you don't think they need. Talk to them about independence and individuality and being happy with what Hashem gives us. If you do a good job at getting the point across with examples and stories, your children will feel less pressured to conform.

If you see that they cannot stand up to it, try not to force them into conflict. Sometimes you might just have to give in. If you really can't, try to empathize, but use your authority to put limitations on how far their resentment will take them.

Kids this age are *baalei taavah* — lustful. Girls should be taught the laws of *tzniyus*, and boys should be trained in *shemiras einayim*. For girls, *taavah* expresses itself many times in the desire for admiration. Lay down the right foundation by teaching them the joy of discipline. Self-esteem comes from self-discipline. Stretching yourself beyond your limitations gives you a feeling of satisfaction. Train them to take pride in overcoming base desires. Teach them *yiras Shamayim* by your own example. Listen to them, be willing to extend yourself if possible, and exert your authority when necessary.

Kavod, honor, is much harder to deal with. Children have an insatiable need for acknowledgment and appreciation. If they feel slighted it will be hard for them to control themselves, and they may react by saying and doing things they shouldn't. The *Nesivos Shalom* writes that insulting a child is like pouring oil on a fire.

Criticizing and devaluing destroys self-esteem. Use acknowledgment, validation, and appreciation generously. If your child feels mistreated, listen to him, restate his complaint, acknowledge that you think differently, state the thing he did, and assert your authority. Children who are hypersensitive will interpret any disapproval as complete rejection. Acknowledge your child's inherent goodness. Help him develop a sense of security, value, and trustworthiness. Then you can credibly say, "A boy like you, who I believe in, shouldn't be doing something like this."

In early childhood, take advantage of your children's desire to follow and teach them the basics of *kibud av*. They should learn to respect and listen to you. In return, you should listen to them and make fair decisions with their interests in mind. In mid-childhood, be an example for your child by treating your spouse and your own parents respectfully. Cultivate a relationship of discipleship and friendship in late childhood and adolescence. Be an empathetic listener, but remain authoritative. Get your decision across in a way that the child feels he's been acknowledged and that it is not your ego speaking, but the Torah.

We've only touched on this topic, which is broad and complex. These ideas should get you off to a good start on the challenging road of teaching your kids respect and honor for elders.

Building Parent-Child Relationships

The teen years are a challenging time. A teenager does not have the self-control and sense of responsibility that an adult has, yet he still wants to be thought of as a grownup. In a sense, teens are in an impossible situation. What they want to be and who they really are is not compatible.

Teens are in the midst of discovering their own identity, as opposed to becoming just extensions of their parents. Sometimes they may in fact resemble their parents with an individual twist, but many times they may become the polar opposite of their parents just for the sake of being different.

Our sages say that *kinah* (jealousy), *taavah* (desire), and *kavod* (honor) remove a person from this world. Teenagers struggle mightily with these forces. *Kinah* plays a big factor in social relationships. Teenagers are insecure and still unsure of who they are and what they want to be. They desire whatever their cool and with-it friends have. Kids who were never materialistic suddenly want brand-name ties and logo shirts so they can fit in with the in-crowd. Kids who were always straight suddenly start cheating in school to gain prestige. Teens beset by *kinah* may do all they can to project a certain image. The more emotionally insecure a teen is, the more *kinah* becomes a factor.

Kinah stems from a lack of belief that the way you are as Hashem made you makes you significant in His eyes. Being secure means feeling that you don't have to be someone else. The more you can impress upon your teen that he is valued and has everything he needs to be what Hashem destined him to be, the less likely he'll suffer from *kinah*.

Taavah comes to the fore when children begin maturing. They may not know exactly what they are experiencing. In boys, there may be a surge of excessive aggressive behavior. They may act out and get angry easily. Find a positive outlet where they can release their pent-up energy, such as packing food boxes for a *chessed* organization or getting involved in sports. Girls are much less self-aware than boys in this regard. They want to feel cherished and beloved, and they don't identify this as *taavah*. In a sense a girl's conscious part is blameless, but her subconscious self is not. If you talk to your daughter about dressing more modestly and she gives you an innocent look, don't take it personally. She is not deceiving you. She is deceiving herself.

What *kinah* is to the emotions and *taavah* is to the body, *kavod* is to the mind. *Kavod* is the desire for acknowledgment, validation, and appreciation. The less a teen believes in himself, the more he will crave external validation. If he doesn't get enough of it from his parents and teachers, he'll try to get it from his peers. For a boy, status depends on success in learning. If he is not making it there, chances are he'll go somewhere else to get that elusive *kavod*. He may also become jealous of others who are succeeding and develop an emotional need to tear down other people or groups who are more accomplished than he is.

With girls, the issue is not so much academic achievement but rather feeling accepted in school. A girl who feels labeled and excluded will rebel.

Kinah, taavah, and *kavod* play out in different ways. *Kinah* results in bad social adjustment, extreme anger, and rejection of parents and Judaism.

Taavah leads to negative interpersonal relationships and disastrous friendships. Sometimes teenagers really don't know what is wrong with their behavior. They may not have been told or were told in a way that they didn't understand. They may have asked questions and were made to feel as if there were something wrong with asking. Once a teenager starts slipping, there is no limit to how low he can fall. *Taavah* can take people very far, because they assume that if they're wrong anyway, they may as well do what they want.

The desire for *kavod* can be the most damaging of all. Many kids will join any group that feeds their craving for validation. *Sefer Mishlei* tells us that the greater the group, the more exclusive they are. The lower the group, the more accepting they are. Well-adjusted people are constantly busy with learning and good deeds. The energy and dedication they have left for social connections is moderate compared to that of street kids, who have nothing else going on in their lives. Often, a teenager looking for acknowledgment will find it much more readily from negative friends than from positive ones.

The first thing to realize is that the most valuable card in your hand is *kavod*. Your role as a parent is to dole it out in huge dollops. If you have a reasonable relationship with your child, your opinion is enormously important. Anything you can say to make your child receive the message "I trust you, I need you, you are important to me" will keep him on the straight path. Show respect by asking your teen for advice and suggestions. Include him in things in which you would normally only include an adult. This will give him a feeling of significance.

Putting teens down when they do something outrageous just adds fuel to the fire. Instead, your weapon should be *kavod*. If your daughter wants to buy an immodest skirt, tell her, "This is cheap looking. I want you to look like a refined, polished girl who dresses with quality." Realize that the bargain basement look is usually the cool look, so be prepared to spend more money on contemporary, classic clothing. Talk to your daughters about the inner beauty and royalty of modesty. The more you can get them to take pride in projecting a certain dignified image, the more the battle over *tzniyus* will diminish.

Boundaries are crucial, but try to keep them clear and limited. Anything you can do to make your teens feel big by being obedient is much better than making them feel small for disobeying authority. Don't be reactive to your teen's sullen or aggressive behavior. It will just draw you into a cycle from which it will be very hard to get out. Talk to him as though he is the child you want him to be, not the child he really is. Treat him as though he is mature and acting appropriately and he'll become that way.

Some parents vacillate with rules. They wonder, Should kids have a curfew? Should they be given spending money? All these rules are individual, but the basic rule is that if you've given your children a foundation where they've integrated the meaning of your demands, you can request a lot less. Don't tell your children what you don't want them to do. This shows that you're admitting that they're capable of doing it. It's much better if you bring them up in a way that you can trust them. If you haven't and you want them to feel trusted anyway, don't ask too many questions, but be on top of them in a subtle way.

A huge problem with boys is their insatiable desire to sleep. The first thing to do is to try to get out of the picture. When your son is in a good mood, take him to the store and tell him, "I don't like the morning hassle. Pick an alarm clock. You're old enough to take care of yourself." If he takes responsibility for getting up, then it's off you. If he won't take responsibility, then it's on you, because you're liable for his future. You can't let him be thrown out of yeshivah any more than you can let him hitchhike to Timbuctoo, just because he loves adventure. The big question here is how much credible authority you really have. Unfortunately, this is one of those unsolvable problems. You have to try to do your best. There may be a physical component, or it may be an emotional escape. If a boy isn't succeeding in yeshivah or he finds davening too long or boring, he may not have a reason to get up.

It is important for kids to feel successful in the framework they're in. If your son is not succeeding, you may want to consider a different option. Be careful though. Grouping problems doesn't work. If the critical mass of a group is kids who are failing, the energy will be that of a group of failures, which can easily turn into a group of rebels. Think five times before you place your son in an alternative environment. However, if you've gone there and seen that the Rosh Yeshivah, by dint of his charismatic personality, has succeeded in creating a positive environment in a non-exclusive setting, then it may work out fine.

For girls, academics should not play a critical factor in choosing a school. If your daughter would be happier in a school where all her friends are or where the teachers are nicer, let her go. If she's failing in the school she chose and you really think she could succeed elsewhere, look very carefully and see if the critical mass is positive before making the switch.

Choose your battles. A significant number of students in Neve Yerushalayim in Jerusalem are girls who went off the *derech* and are now coming back. An unbelievable proportion of these girls have mentioned that the most significant source of their conflict with their mothers was over keeping their rooms clean. This is definitely not worth pushing your daughter off the *derech*. A good rule to keep in mind is that anything that won't matter in 30 years shouldn't matter today. Your daughter will learn cleanliness and neatness eventually. Don't expend your energies over it now.

Summer vacation can be daunting with teenagers. My view is that kids have to be busy. I tell my own children that during their break they have to divide their day into three parts: work, doing mitzvos, and having fun.

Teenagers can work as camp counselors or do temp work in offices. Be careful about putting your child in an environment that's less than perfect. It is your responsibility to check things out beforehand. Earning money gives teenagers a sense of achievement. Let them have the pleasure of giving *tzedakah* and deciding where their *maaser* will go. This is very good for their development. Let them spend their money on fun and extras, not on necessities.

Join them on excursions and trips. If you can't, have someone you trust go with them if possible. When they go on the sort of outings that a teenager can manage on his own, try to be a safe person to whom they can relate their adventures. Show interest and approval.

Often you will need to be the one to find them *chessed* and mitzvah opportunities. Invest effort to match up projects with their talents and abilities.

People sometimes discredit a prevalent problem among today's teenagers. When children are young, they are taught fundamental tenets of *emunah* on a simple level. When they grow older, they no longer want to accept these ideas without deeper understanding. Sometimes teenagers may be doing very well in school intellectually, but their *emunah* is much like loose sand — the particles are there, but nothing really holds them together. Although principles of *hashkafah* may be taught in school, if they are not presented in question-and-answer form, students are bound to tune out. In some schools, the teachers aren't confident enough to teach these concepts. They worry that students will ask questions they aren't equipped to answer. It is important that foundations in *emunah* be firmly established and reviewed in greater depth in the later teen years.

Your child should hear you say, "I don't know," and observe you asking *shaylos* to a Rav. This tells him that he doesn't have to battle against his parent's *gaavah*. His parents know they don't know, and there's an authority above them who can be trusted.

Capitalize on your children's idealism. Expose them to what's right and good and worthy of imitation. As children get older they will have what I call Hallmark birthdays, birthdays that they'll only remember a few days later. At the risk of sounding like a teacher, talk to them on their special day about what life's all about and what's really important.

Treat your teen almost like a friend. Provide positive outlets for their strengths. Taking an idealistic child to *mekomos hakedoshim* or to a round of *tzaddikim* can be life transforming. Including a child in the mitzvos you do can be enormously positive.

Find out what your kids like to do and spend time together enjoying these activities. Some girls like the creativity and energy of the kitchen. Find occasions for your daughter to use her talents. Have her bake a cake for a *sheva berachos*. The compliments she will receive will satisfy her desire for *kavod*. Some girls like social things. Have them organize a *melaveh malkah* or a Chanukah party for kids with special needs. There are girls who enjoy *chessed* and will sleep over at the hospital with a sick child or visit homebound seniors. There are boys who are wizards at organizing. Have them pack and deliver food packages to needy people. Other boys excel at learning and enjoy being called a *masmid*. Spend quality time studying together.

Almost all teenagers turn out fine in the end. Even the ones who gave their parents a terrible time usually come around eventually. The teenage years are a period of exceptional growth. It's a time of discovery, *deveikus*, spiritual maturity, *taharah*, and an opportunity to develop a profound, almost discipleship connection with one's parents.

Teens have enormous capacities. They're idealistic. They love justice. They have lots of physical energy. There's a certain *temimus* and purity in their ability to learn. Find your child's strong point, give it a place to shine, acknowledge and validate his or her efforts, and with Hashem's help you'll reap the *nachas* for which all parents pray.

Meaningful and Productive Summers for Our Children

Summer vacation with children can be very challenging because of the long, unstructured time that needs to be filled. There are only two directions in which vacation time can go, either up or down. What appears to be just "vegging out" usually means moving down. Many teachers have told me that so much of what is taught during the year is lost during vacation. It doesn't have to be this way. There are enormous possibilities for progress during the summer, but it will involve incorporating structure into your child's day.

Children age 4 to 7 are accustomed to a day with a defined beginning and end filled with planned activities. Often, these children have younger siblings, which makes vacation time even more challenging. Although a mother may want to give her older children structure, she may be too busy with her young kids to do so. Set goals for the summer. As Rav Tzvi Meyer Zilberberg says about every holiday, the main element is being prepared. What do you really want your kids to get out of their vacation? You may want to acquaint them with relatives they hardly get to see during the year. You can do creative activities together. Play things by ear, but have some kind of goal in the back of your mind. Otherwise things tend to disintegrate quickly.

Let's explore some realistic plans. If your kids are not in a framework, it's good to schedule an outing at least once a week. Kids get "cabin fever" by being cooped up in the house too much. Share fun time together. It heightens closeness with your children. Having picnics in the park, going out for pizza, swimming at a kosher beach if you live in Israel, or at a local swimming pool are all great activities. Go with friends if possible. You and your kids will have company, and organizing the trip will be easier.

Plan in a way that is not overwhelming or difficult. Decide when to go, how to travel, what to do when you get there, and when and how to get home. Going out in the early afternoon may leave you with tired, cranky kids complaining about the heat. I would recommend leaving at 10 a.m. for a noon picnic or considerably later in the day, after the children have napped, for a picnic supper.

Plan how to get there. Will you drive, walk, take a train, or travel by taxi? Decide what you will do once you get there. This would include food, games, and private time with your kids. Take along easy-to-eat meals and snacks that your kids will enjoy. Pack wipes for quick clean-ups. Kids get ravenous outdoors, so make sure to load up with *nosh* for the way and for when you get there. If you'll be visiting a park, it's good to take along a disposable tablecloth, as wooden park tables tend to get tacky. Eat right away when you get there. This way you can get rid of the food, and the kids will be in a calmer state of mind.

Plan different activities for different age groups. Physical games such as ball and jump rope are great. If you have another mother with you, you may want to switch off and leave your younger kids with her while you take the older kids into the forest for a nature walk. Explain how trees grow and rejuvenate with the changing seasons.

Point out the different species of wild flowers and vegetation. Let them dig for earthworms, and talk a bit about their fascinating life cycle. For younger kids, take along books and schedule storytelling time after they have had a chance to run around and play.

Don't spend too much time at your destination. Two to three hours should be adequate for snack time, playing, dividing the kids into age groups, eating a meal, singing *bircas hamazon*, and telling stories. You want the kids to be reluctant to leave, not bored. This way they'll want to go again the following week.

Prepare dinner ahead of time for your husband so you don't go right to the kitchen when you come home. If it was an afternoon trip, focus on baths, pajamas, and bedtime. If it was a morning trip, you'll find yourself in a funny situation. The kids are fed, tired, but still stimulated, so they won't want to go to sleep right away. Play quiet games or read them a story to keep them busy.

Factories often welcome young visitors. Kids find it fascinating and exciting, and admission is sometimes free. Going swimming is another fun way to spend the day. However, pools tend to be expensive and crowded and are never easy on mothers. If you still think you'd like to go, realize you'll be doing this for your kids; you won't get much fun out of it yourself.

Plan creative activities and projects. Crafts are great and can keep kids busy for hours. It's also a fun way to spend time with your kids in a structured way. It's a good idea to get together with friends. You and the kids can socialize and alternate doing activities at a different friend's house each time.

Though people tend to slow down and relax during vacation, be sure to maintain your child's routine. This gives him a sense of security. There should be a defined time for getting up in the morning (it doesn't have to be as early as during the school year), davening, and going to sleep. Serve breakfast and have your kids plan how they'll spend the day.

There doesn't have to be strict structure, but you should stay on top of things. Suggest activities such as board games, imagination games, and toys to play with. Your goal at the end of the summer should be to improve your child's social skills, self-expression, and *middos* development.

Children somewhat older will do better in camp than at home. Personally, I prefer day camp to sleepaway camp, although my own experience at sleepaway camp was marvelous. Structured activities, wonderful role models, and exciting night activities are part of the magic of sleepaway camp. However, it is expensive, so unless you can easily afford it, try to find a good day camp instead that will offer your kids exemplary counselors, great activities, and bonding without bankrupting you. If there isn't an available day camp where you live, or you can't afford it, or it only runs for a few weeks, you can make your own day camp. My daughter-in-law did that with her kids. She got them to help her around the house during the day, and planned exciting night activities reminiscent of her own camping days for the evening.

Bonfires, treasure hunts, and storytelling are a great way to bond with your older kids. If your children are talented, you can have them get together with cousins or friends to put on a play or form a choir. It's worth spending some money on good props, although the production doesn't have to be professional. The main thing is for your kids to enjoy themselves and to use their time constructively by developing their self-expression and latent talents.

Teenagers and unstructured time equals disaster. When my children reached late childhood (I didn't wait till they hit their teens), I had them divide their summer into three segments. Part of the summer was dedicated to doing *chessed*, another segment was for working and earning some money, and they could spend the last few weeks having pure fun. I would find the *chessed* jobs based on each child's interests and abilities. My children volunteered for organizations such as Zichron Menachem and Yad Eliezer. Sometimes they would do *chassadim* that involved more adult supervision, such as helping large families with children (which means you have to know the family well) or delivering food to the elderly. The *chessed* segment can be two to three weeks long. You'll still have to plan the rest of the day, but doing a daily *chessed* will help your kids release their energy in a positive way and add structure to their routine.

The second segment of vacation would be holding down a job for pay. For girls this could be working as a counselor in a day camp or babysitting. Older teens can help out in a store or temp at an office. You'd have to check out the work environment beforehand. It can be difficult to find suitable jobs. Many times, out of desperation, I would actually pay people to employ my children (of course they didn't know), because I felt it was wholesome for them to work and earn money.

Boys often have a shorter summer vacation, which makes working unnecessary. But there are boys' schools whose vacation is as long as that of the girls. In that case, being a camp counselor or helping out in a store owned by friends (whom you may have to pay) are good ways to fill extra time.

The third part of the summer can be first class fun, such as kayaking, sports, trips, and games. Stay on top of things by making sure you know exactly where your teens are going and with whom. Don't leave it all up to your kids, but don't let them know that you're watching them either.

For boys, there are excellent learning camps, which are wonderful for kids who enjoy learning. My boys were great enthusiasts of Yeshivas Bein Hazemanim, because they got paid for going and there was an exciting trip at the end. If you can, organize something like that in your area.

You may encounter problems with getting your teens to do what they have to do. Getting boys out of bed on vacation mornings can be challenging. Some boys can easily sleep till 10:30 a.m. and miss all the *zemanim*. It's not always the late nights. Teenagers do need a lot of sleep, and they want a break from the rigor and regimentation of the year.

There are several ways to handle this. Buy your son an alarm clock and make him responsible for getting up on time. This takes you out of the picture. Another option is to offer a semi-weekly or weekly reward for getting up on time. A third possibility for the right kind of child who is sensitive and intelligent is talking to him honestly about the importance of getting up on time. Let him understand that he is not doing it for you. Sit down with him and show him the Gemara in *Berachos* that discusses the *Avos* and *tefillah*. This way it's not you doing the talking, but the Gemara. Encourage your child to emulate Avraham, who saw the potential of a new day. Have them look up descriptions of *avodas haAvos* in *Mesillas Yesharim* or any of the other inspiring *mussar sefarim*. If you're training your child to get up for the right reasons, it's bound to work.

The "proper dress" problem commonly sets in during the teen years. This can be a challenge with boys and certainly with girls. Girls who are careful how they dress and behave during the year sometimes let things slide in the summer. Here planning helps too. At the beginning of the summer, take your girls on a shopping trip. Buy them casual, nice things and go out for a soda and ice cream afterward. If things have been reasonably good during the year, having your girls pick some clothes for casual wear will prevent you from later noticing that what they're wearing isn't okay. Remind them that Hashem is with us wherever we go. The way He sees us and rewards us in the fall is the way He'll do the same in the summer.

Swimming is a great activity for teens, but you'll need to check out all the *tzniyus* issues beforehand.

Sometimes out of laziness and casualness boys will skip some of the formal wear in the summer. If your son normally goes to davening with a hat and jacket, make him maintain this. Talk to him about *kavod hatefillah* so he appreciates what it's all about.

You can't observe your teenagers all the time, and they certainly don't want you to. The values you inculcate within them during the year are the values that will accompany them in the summer. Give them plenty to do, and talk to them every so often about where they want to be, who they really are, and how they can positively affect others.

Enjoy the golden days of summer with your children. The fond memories you create together will stay with them forever.

Tefillah: Opening the Gates

The roots of *emunah* begin in very early childhood.

Young children between the ages of 3 and 6 are concrete thinkers. Abstract ideas such as the concept of a Creator are difficult for them to grasp. Is making *tefillah* a central part of their day doing them harm or good?

There are two views. One opinion maintains that giving *tefillah* central importance is detrimental because it makes it almost impossible for a child at a later stage of development to shake the superficial, robotic *tefillos* of early youth. Even Israeli children who understand Hebrew are so tuned out that *tefillah* becomes like a reading exercise devoid of meaning.

At this age, little children enjoy parroting. Nursery rhymes make no sense to them, yet they like reciting them. To that end, the second opinion holds that when a young child learns the *tefillos*, the part of him that loves repetition absorbs the words of the prayers into his soul. There is so much *kedushah* in *tefillah* that taking it in like mother's milk has enormous benefit, as it creates a positive backdrop for a later reality.

What about the present? How do we help our children create a connection with Hashem?

Young children are superficial. If they hear that they can please Hashem with their *tefillos*, they feel empowered and connected, especially if *tefillah* is done rhythmically or set to a tune. Song gives them a sense of security, stability, and connection, which is important.

When you teach a child to daven, you are setting the stage for him to feel good about being Jewish. If you expect him to say every word perfectly, or repeatedly admonish him to sit straight or pay attention, the child may come to associate davening with feeling inadequate and disconnected.

Don't kill a child's love for davening by being overly focused on externals.

I once had a charming book about the Baal Shem Tov. It had a beautiful picture of a young child holding a *siddur* aloft while davening in the forest. When my children saw this drawing, they became the Baal Shem Tov for a moment. They could understand talking to Hashem, because the picture concretized it.

If a young child davens and his prayers are not answered, he needs to be told very plainly that Hashem said no. You can bring examples from *Tanach*, such as when Hashem rejected Moshe's *tefillos* to enter Eretz Yisrael because it would not have been good for him or the Jewish people.

Tell your child that Hashem had reasons for saying no that we may not see at the moment, but may understand later on.

Don't take young children to shul. If you want to daven, find a girl who is willing to watch them. If the shul is tolerant about kids disturbing, don't frequent such a shul. A child should be taught that *kavod* and decorum must reign in a *beis knesses*.

Children in mid-childhood can begin to grasp the concept that *tefillah* is about expressing gratitude to Hashem. It's also recognizing that He is the source of blessing and salvation. This is a great age to tell a child, "Look at this delicious orange. Let's make a *berachah*." Or "The neighbor's baby is very ill. Let's daven together." The real enemy of davening is boredom — not understanding what the words mean, and not being able to relate to the prayers. Children understand the concept of davening, but not from a *siddur*. You have to provide them with structure and create a vision in their minds where they see that their *tefillah* is accomplishing something.

At this age, children begin formal *davening*. When they say *Birchos HaShachar* and the *berachos* of *Poke'ach Ivrim* and *Mattir Asurim*, point out that their ability to see and to get up in the morning are gifts from Hashem. We say thank you because we hope Hashem will continue giving us all these great blessings.

Try to reach your children on their level. Talk to them about the story of Yaakov and his sons and the first *Shema*. Teach them that when we say *Shemoneh Esrei* we are like troops standing in front of a general, ready to do his bidding.

It's important to take a child to an inspiring shul where everyone is serious about davening so they can see what real connection is. It's crucial for them to understand the *tefillos*. Teach them that prayer without *kavannah* is like a body without a soul. They may be blocked by the archaic nature of the words or Hashem's abstractness, but don't let that become an insurmountable obstacle. They can still talk to Hashem and mean what they say. Today there are excellent translations of the *siddur*. If it's difficult for them to follow the interlinear translation or they can't get the stilted English, encourage them to attend a class either in school or out of school where the *tefillos* are explained line by line so that they can understand the prayers on a simple level.

Children need to know that their *tefillos* make a difference and that when they daven they are creating a relationship with Hashem. It's good to teach a child *hisbodedus* and that he can talk to Hashem in his own words. Tell him that Hashem loves us, listens to us, and answers our prayers.

Children should hear lots of stories, especially about people they know who were helped through *tefillah*. Prayer brings down *shefa*. It's electric; it changes things. Let them hear that miracles happen a lot of the time but not all of the time, because ultimately Hashem makes the decision. However, our *tefillos* do make a difference, even though we may not always see it.

An inherent part of teaching children *tefillah* is improving your own *tefillah*. If your *bentching* looks bad, your child will get the message that you don't really believe that Hashem is listening to you. The same way your child should know what he is saying, you should too, and with a reasonable degree of depth. There are many excellent books available on the subject. The Maharal teaches that the realization of our vulnerability and our attachment to Hashem is the core of *tefillah*. Teach your children from an early age that we are completely dependent on Him. He is the only One Who can give us what we desire. Tell them that Hashem can send us health, success, sustenance, and insight, if we only ask. This will improve the sincerity of their prayers.

If you live in Israel, going to *mekomos hakedoshim* is wonderful for kids. Picturing Rachel Imeinu as a tangible person makes the idea of Hashem more comprehensible too. There are almost always people at these sites praying with fervent *kavannah*. This is good for kids to see. It gives them a sense of Hashem's Presence.

Teach your children decorum when they daven. Tell them that when they talk to Hashem, they and their surroundings must be clean. They must refrain from talking to others. This makes Hashem real to them. If parents look away and say to themselves, "He's only a child," they lock their child into a juvenile state of development.

Decorum in some schools means davening *together*. This is good, because it gives a sense of group energy to *tefillah*. Because of this, when appropriate, it's beneficial to take children to shul briefly.

May all our prayers be answered *l'tovah* along with all the pure and heartfelt *tefillos* of our children.

Relating to Torah Leaders

Unfortunately, today's generation has seen an enormous erosion in *emunas chachamim*. Adults who openly voice their negative opinions about Torah leaders cannot realistically expect their children to have pure *emunas chachamim*. Therefore, before we educate our children, we have to first inculcate within ourselves respect for Torah leaders. This does not mean thinking that Rabbis never make mistakes. They are human just like we are. It means trusting that our *chachamim* have the ability, through their outstanding Torah knowledge and *middos*, to see truth through a higher, deeper, more inclusive lens than we can. Anyone at a less exalted state is not in touch with perfect *emes*. The real *chachamim* are. That is the difference between them and us.

How do we teach *emunas chachamim* to very young children? It says, "*V'hayu einecha ro'os es morecha* — Let your eyes see your teachers." This can begin in babyhood. An easy way to start is to place cardboard pictures of *tzaddikim* in your infant's crib.

Let them hear you express your faith. When terrible things happen, pray to Hashem out loud, "Hashem, in the merit of our *Avos*, save us." This shows your children that your *emunas chachamim* is real and tangible.

Children from ages 3 to 6 are more verbal and can begin to understand. It's a great age to plant the seeds of *emunas chachamim*.

Simple stories of *tzaddikim* are an excellent medium. Many of the children's books for this age have the same plot: A family is faced with an insurmountable challenge, the wife suggests that the husband go to a *tzaddik* for help, at which point the *tzaddik* usually saves the day. Let them hear these stories again and again. Choose books with beautiful pictures. For young children, words are less important than images, which have a way of speaking to a child's heart.

Talk to them about the photos of *tzaddikim* in your living room. Tell them about the Steipler's dedication to Torah and about the Chofetz Chaim's *ahavas Yisrael*. You may know some Rebbe stories, but be sure to keep these stories simple. Don't tell them stories with ten subplots, as they will get wrapped up in the drama of the tale and forget about the hero. Help them understand that *tzaddikim* are not just people who live good lives but that they also benefit us. Relate stories of people who received a blessing from a *tzaddik* or who went to *kivrei tzaddikim* and were saved. Kids should know that *tzaddikim* are actual people. Make an effort to take your children to a *tzaddik* from time to time so that they become real to your kids.

Children from ages 7 to 11 should graduate from hearing tales about *tzaddikim* to actually seeing you ask advice from a Rav or a *tzaddik*. Additionally, watching you consult *sefarim* is good for kids.

At this age, they may hear *chillul Hashem* stories and come to you for an explanation. There are several ways to deal with this. First, investigate if the story is actually true. If there is a reasonable doubt about the veracity of the scandal, protect your child by not talking about the story but about the people who made up the story. Tell them, "Just because someone told you this does not make it true. People say these things when they're jealous. Maybe someone was envious of this person."

If the scandal is true, you could say, "Everyone makes mistakes." Explain to your child that people in desperate situations can sometimes make terrible errors and then regret their actions and change. Talk about the child's past mistakes and your mistakes. Tell him that you are sure the person has already repented or will eventually do *teshuvah*.

When the scandal is not only true but the child himself was victimized, you are walking on very thin ice. This is because if you make the perpetrator the hero, the child subconsciously becomes the villain. Tell him the story of Korach. Talk about the *tzaddik* who could have been holy but made an awful mistake because his ambitions blinded him. He made other people suffer, and in the end Hashem punished him.

With kids in later childhood and adolescence, you can teach *emunas chachamim* through having them read about *tzaddikim*. Buy them biographies of *tzaddikim*. These books are vivid and so full of *mussar* and *hashkafah* that the child will automatically grasp what a *tzaddik* is without having to hear you preach about it. They will want to be like the *tzaddik* and will admire people like him.

If your child's reading level is not that advanced, give him simple but detailed *tzaddikim* stories. At this age stay away from the magical *tzaddikim* tales. Tell your child stories that relate to the character of the *tzaddik*, such as his *hasmadah* and *tzidkus*. *Emunas chachamim* doesn't necessarily mean that every *berachah* or piece of advice will necessarily be on target. This is because ultimately Hashem rules the world. However, it does say, "*Tzaddik gozer v'Hakadosh Baruch Hu mekayem* — A *tzaddik* decrees and Hashem fulfills." This means that the *tzaddik's* decree may be a reason for something happening that had no reason to happen. For example, someone doesn't necessarily deserve a *refuah*, but it isn't time for him to die; he just needs the suffering and is therefore afflicted with terrible pain. It could be that the spiritual level the person will attain by believing in the power of a *tzaddik's berachah* will take him beyond the need for suffering, and he will miraculously recover. Anything is possible. However, don't let your children think that a *tzaddik's berachah* is a guarantee. This will erode their *emunas chachachim*.

At this age, if you've done a proper job of educating your children to respect Torah leaders when they were younger, it will stick with them now. I've seen teenagers make life decisions based on the advice of *tzaddikim* and *talmidei chachamim*. If you have a history of having failed with *emunas chachamim* in your child's younger years, it's almost impossible to fix in the teenage years. However, if you attempt to expose them to real *tzaddikim* now, they may develop *emunas chachamim* on their own.

Help your kids gain an honest appreciation of *tzaddikim* and *chachamim*. This means demystifying these leaders to some degree. Explain that a *gadol* with *daas Torah* is someone who is attuned to the Torah's outlook — Hashem's Will and wisdom.

At this age, your children are more likely to hear about sensational scandals. This requires an enormous amount of sensitivity. Your goal is to evoke a very delicate combination of revulsion for the act and compassion for the person so that your child does not associate this Rabbi's failures with all Rabbanim.

Introduce your child to the idea of communal consciousness. Make him understand the motivation for keeping scandals under wraps, but don't justify the evil act. A person who loves his fellow Jews will try to cover up their mistakes because such a person does not want other Jews to be degraded, especially in front of non-Jews.

We pray every week in the *Techinah* of Motza'ei Shabbos that Hashem should help us attain true *emunas chachamim* so that our children will grow up to emulate the living examples of our great Torah leaders.

The Value and Sweetness of Torah

How can we teach our children the value and sweetness of Torah?

Children between the ages of 3 and 6 develop a strong sense of what we value and what we don't. No matter how many rhymes and songs they've learned, if they don't see anyone in their own life appreciating Torah, they will pick up the worst possible message, namely, that what you say and what you do don't have to be consistent.

Let's look at three different home scenarios:

In one family, the father comes home from work, eats supper, interacts with his wife and kids, and then may or may not go out to a *shiur*. However, if every so often, the father does go to learn, the children should be aware of it. The mother should tell them, "Say goodbye to Abba. He's going to learn Torah." Torah learning should be part of the child's sense of normalcy, just as eating with utensils or putting on shoes are.

In another home, the father almost never goes out to learn. Here, the mother needs to make sure that at least on Shabbos there is Torah at the table. Even if Torah comes into the home only once a week, it is visible and treasured.

In the third kind of home, the father learns a lot. Maybe a *chavrusa* comes to the house every night, or the father teaches in yeshivah or is a full-time *kollel* member. The child knows that Abba learns Torah. However, he can make the mistake of thinking that Torah belongs to Abba and has nothing to do with him. The child can even reach a point where he views the Torah as a rival that cuts him off from his father. Here the father should, at least occasionally, invite his child to join him in Torah learning. This can be through telling a story at the Shabbos table or learning with the child daily, even if it is only for a short while. This way the child won't feel locked out of his father's world, which can result in serious problems later on.

There has to be time set aside for Torah, even if it doesn't happen every day. A child should know that whenever possible, Torah learning takes priority. Additionally, the child should see that there are Torah books displayed prominently on the shelf. Children must imbibe the feeling that Torah is important and valued.

Girls should see their mothers involved in spiritual pursuits. A mother must make it her business to go out periodically to a *shiur* or to read an inspiring book so her Torah becomes a part of the home too. If she bakes *challah* or gives *tzedakah*, her daughter should hear her say, "I am doing this mitzvah because this is what the Torah teaches."

There are wonderful Torah books available for kids today. There are *sefarim* on the *parashah* and *Pirkei Avos*, and stories about the sages. If longer stories are too difficult for your child, you can compensate with pictures. Show your child an illustration of Hillel lying on the roof in a snowstorm. Point out, "Do you see how hard Hillel tried to learn? Even though it was cold and snowing, he climbed on the roof to listen to Torah." This will teach your child that learning Torah is possible in every situation.

Serious *chinuch* starts with children from ages 6 to 10. This is when formal schooling begins. While the main component of a good preschool is a warm, loving atmosphere where the right values are imparted, elementary school requires more. The essential keys are the personal example of the teachers and the good feeling that is imparted about learning. Study material can be supplemented by the parents, but it is important for your children to be in an environment where learning is a delight. This will give them the desire to continue with intense learning later on.

Another thing to consider before choosing an elementary school is the graduating class. What do the students look like? Are they happy and well adjusted? Do they walk around with a certain air of knowing who they are, or is there overt rebellion? Where will they go for high school? At this age it is difficult to know your child's abilities and what style of learning will appeal to him.

Another aspect to consider when choosing a school is your own lifestyle. As much as possible, it is best if the school and your home are on the same page. Even if the school is academically superior, if the other students come from homes which are more fun or family oriented and where it's strange for the father not to be home all evening, it will devalue Torah to your child. Conversely, if your husband will be the only father who doesn't learn full time, it will devalue your husband in your child's eyes.

An additional aspect to look at isn't how much the kids are learning, but what their attitude is. What do they do when they have free time? What are their life goals? Whom do they admire and aspire to be?

I'll never have enough praise for *Avos U'Banim,* the father-son learning program. If you don't have one in your area, it's time to start one. All it requires is a shul with space to learn and a group of fathers who care about their kids. Fathers and sons get together to learn weekly, either late Friday afternoon, Shabbos afternoon, or Motza'ei Shabbos. The kids are marked for attendance and receive prizes for learning. This program has bonded fathers and sons in an amazing way.

Learning difficulties sometimes emerge at this age. Many times children are labeled unnecessarily. Testing helps you know how to take care of the problem. However, as soon as you label a child and change your expectations on that basis, you're walking on very thin ice. Try to keep the label small. Do what you have to do to take care of the problem, but don't let your standards change because of the label. Sometimes a therapist may recommend medication. Adjustments in the child's diet can at times take care of the problem. However, if after several months the diet does not work, you will have to consider medication. It can change your child's attitude, learning, and life forever. The difference between a child who can sit through class and shine and a child who can't do it and hates himself for it is vast. Don't skip the medication if it's needed. Just make sure it is solving a defined problem and is not just a band-aid to cover up other difficulties.

Your relationship with your child's teacher is crucial for your child's growth and success in school. Every teacher wants to succeed. They're working hard to achieve their goals with their students, and they want parents to respect them. Even if your child's teacher says critical things about him, possibly unjustly, don't develop an adversarial relationship with him. If your child says that his teacher punished him unfairly or humiliated him, listen to your child, repeat what he said so he knows you heard, and then say, "Wow, that does not sound good. We have to fix this. I'll call your teacher and we'll discuss how to make things better." This way your child sees that he was heard but that you still view the teacher as an advocate.

When you talk to the teacher, ask him what actually happened and offer to work with him to help correct the problem. If you approach him in an accusatory manner, he'll be hostile, and you will only be hurting your child in the long run. After discussing the problem, deal with it and be sure to follow up. Talk to the teacher at least once a month or biweekly. This way you can get his perspective on where your child is holding and how you can further help him.

If your child tells you that his teacher was physically violent or if there is repeated humiliation, you need to speak with the teacher immediately. You must be certain of the facts. Realize that it isn't unheard of for children to exaggerate, especially if they "know" they will be believed. The truth is sometimes painful and a great deal of care must be used in simultaneously making it safe for a child to confide in you and expect you to take his side, and finding out where the facts actually lie. The teacher may be in a difficult classroom, but that doesn't excuse abuse. If it seems that there is real abuse going on, or if the teacher is not responsive to your child's concerns, you will need to go over his head. However, don't do this before trying to speak with the teacher directly. Most teachers do want things to run smoothly, so you'll most likely gain cooperation.

Some schools are very creative in the way they get the kids to live what they learn. Other schools don't emphasize this, in which case you'll have to work a little harder to fill in the gaps. You can do all sorts of activities to enhance your child's learning and make it come alive. If your child is studying *Vayikra*, you can take him to the zoo and show him the different animals that were used for *korbanos*. If he learns about *chessed* or *hachnasas orchim*, you can invite a guest and include your child in the mitzvah. Invest effort in igniting your children's love for mitzvos by creating real life experiences that will stay with them forever.

With girls the focus is far more on seeing that they enjoy actualizing what they learn, rather than on learning more. If your daughter is intellectual, you can supplement her learning with books. Try to move your daughter's interests to things that will find expression in real life. There is nothing wrong with her learning, but make her realize that it is a means toward an end.

If your daughter doesn't particularly care for academics, it's not the end of the world. However, she has to make it through the school system. In order to do that with reasonable self-esteem, you have to be there for her. Offer your help with homework and school projects.

Some schools put extra emphasis on secular subjects and passing State-mandated exams. Be sure your kids see that *limudei kodesh* comes first by the way you talk about it and value it.

Children from ages 10 to 13 are at a critical juncture in their lives. These years will determine what will happen to them in the next 10 years. This stage is particularly difficult, because it is when boys transition from learning relatively easy subjects to studying serious Gemara. As a parent, you need to do everything possible to make learning delightful. When boys fall apart and become kids at risk, it is almost always the school or the child's relationship to learning that triggers their downfall. For boys, achievement is very important, and if Gemara is not exactly your son's best friend, it will wreak havoc with his self-esteem.

Try to find another Torah subject that your son can excel in, and shower him with compliments and *kavod*. Assist him with his Gemara learning by being in touch with his rebbi frequently and hiring tutors to help him. Show appreciation for the rebbi by sending him occasional gifts and complimenting him on his hard work. People work a lot differently when they feel their efforts are valued. Try your utmost to help your son through these years. Realize that you are not only buying learning but *yiras Shamayim* and adherence to the *derech haTorah*. If your son has a good feeling about learning when he is in *yeshivah ketanah*, he more than likely will stay on the right track.

Girls at this age are affected differently. Although the problems that can lead a girl off the *derech* may be aggravated by what happens in school, it generally begins with the relationship she has with her parents. If a girl feels valued and understood at home she will be okay. School usually won't make it or break it. Nevertheless, since there are a lot of temptations out there, she may begin to question things. She may feel that her individuality isn't being acknowledged sufficiently. You need to make her feel good about actualizing what she's learned. Do this by being a living example of this.

At this age, she will begin seeing herself as a person with spiritual values. If your daughter is very bright, every so often ask her for a *d'var* Torah that you can share with your *chavrusa* in Partners in Torah. When you prepare your lessons, try to involve her by asking her what she thinks are the most important points to cover.

If your daughter is not intellectually inclined, you can still make her aware that the Torah has *penimiyus* and *chitzoniyus*. *Chitzoniyus* is knowing what the Torah says, while *penimiyus* is understanding that it's all from Hashem and that this is what He wants His world to look like. Explain that Torah connects us to Hashem and that the halachos that come forth from it form us into spiritual beings.

Children at the yeshivah-ketanah and high-school age are idealists. They crave meaning and love fairness. When you are helping your child choose a school, try to see that these two values are there. Don't push your child into the top-notch yeshivah of your dreams. See first whether he'll be inspired and whether he'll be able to learn successfully there. Examine the school's graduates carefully. Where do they go when they finish? Do they go on to *beis medrash*, or do they close their books and never open them again? How do they regard their teachers and rebbis? Are they happy and do they sweat the long hours with joy? Is the learning challenging? Are they close to the Rosh Yeshivah? The reality may be that because schools today are so exclusive, you may not have that many choices, but you should still ask these questions.

For girls, look for a high school where the students appear happy, where your daughter will feel understood, and where there is someone to talk to if things aren't going smoothly. Choose a school where the staff believes in the girls and where they are given guidance in a firm and loving way.

Teenagers often find themselves torn because the world is so full of temptations. Often, they hear double-standard talk or need to stand up to social pressures. Taking your sons to *gedolei Torah* for a *berachah* or just to be in their presence can counteract this. Seeing the *chashivus* and *kavod* that our Torah leaders are given can leave a lasting impression.

May we guide our children on the straight Torah path so they can grow into proud *bnei* and *bnos Torah*.

Glossary

Glossary

acharis ha'yamim: end of days
achdus: unity
ahavas reyim: friendship
ahavas Yisrael: love of Israel
akeres habayis: mainstay of the house
am hanivchar: the chosen nation
anavah: humility
anshei emes: men of truth
arba minim: four species held during Succos prayers
asarah harugei malchus: ten martyred rabbis killed by the Romans
aveirah: sin
avodas hamiddos: working on perfecting one's character traits
avodas Hashem: service of G-d

Avos: Forefathers (Abraham, Isaac, Jacob)
ayin tovah: lit. a good eye; generosity of spirit
baal teshuvah (fem: *baalas teshuvah*): one who returns to Torah observance
baalei batim: working men
bachur: unmarried yeshivah student
baruch Hashem: thank G-d
bas Yisrael: lit. daughter of Israel; a Jewish girl
bashert: destined
bechirah: free choice
bechor: firstborn son
bein hazemanim: vacation time from yeshivah

beis din: Jewish court of law
Beis HaMikdash: the holy Temple
beis medrash: study hall
ben sorer u'moreh: rebellious son
Beni bechori Yisrael: My (i.e. G-d's) firstborn son, Yisrael
bentch: to say Grace after Meals
berachah: blessing
bedi'eved: post-factum, after the fact
bikur cholim: visiting the sick
binah yeseirah: extra measure of understanding
bitachon: trust (in G-d)
bris milah: circumcision
chacham: wise man
chasan: bridegroom
chasunah: wedding
chavrusa: study partner
Chazal: Sages of the Talmud
cheilek: portion
chesbon ha'nefesh: spiritual accounting
chessed: lovingkindness
chillul Hashem: desecration of G-d's Name
chinuch: education
chizuk: encouragement
Churban: Destruction (of the Temple)
chutz la'aretz: lit. outside the land; any place but the Land of Israel
d'var Torah: a short Torah insight
daven: to pray
dayan (pl. *dayanim*): judge(s)
derech ha'teva: through the laws of nature
derech: path
deveikus: closeness to G-d
dikduk halachah: scrupulous care in observing Jewish law
Elokus: G-dliness
emes: truth
emunah: faith
emunas chachamim: faith in the Torah sages
Eretz Yisrael: Land of Israel
ezras nashim: women's section of the synagogue
frum: (Yiddish) observant
gaavah: pride
gadlus: greatness
gadol (pl. *gedolim*): a great Torah leader and scholar
galus: exile
Gan Eden: Garden of Eden
ganenet: pre-school teacher
gashmiyus: physicality
gemach (pl. *gemachim*): free loan fund
geulah: redemption
gevurah: the trait of strength and self-discipline
gezeirah: decree
giluy Hashem: revelation of G-d
hachnasas kallah: the mitzvah of helping needy brides

hachnasas orchim: the mitzvah of hospitality
halachah: Jewish law
Har HaBayis: Temple Mount
Hashem: G-d
hashgachah: Divine Providence
hashkafah: perspective, point-of-view
hasmadah: diligence
hefkerus: wild, undisciplined behavior
hesped: eulogy
hevel: in vain
hiddur: beautify
hisbodedus: solitary meditation
hishtadlus: effort
ikar and tafel: more important and less important
Imahos: Foremothers (Sarah, Rebecca, Rachel, and Leah)
ish: man
ishah: woman
k'ish echad b'lev echad: like one man with one heart (said of the Israelites at Sinai)
kallah: bride
kaparah: atonement
kavannah: intent, fervor
kavod: honor
kevod Shabbos: honor of Shabbos
kedoshim: holy ones, martyrs
kedushah: holiness
kefirah: apostasy
kesubah: marriage contract
kever: tomb
Kibud av va'eim: mitzvah of honoring one's father and mother
Kiddush: sanctification (of Sabbath or holiday), usually made over wine or grape juice
kiddushin: betrothal agreement
kinah: jealousy
kiruv: Torah outreach
Klal Yisrael: the Community of Israel
Kohen: male descendant of Aaron, brother of Moses, who performed certain priestly functions in the Temple
Kohen Gadol: High Priest
kol hakavod: exclamation of approval: Good for you!
Kollel: Torah study program for married men
korban (pl. *korbanos*): sacrifice(s)
Kosel: Western Wall
krias haTorah: public reading of the Torah in synagogue
l'shem Shamayim: for the sake of Heaven
lashon hara: gossip and malicious speech
maaser: tithes
madreigah: spiritual level
makah (pl. *makkos*): plague(s) of Egypt

malchus: kingship

mamzer: child of an adulterous relationship

mashgiach (pl. *mashgichim*): supervisor of students in a yeshivah

Mashiach: Messiah

Matan Torah: the giving of the Torah on Mt. Sinai

matanos l'evyonim: gifts to the poor (a mitzvah observed on Purim)

mazal: destiny, luck, astrological sign

mechazek: to strengthen and encourage

mechilah: forgiveness

mechitzah (pl. *mechitzos*): barrier(s)

mekabel: one who receives

mekadesh shem Shamayim: one who sanctifies G-d

mekomos hakedoshim: holy places

melachah (pl. *melachos*): activities prohibited on Shabbos

meshulach: collector of charity funds

mesibah: party

mesirus nefesh: self-sacrifice

mesorah: chain of Torah transmission

metzora: someone who suffers from *tzara'as*, a spiritual disease with physical manifestations

middah k'neged middah: measure for measure

middah (pl. *middos*): trait

middas hachessed: the trait of lovingkindness

minhag: custom

minhag hamakom: the custom of a specific locality

minyan: quorom of ten adult Jewish men needed for certain specific communal prayers

Mitzrayim: Egypt

mitzvah (pl. *mitzvos*): commandment(s)

mitzvah d'rabbanan: rabbinic mitzvah

mussar: study of ethics and personality development

mussar vaad: group that meets to grow spiritually

Na'aseh v'nishma: "We will do and we will hear" – said by the Israelites before receiving the Torah

nachas: pleasure (esp. from children)

nachash: snake

nechamah: comfort

neginah: music

nes (pl. *nissim*): miracle(s)

netz: sunrise, the first moment when one may pray the morning Amidah

nisayon (pl. *nisyonos*): test(s), ordeal(s)
off the derech: straying from the Torah path
olam haba: the next world
olam hazeh: this world
ona'as devarim: harsh, hurtful speech
oneg Shabbos: delight in Shabbos
oved Hashem: a servant of G-d
parnasah: livelihood
pasul: invalidated
penimiyus: the internal content
posek (pl. *poskim*): halachic decisor(s)
ratzon: desire, will
refuah: recovery
refuah sheleimah: a full recovery
ruach hakodesh: Divine inspiration
same'ach b'chelko: happy with your lot
sefer: book
sefirah (pl. *sefiros*): manifestations of G-d's Will
sefiras ha'omer: counting of the omer; 49 days from Pesach to Shavuos
semichah: rabbinic ordination
seudah: meal
shalom bayis: harmony in the home
shamor: guard (as in, guard, or keep, the Shabbos)

shaylah (pl. *shaylos*): question(s) of halachah
Shechinah: Divine Presence
shechitah: ritual slaughter of poultry and meat
shefa: G-d's bounty
sheitel: wig
sheker: falsehood, lie
sheleimus: wholeness
shemiras einayim: guarding one's eyes (from forbidden sights)
shemiras halashon: guarding one's tongue from forbidden speech
shemitah: Sabbatical
shevet (pl. *shevatim*): tribe(s)
shidduch (pl. *shidduchim*): match(es)
shiflus: humility
shiur: Torah class
shleimus: wholeness, perfection
shmattah: (Yiddish) rag
shmuess: talk
shul: synagogue
siddur: prayer book
simchah: joy, also a joyous event (e.g. marriage)
sinas chinam: baseless hatred
siyata d'Shmaya: Heavenly assistance
taavah: lust, desire
tafkid: purpose in life
taharah: purity
taharas hamishpachah: laws of family purity

talmid (pl. *talmidim*): student(s)
talmid chacham: Torah scholar
techiyas hameisim: revivification of the dead
tefillah (pl. *tefillos*): prayer(s)
teshuvah: repentance
tikkun: rectification
treife: unkosher
tzaddik (pl. *tzaddikim*): pious and saintly individual(s)
tzedakah: charity
tzelem Elokim: the image of G-d
tzibur: congregation
tziyun: tomb of a *tzaddik*
tzniyus: modesty
vatran: Someone who yields before another
vatranus: the act of yielding before another
yeridah: descent
yetzer hara: evil inclination
Yiddishkeit: Judaism
yiras Hashem: fear, awe of G-d
yishuv: settlement
yissurim: suffering
yissurim shel ahavah: suffering that reflects G-d's love
Yetzias Mitzrayim: Exodus from Egypt
yom tov: Jewish holiday
yotzei: having fulfilled the halachic obligation
zachor: remember (as in remember the Shabbos)
zechus: merit
zemiros: Shabbos songs
zerizus: alacrity
zivug: destined spouse
zivug sheini: spouse of a second marriage